Are you wondering...

How
E.T.
Phone
Home
Made Me a Millionaire
Twice!

The first million is self-explanatory in this book.

The second million? I hope will come from you and all your friends buying and reading this book. LOL!

Copyright © 2023 Wendell Parnell

All rights reserved. No part of this publication may be reproduced, distributed or transmitted in any form or by any means, including photocopying, recording or other electronic or mechanical methods, without the prior written permission of the publisher, except in the case of brief quotations embodied in critical reviews and certain other non-commercial uses permitted by copyright law. or permission requests, write to the publisher, addressed "Attention: Permissions Coordinator" at the address below.

ISBN 978-0-6455695-9-9: First printing edition 2023

Madhouse Media Publishing | www.madhousemedia.com.au

Written and distributed by Wendell Parnell

My Notes

Most names in this book are real. Other names have a slight twist to them. I have written everything I can remember. I am sure most of the events are true and correct. I have a very dark sense of humour which you will easily pick up, especially in some of my 'Nutter' and 'Con Men' stories.

I say a lot of things *'tongue in cheek.'* I've been advised to change certain words and stories, but I can't. It is what it is, including the obvious typing errors too! I haven't written anything that should offend anyone. Well, I hope I haven't! My apologies if I have. I don't think any of my contemporaries who were working for Telstra back then are still working for Telstra today.

They are possibly working for other companies, paying off their mortgages, and may even wonder how Ben and Wendell are faring.

"As a matter of fact, extremely well. Both are retired and enjoying life, thanks to all of you," says two Naïve Greenhorns.

ACKNOWLEDGMENTS

I am dedicating this book to my loving and hard-working wife, Deirdre Parnell, and my 'dodgy' business partner Ben Stuckey. Without these two, I probably would still be singing, "It's a long way, to the top, if you want to sell mobile phones!" Their unwavering and tireless support has helped me achieve my retirement fund sooner than expected.

Both Deirdre and Ben have been an integral part of this endeavor.

We celebrated Ben's 50th birthday in Bali in March 2023. He has also laid many golden eggs for his retirement fund. Thank you, Deirdre, and Ben.

BEN, DEIRDRE AND WENDELL AT BEN'S 50TH IN BALI 2023.

Preface

I sent the following message to Ben Stuckey on Sunday 13 November 2022 at 10:20 pm. He was in Bali, and I was in Perth.

"Hey Ben, remember the Lord Alan Sugar book you gave me to read in Bali last October? Well, I am halfway through reading it. Funnily enough, you and I have remarkably similar stories to his story. Sadly, you and I ended up as mere 'Yobbo Millionaires' compared to him being a 'Lord Billionaire'. I am now going to write my own storybook:

How E.T. Phone Home Made Me a Millionaire, TWICE!

I am damn sure this book will be enjoyable reading for young and old business-minded people. Especially for new entrepreneurs wanting to try their luck in business.

Thirty years have flown past so quickly. It is only now writing this book, that I am recalling all the fun we had and all the risks we took. If I could only turn back time.

Table of Contents

Forward
Street Level Advice for Young and New Entrepreneurs........xv

Part 1

Chapter 1
Myanmar to Australia 1963...1
    Perth 1963-1967..2
    Drumming days, Music Australia 1967-1990...................3
    Music Perth 1983-1990..10

Chapter 2
Music Kuala Lumpur 1991-1994..12

Chapter 3
A Second Career, Tele-Communications............................16

Chapter 4
Meeting the Industry..22

Chapter 5
Meeting Charles...26

Chapter 6
Luck and Risks...30

Chapter 7
With A Little Help from my Friends..................................33

Chapter 8
Naming the shop 'E.T. Phone Home'...............................39

Chapter 9
E.T. Phone Home Opening Day 1st July 1994....................42

Chapter 10
First Break-in...47

Chapter 11
Damage Control via Media..51

Chapter 12
Ben and I Wore Cheap Suits..57
   Our Patch...59
   Back to the Story...61
   Our Lord and Masters..63

Chapter 13
These are two delightful stories: The Beatles Dolls..............64
   Topolino and the Armani Leather Jackets.....................66

Chapter 14
Dirty Deeds, Done Dirt Cheap...69

Chapter 15
Customer Service..73
   Amy, the Bikie's Girlfriend..74
   Mobile Phone Disappearing in Shop............................77

Chapter 16
Second Break-In...79
   Third Break-In..81

Chapter 17
Charles my Landlord..84
    Theevin - My Security Guru..................................87

Chapter 18
Adelaide Grand Prix 1995..91

Chapter 19
Spielberg shuts down E.T. Phone Home....................98
    Newspaper Ads read: Phone Shop ex E.T. Phone Home..106

Chapter 20
Buying Phone Shop Garden City 1996...................108
    This is one story that changed the course of my business..108

Chapter 21
The Dudes from One-Tel..120

Chapter 22
Deirdre Comes Aboard..130
    Director Deirdre..132
    Deirdre Robbed and Bashed..................................133
    Nurses' Version of Bashing....................................134
    Ambulance Officer..135
    Deirdre's Version..135
    Hello Darling Novelty Phones................................138
    Fair Work case with the Twins..............................141
    Coloured Girl's Big Breasts....................................143

Chapter 23
TV Radio and Newspaper Advertising 1997............147

Chapter 24
Nutters and Con Men Stories: Electro Magnetic BOX......151
    The Lebanese Connection......................................154
    Black Dollars..158

Chapter 25
Meencomm Takeover 1998 165
    Eyelevel Communications Takeover 1998 171

Chapter 26
Subiaco Business Central 1997 173
    Panasonic Court Case 175

Chapter 27
Melbourne Cup Competition at Garden City 1999 179

Chapter 28
Belmont Forum Little Shop 183

Chapter 29
Telstra Opening at Garden City 189

Chapter 30
Becoming Disillusioned with Telstra 193

Chapter 31
Had Some Big Wins 2001: Smashing Telstra's Glass Window. 195
    We Had A Telstra Win 199
    A Big Brightpoint Refund 201
    Citibank 203
    Dharma and the Tax Office 205

Part 2

Chapter 32
The Tide Turns 207

Chapter 33
Belmont Forum New Refit 2002 212

CHAPTER 34
    Ben growing wings 2002...................................216

CHAPTER 35
    Sean was Popular in Belmont.............................223

CHAPTER 36
    Belmont Forum Ending 2010..............................226
        Buyer 1...227
        Buyer 2...227
        Buyer 3...232
        Buyer 4...234
        Fonezone...238
        Buyer 5...238

CHAPTER 37
    Where Are They Now? - Ex-Staff Doing Well...................241
        Ben Stuckey...241
        Tim Guest..241
        Neil Randle..242
        Charisse Parnell....................................242
        Tasha Jane (my other dodgy daughter).......................242
        Shane Durrant......................................243
        Mathew Wall...243
        Siska Presila Fletcher............................244
        Kathy Russo..244
        Danny Wilder..244
        Laura Shockthorap..............................245
        Mosharraf Hossain...............................246
        Sickies..246
        Ratbag Staff..247
        Mobile Phone and Accessory Wholesalers...................247
        Accessory Wholesalers.........................249

Chapter 38
Miss Maud's My Head Office..................................251
    Saturday Breakfast..................................252
    Uniforms & Choosing the Right Workers...................253

Chapter 39
Things That Made Life Hell..................................255
    New Design Chiefs Telstra Didn't Need.......................255
    ICE-Tech, IT Programmers Telstra Did Need.............256

Chapter 40
Interesting Short Stories – Telstra Woo Us.....................258
    Bledisloe Cup Melbourne 2001...................258
    The 2000 Sydney Olympics.....................259
    The Olympics..................................262
    Day 1..................................262
    Day 2..................................264
    Day 3..................................264
    Day 4..................................265
    Day 5..................................265
    Day 6..................................266
    World Master of Business Conference 1999.................266

About the Author
..................................275

Forward

Street Level Advice for Young and New Entrepreneurs

When I was 43 years old, I was unemployed, had no superannuation fund, not one cent saved for my retirement and had very little money in the bank. Luckily, I half owned a house in Dianella, a northern suburb of Perth. The house was worth $220,000. Therefore, I was not doing too badly, but not doing too well either.

Then for the next twelve years, from the tender age of 43, until my younger age of 55, I discovered a good business opportunity staring me in the face, a rather risky one at that. I saw a chance to secure my retirement fund. So, I jumped in, following my gut instinct but cautiously. I worked ridiculously hard in the unknown world of telecommunication retail sales. Later as I learned more, I took on more risks in expanding that business and the best part of this story is that I crossed the line and made it.

I ran with the telecommunications industry, which was in its infancy. It was certainly pure good luck to have found it. My story is all about **luck**, **risk-taking,** working diligently and following your gut instincts.

What I am about to tell you, most people find hard to believe at first, but it is all true. When I tell anyone that I only went to high school in Australia for six months, they go: "Really, yeah sure, whatever!" I never went to primary school in Australia. I am talking about my first year of high school here in Perth, Western Australia. The average student spends five years in high school before taking up a trade or general work. Some students opt for higher education or go on to university. I gave up school the day I turned 14, against my parent's wishes. God love and bless them both (RIP).

When I arrived in Australia in December 1964, I was 13 years old. I soon found out about money and wages in Australia, by talking to the boy who sold the Daily News, Perth's afternoon newspaper in the city. He earned more money in a month than an average adult in Burma/Myanmar in 1963. This was only a part-time job for him after school. I convinced myself not to attend school anymore after the day I turned 14. Instead, I'd sell newspapers all day, every day in the city. I figured out I could earn or make twice as much per month as the average adult back in Burma (calculating on the black-market money exchange rate). I would be extremely rich soon, that was, according to my calculations. This was the dream of a mere adolescent, determined to succeed in life.

In theory I was right; but one couldn't live on 12 pounds a month in Australia in 1964. You could easily do that in Burma back then, especially with the black-market money exchange rates that went on there. I thought I had all the answers, I knew it all at my young pubescent age of 14. Today I would not advise anyone to quit their education as I did.

Education requirements, economic conditions and working circumstances are very different nowadays. The world has changed, and you need a good education. I mean, go to university level if possible. Then if you're lucky enough, you might find a suitable job to survive and enjoy the rest of your living days. It's tough out there in this 'IT' world. Think very carefully about your future, don't do what I have done, as not many make it, doing it my way.

If you are asking yourself, what can you learn from this book, keep reading. There is a lot to be learned here. My advice is simple. Get educated first, but if you see an opening to improve your future, go for it. Don't be scared. Life is one big **risk**.

If somebody wants to sell you a restaurant for $250,000, don't jump into it unless you are a well-qualified chef with a big following, at the very least. I can name lots of Australian and overseas chefs, who have failed when they opened a restaurant. We all know at least one. There are some well-known successful TV personalities like Jamie Oliver and Manu Feildel, just to name a few. It's not easy to operate a restaurant. You almost need to be there personally 24 hours a day, or you'll go bust. Now, that is a fact, ask any chef.

Most inexperienced young people think that by opening a small coffee shop or café and investing around $100,000 to $150,000, they are going to be successful and rich. This is rarely true. Unless that coffee shop was selling about 300 coffees or more per day, don't touch it. Once you lose that type of money in a failed venture, your whole life will be ruined, especially if you start at a young age.

You read regularly on Facebook, on Instagram or anywhere on the internet, 'that by investing $250 in some Ponzi scheme they advertise, you will get a return of $1,450 in eight weeks.' It's bullshit. It's a scam. Ask parents for advice, ask other people in business, ask people who have gone bust, speak to your accountant, and ask him to look carefully into all your business ventures.

For every 100 businesses that are up for sale, only 20 percent of the businesses sold will survive if that. Sadly, most people lose their money quickly by jumping into business without understanding numbers.

Do the numbers stack up? Why would someone offer you 11% interest on a term deposit when the big banks are only offering you 3%? For lessons one, two, and three, there are no free lunches because they are not free. The get-rich Bitcoin or Crypto-related Ponzi currency schemes are rampant out there. Most internet get-rich schemes and offers are scams. They use photos of Elon Musk and Gina Rinehart to lure you in. See the photos below. They are not going to make you rich. If anything, it will make you poorer. Unless you first bought into it when it was first offered on the market years ago, it's too risky now.

SHOTS TAKEN FROM THE INTERNET

SHOTS TAKEN FROM THE INTERNET

Here's one sad story I will share with you. To save embarrassment, I won't mention their names as they are still my good friends.

The lady of the couple was constantly being told what a good cook she was. I have eaten her cooking many times and she was. An opportunity arose for her to open her own restaurant. She signed a five-year lease at some B-grade shopping centre for a rental cost of $74,000 per annum, plus outgoings. All she got was a shell of a shop. She had to fit it out to her desired requirements by putting in a new kitchen, tables, chairs, etc. The shopping centre gave her three months rent-free. She was happy with that. At least with no rent for three months. She thought that was a good deal to start her new venture.

They borrowed from the bank, $150,000 against their house to start their new business. Without any experience, they sailed out into a storm without life jackets.

The restaurant looked good, food was fantastic, but the customers were few and far between. So, what happened? Well, they closed after 18 months because it was costing them money to stay open. Their weekly income was roughly $3,500: outgoings were $4,000 plus a week. They both worked seven days a week, only to lose $500 per week! A no-brainer here. It's that easy to lose money.

They never asked, "How many plates of food do I have to sell per day to break even?" They eventually closed the restaurant and had to settle and buy their way out of the five-year shopping centre lease. That cost them $70,000 and that was a cheap way out.

They sold their house for $390,000. They paid out their remaining $170,000 loan which was owed on their house. They paid off the bank shop loan of $150,000. They paid the shopping centre $70,000 and ended up with $20,000 after selling all their restaurant furnishings and equipment.

They vacated their family home and went into a rental property. To my knowledge, they are still in it today. There are thousands of these stories or similar ones out there.

Tread very carefully Mon Ami. If you really get desperate, try your luck by buying a Lotto ticket.

DO YOU STILL WANT TO GO INTO BUSINESS?

PART 1

Chapter 1

Myanmar to Australia 1963

I vividly remember when I was 10 years old in 1961, my dad, George Andrew Parnell and my mother, Doris Margaret Parnell gathered our family together for a meeting. My dad announced that we were migrating to Australia. In his wisdom he explained, because we were fair in colour, our future standing in business or in the workplace was going to be limited. Burma (now called Myanmar) gained independence from the British in 1949. By 1961, they had had enough of the white man ruling them.

My paternal grandfather was Spanish (Dominic Viagus) and my paternal grandmother was a Pho Karen, a native tribe living between Myanmar and Thailand. My maternal grandfather was French (Leon De Clozet) and my maternal grandmother was British. Dad looked Asian. My siblings and I took after Mum and looked more European.

Because of this logic, my parents applied to migrate to Australia, and they had to borrow all our airfares from a loan shark. This crook charged us a total of $5,000 in return for a $2,000 loan. It took all of three years to get our visas and documents together to migrate to Australia. During these three years, my dad insisted I learn a musical instrument, and I chose drums. Poor dad gave up most of his leisure time to accompany me weekly to my drum lessons, which were conducted by a blind drumming instructor, (ensuring I did not wag the lessons).

I was not happy about the news my parents presented to me at the tender age of 10. I was quite advanced in the knowledge of 'social activities' including being able to travel vast distances from home. My friends were usually much older than me and I was sometimes used as a 'matchmaker' for them. They trusted me to hand-deliver their love letters to their sweethearts, (for a fee of course).

That was the way matters of the heart were handled in those days in Myanmar. Usually behind their parents' back (of course). Many a time, this task meant I had to travel far from home and negotiate the rigors of daily hustle and bustle of life, buses, bike rides, to deliver these important, life changing letters. Consequently, I was exposed to many more things than most 10-year-olds in Australia would usually have to wait until they were 18 years or older to experience. Say no more!

After the neighbourhood heard about our decision to migrate, most were disappointed, and some even said, "You have a home here, friends, and plenty of food, so why are you leaving?"

I agreed with them. Why? I even contemplated being kidnapped by some of my older friends just days before departing Rangoon. In the end I reluctantly went with the family to Australia, instead. I had no choice in the matter. This secret is something I have never made public.

Perth 1963-1967

We arrived at midnight in Perth, in December 1963. There was no one to greet us. My dad was given an address for the Salvation Army in Pier St in Perth. He ordered two taxis to take us there. It was about 3am when we got to Pier Street and the place was in total darkness, so dad refused to wake anyone up. The driver suggested a backpacker hostel close by in William St called Britannia Hostel.

Dad was happy, it was one pound per room per night. We had three rooms for five nights. We then found a house to rent in Balga. I think we had 150 pounds for the whole family to start life in a new country. What a beautiful country.

My 14th birthday was on the 25th of June, so it was still high school for me; not getting a job working as I had hoped. My parents had different ideas for me, but I was a naughty boy. I hardly went to school as expected by my parents. When Dad found out, I got a good old belting. Remember them?

I made friends with the neighbourhood boys and was soon leading the gang. Because I played drums and formed a schoolboy band, I was invited to play at everyone's birthday party and any other parties that came along. I then joined a band more professional. I was more interested in music than stealing cars and petrol as my friends were doing. We were living in Balga, a rough state housing commission suburb.

Drumming days, Music Australia 1967-1990

When I was 16 years old, I was playing in commercial pop bands professionally. I played drums in a band called 'Karma'. We travelled around Australia extensively for about 18 years, working six nights a week, without a break. We never had a Christmas Day or a New Year's Eve off, ever. We were doing what came naturally, playing music and loving it. By the age of 40, I was a fully-fledged music promoter in Sydney Australia.

On reaching my 30th birthday, I started to realise that I needed to earn more money for my future. So, I replaced myself in the band with another drummer. I now became the band's manager and doubled as the band's sound engineer, all for the same wage. It was my beginning towards bigger things. I had always handled all the band's affairs from day one, but never got paid for it.

In those days, we split the money equally between the band members after expenses. Those expenses were the sound system, lights, truck, petrol and roadies. That was my first duty each week on Mondays. I forgot; I was the unpaid accountant too.

During our touring days over the years, we travelled all-around Australia playing music. On the road, I met and made many friends and contacts, with owners and managers of hotels and nightclubs. We regularly had drinks with these guys, usually most nights after the gigs. During these free-drink sessions, I would hear similar cries from all these hoteliers and nightclub owners. They all had similar stories; they wanted more good bands on a regular basis. I saw an opening and a good opportunity there, so I negotiated to act as an agent for some of these guys nationally. Not all, but some agreed.

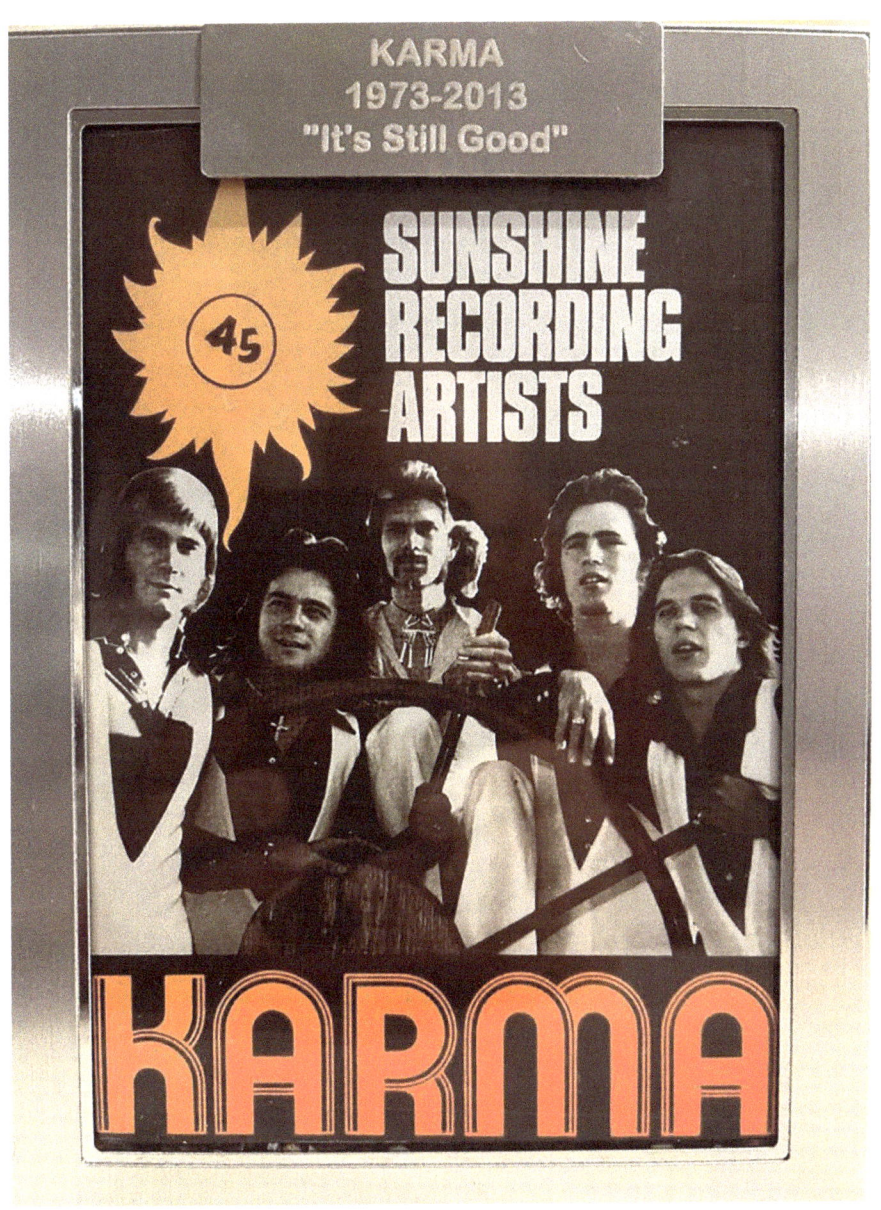

'KARMA' TOURED AUSTRALIA EXTENSIVELY

I tried my luck, and used my knowledge of good bands I'd seen and knew around Australia. I supplied the venues with bands and various other artists. To my luck, it took time to establish, but I slowly got there and it worked. I was now earning extra money on the side.

After a few years of being an agent, most of my bills got paid so I decided to settle down in Sydney. After years of learning how the music industry ticked, I somehow managed to graduate and become a music promoter in Sydney, Australia. Forming my company 'Parnell Music Promotions', was a giant step to take, and I took it. A really big risk.

One day I heard that the Maroubra Seals Club, a water sports club in the Eastern Suburbs of Sydney, was having some difficulties in growing their membership base, which in turn was affecting their finance department. Their membership was declining, and business was not looking that good for them. My band Karma was always a big hit when we played at the Maroubra Seals club over the years. I was very well known to them through the Karma band days. It was I who negotiated all the work for the band at that club. As I said, I was the official unpaid manager, even in those days.

I took the courage and approached the Maroubra Seals club management behind the backs of their long-term club agent, Ceema Promotions. Ceema Promotions was run by Marlene Hutchinson and her brother Colin. It was through them that I initially got all our gigs at the Maroubra Seals club.

Even though I felt a little bad doing this, I thought 'What the hell, nothing to lose'. I was entering the music-promoting world, and that's what you had to do; take risks and face the consequences when they arose.

One day I arranged a meeting with John McCormack the General Manager, together with his duty manager Peter Reid (Peter is the General Manager now, since 1995). At this meeting, I suggested they look at putting on some very big rock and roll bands at the Maroubra Seals Club. I mentioned to them bands such as the Angels, Mental As Anything, Cold Chisel, INXS, Little River Band, and bands of that calibre.

Their immediate reaction was "Wendell, we don't know anyone who can get us these bands. Can you help?" Just the words I needed to hear. "Watch me," I said, "I'll be back next week with good news, I hope."

CHERYL IN ACTION IN 'HANDS OFF' SUPPORTING COLD CHISEL

At that time in Sydney, I was managing a band called 'Hands Off'. An original band fronted by the very beautiful, talented and dynamic singer, Cheryl Hoogwerf. I had them working through the **Harbour Agency** and the **Frontier Touring Company** (they toured ACDC, The Rolling Stones, Elton John, and more recently, Taylor Swift, Ed Sheeran, etc). These companies were owned by Australia's big-gun promoters Michael Gudinski (RIP) and Michael Chugg. They seemed to like 'Hands Off' and gave us lots of gigs including support to KC and the Sunshine Band and many more big bands of that calibre.

Hands Off were very successful, and I was quite liked by Sam and Robbie, the two guys who were running the Harbour Agency back then. They were the No 1 agency then, and still are now in 2023, the biggest agency in Sydney, so I am told. The Harbour Agency had an offshoot company called **Australian Variety Artists** specialising in cover bands. They asked me to help run this division for them. I did this for twelve months.

MY AVA BUSINESS CARD

In Melbourne, their sister agency is called **Premier Artist/Mushroom Records**, managed by Frank Stivala, another big name in the Victorian music industry.

I approached Sam and Robbie about using the Maroubra Seals Club as their Eastern Suburb's venue. There was another big well-known venue in the Eastern Suburbs called Selinas at the Coogee Bay Hotel. That was the "IN" place to go to. All the big-known bands played there.

To my luck, the Harbour Agency agreed to help me place some of their larger bands at the Maroubra Seals Club. Some of these bands were Little River Band, Noiseworks, Australian Crawl, The Radiators, Men At Work, INXS, Hunters and Collectors, The Angels, John Farnham, and a whole host of international acts like The Cure, George Thorogood, Tina Turner (RIP), (way before her career took off), Bo Diddley (RIP). Too many acts to name all.

That punt I took paid immediate dividends. That bold move I made, brought thousands of music lovers to the Maroubra Seals Club weekly. It launched me successfully as the new up-and-coming promoter in Sydney. Then of course, other big band managers from bands like Cold Chisel, etc, and other big agents started to approach me to put their bands and acts into the Maroubra Seals club. And yes, I welcomed them with open arms. The risk of being 'a Promoter' is you have to have the capital to cover expenses before you make any money selling the shows.

Everyone was very happy at The Harbour Agency with the success of the new Eastern Suburb's venue. The bands that played there were happy too, and especially the Maroubra Seals Club, they were most impressed with me. After I introduced the big acts to their club, they were getting 1,200 to 1,500 people every Friday and Saturday night, compared to the 200 to 300 people they used to get on good weekend nights in the past. It was a sweet success.

This success naturally led me to expand my wings a little. I went and explored a bit further out to the country areas, to larger towns like Lithgow, Orange, Bathurst, Young, Parkes, Dubbo, and many larger towns nearby. Again, another success story in the making. The country

RSL, Bowling, and Football Clubs were starved for big bands. They loved me bringing these big bands out to them, especially mid-week like Monday, Tuesday, Wednesday, and Thursday nights.

I believe I was one of the early rock and roll music promoters who successfully had a New South Wales country circuit. Soon most managers and other agents started to approach me to take their Acts on the road too. This I also did. I finally stamped my company's name 'Parnell Music Promotions' on the Sydney music scene. That was 1978-1983. Thanks to Sam and Robbie.

Music Perth 1983-1990

I then decided to move to Perth in 1983, to be close to my daughters. I had saved enough money to buy a house in Perth. I'd had a satisfying time in my career playing drums in bands and I would do it all over again at a drop of a hat. They were the best years of my life. Not discounting my success days as a Sydney music promoter.

In Perth, the Music scene was raging. Cover bands like the Jets and V-Capri were pulling huge crowds in beer barns like The Raffles, Nookunburra, Morley Park, and the Herdsman.

The Rock Agency headed by Des Jose (RIP) had the town sown up big time. There was no room for any new agents or promoters to open shop there. I was intimidated, but I was a big boy from Sydney and opened shop without fear. Everyone was waiting to see me fall flat on my face. I didn't.

The first thing I did was, I got the Sydney band I managed (Johnny Demon Band) a week's support to Dragon (with the hit single 'April Sun in Cuba') in all these Perth beer barns. This established them in Perth overnight. I brought them back a month later for a twelve-month stint. I then started the 'Battle of the Garage Bands.' This was an instant hit. I then took over management of the Queensland band 'The Toys', another hit in town.

I then formed, managed, and toured 'Tora Tora' from the Garage Bands era. They toured Nationally for me and were a hit with the Harbour Agency in Sydney. They were my number-one band in Perth. Unfortunately, these boys were spoilt in Perth with the best sound and lighting money could buy, plus a full road crew. In Sydney they had to do it tough, (so did INXS, another hugely successful Perth band) carrying their own equipment and sharing rooms on the road. Nothing like being home with Mum's cooking. If only they had stayed on in Sydney, they had a good chance of breaking through and becoming another INXS.

To get a gig through the Harbour Agency was like winning lotto. Tora Tora worked through this agency and were liked by Sam and Robbie. They were already halfway there to success in the music scene. But they weren't ready for it. So they decided to stay on in Perth and broke up a few years later. David Gough, the bass player, passed away recently in Cairns Queensland (RIP).

I had at least a dozen bands working for Parnell Music Promotions in Perth. I also brought the ABBA tribute band Bjorn Again to Perth several times. I also toured them through Singapore and Malaysia. Then I managed to finish off my promoting days in Perth with the last Sherbet tour ever which ended in Perth. Daryl Braithwaite enjoyed playing cricket in my backyard many times. I have loads of 'music world' stories to tell but it will have to wait.

Chapter 2

Music Kuala Lumpur 1991-1994

I will tell you a little more about my music exploits in Malaysia, so that this **E.T. Phone Home** story will make more sense. I had to reinvent myself again, this time in Kuala Lumpur.

I spent three years in Kuala Lumpur, building up a music promotional business and I successfully did so, right under the watchful eyes of the local music agents and promoters. Once again, I was the new kid on the block. I was there between 1991-1994.

I had dropped into Kuala Lumpur on my way to London, Paris, and Zurich in 1991. I was taking my daughters Tasha and Charisse on their first European holiday. They were on their university holiday break and I had had enough of the Perth music scene.

I had a good friend by the name of Subramaniam Thanapathy (Thana), living in Kuala Lumpur. He had an apartment right across the road from the Bangsar Shopping Centre, which housed a huge pub called Network. Different local bands played there six nights a week.

On my first night in Kuala Lumpur, Thana and I had dinner and beers at his favourite Chinese restaurant at the Bangsar Shopping Centre. He then took me to his local pub; 'Network'.

He had a bottle of Johnny Walker Black Label there, which was his favourite drink. He mentioned that this bottle was left over from the night before. He insisted we go and finish it. Probably more than 75%

of the bottle was left; at least that was what I saw. You can buy spirits by the bottle, leave what you haven't drunk, and come back another night to finish it off. They put your name on the bottle, mark it, store it, and give you a month to finish it.

The band playing there that evening was local and not quite what one would call 'fantastic', but they were acceptable. Towards the end of the evening in his half-drunken state, he said to me, "Wendell you are supposed to be a music promoter and I live across the road from this pub and have to listen to this rubbishy music, week in and week out. What type of a friend are you?" I knew where this conversation was leading to.

Thana yelled out over the loud music, "Why can't you get some decent bands from Australia to play here?" He went on to tell me that the manager of Network was a good friend of his.

He said, "How about meeting him and discussing bringing some bands from Australia to Kuala Lumpur?" Stupidly, and only because I was also half-cut that night, I agreed.

The next day I had lunch with Premesh, the manager of Network. He was open to having bands from Australia and from the Philippines and was happy to give it a try. I promised him nothing, except saying I'd let him know in a few days' time.

Later that day I met Thana and the first thing he asked was, "Did you ring your friends in Sydney to see if you can organise some good bands?"

I replied, "I will do that tomorrow, Sydney is two hours ahead of Malaysia. It is now 7 pm in Sydney and I'm still suffering from the hangover from last night, so tomorrow I will try my hardest," I promised Thana.

As a man of my word, the following day I rang my friends at the Harbour Agency in Sydney and explained the situation about the Network Pub in Kuala Lumpur needing a band to play there six nights a week, for at least 4 weeks at a time. They rang back and had good news for me. To my luck there was a band from Melbourne called the 'Mal Eastick Band' who were available for a 4-week stint. I organised everything as quickly as I could from Kuala Lumpur, and I continued to negotiate the rest of the deal from London, Paris, and Zurich, and it worked.

The band eventually made it to Kuala Lumpur and was quite successful I'm told. Everybody was happy and of course, they were waiting for me to come back to see what else I had up my sleeve. Because of this one good deed I organised for my friend, I ended up moving to Kuala Lumpur and I stayed there for three years 1991-1994.

To finish off and conclude my Malaysian music story, I made many hoteliers happy there and did good business deals over the three years that I lived there. I was starting to become a highly successful music promoter in Kuala Lumpur.

All except for one thing; my poor wife Deirdre and her health problems. She suffered badly from the heat and the humidity in Kuala Lumper. For some crazy reason, her constitution could not bear the humidity, pollution and heat there. The poor girl spent nearly 12 months of the 36 months whilst we were in Kuala Lumpur in hospital, which was not good.

My doctor and good friend Doctor Rama (RIP) advised me, "Wendell, either send your wife home alone or go home with her or you are going to lose her. She will be dead in 12 months under these conditions."

As any good husband should, I gave up everything I had built up in Kuala Lumpur and came back to Perth, Australia feeling flat. As I was the promoter, everything was under my personal name 'Wendell Parnell Presents' or 'Parnell Music Promotions'. The hoteliers would only deal with me and nobody else. I had no business to on-sell. I was going home without a briefcase full of money. All my time and investments in Malaysia went down the drain. But we made many friends there and still managed to have a great time.

I arrived back in Perth from Kuala Lumpur in late March 1994. Ironically, despite not going home rich, I arrived on a British Airways flight, flying first class. Yes, **first class**. Our personal luggage was over 50 kilograms each, plus another 300 kilograms of extra luggage to bring back. We only had economy-class seat tickets. To my luck, my cousin Patricia's husband worked for British Airways in Kuala Lumpur. He was the Customer Service Manager. His name is Said Abubakar, he is a Muslim and a wonderful man. He was so kind and helpful to us. He upgraded us from economy to first class which was within his power. This in turn solved my excess luggage weight problem. I think he knew my financial situation. At the check-in counter, they ignored my excess baggage weight. They gave me two seats 1A and 1B. I looked at the tickets and looked at my wife and couldn't believe my luck! Flying on a Boeing 747 to Perth Australia, drinking French Champagne, and dining on the best food all the way home. I can get used to this. Thank you, Said.

MY PARNELL MUSIC PROMOTIONS CARD IN MALAYSIA

Chapter 3

A Second Career, Tele-Communications

So here I am back in Perth in 1994, with no job and no spare cash. Being away from the Perth music industry for three years didn't help. I felt a bit embarrassed. I had returned to Perth without lots of extra money. My business venture in Kuala Lumpur was a success, not a failure. Large corporations/hotel groups kept on ringing me for months after my return. They kept asking me for acts and bands, and when was I returning? One had to live and be there to run the business if one wanted it not to fail. Like most businesses, you need to be there, hands-on, talking to, seeing, meeting, and selling your acts to the buyers almost daily. That was a sad end to see three years of successful networking in Kuala Lumpur going down the drain. Finished, all gone, goodbye Kuala Lumpur.

I was now restless and wanted some action; I never could sit still for too long. So, after being back in Perth for only a few days, I rang up John McLeod, a friend of mine from the music industry, and said, "Let's have lunch."

John managed several bands in Perth before I moved to Kuala Lumpur. I was operating in the Perth music scene for a few years. He then managed a band called 'Spinfx', who also worked through my Parnell Music Promotions agency in Perth. John and I got on well before

I left for Malaysia. During our lunch, I asked him what he was doing nowadays. He said he was working for Telecom. We know Telecom today as Telstra.

He said to me, he was selling pagers. "Do you know what pagers are?"

I replied "Of course I do. It's one of those things that you carry around and will beep when they want you to call the office, or something like that."

He said, "Correct."

He went on to tell me that selling pagers was a very profitable business, especially if you were a retailer. New on the market, pagers were running hot in those days.

John said, "The next big thing on the market is mobile telephones. What do you know about mobile phones?"

I said I did not know much about them; I have never owned one. What would I know about mobile phones anyway, I'm a bloody musician. I know nothing about mobile phones or the retail industry for that matter.

John went on to tell me that there was a big retailer by the name of Tony Raj who owned three big retail shops, in and around the metro area. He said Tony Raj was looking for a General Manager urgently to take his place running his business. He was too busy with his racing cars and running around Asia doing other things of more interest to him.

"Are you interested in a job?" John asked.

I said to John, "I know nothing about retail business, however, I'm quite happy to have a chat with this Tony Raj fellow and see what's cooking." The music industry in Perth was not doing very well at that time, and I had no cash which was needed to promote big acts; I had to do something.

The next day John rang me at home and said, "Wendell, Tony Raj wants to meet you at 3 pm this afternoon for an interview, only if you're free."

Yes of course I was free.

I said, "Yep, I'll go see what he has to say, or better still, what he had to offer me."

I went to the meeting at 3 pm that day. Tony Raj was an Indian Singaporean fellow. A very charming man. The meeting went well and all he wanted to tell me was how he needed somebody just like me, someone who had some sort of Asian background and culture, who had to be around my age. Someone who had travelled and worked in Asia, someone with experience in life.

He then looked at me and said, "You look like a very honest and trustworthy person." At least he got that one right. The rest of the interview was all cliches.

Hmmm! I thought! He sounded a little insincere, but not as intimidating as I was expecting. How do you pick an honest and trustworthy person you just met for only half an hour? The penny should have dropped right there and then. There were red lights flashing in my head, but I was a bit desperate and chose to ignore my gut feeling about this guy, for the time being, that is. I thought what the hell, what have I got to lose? I might as well give it a go. You never know, something new and exciting might come into my life. I thought wow, okay, a new challenge and why not? I was just needing to make some money and have a job, that's all. I told myself, just ignore all the sweet talk and flattery he was dishing out to me and accept the job.

During the interview, Tony Raj told me that he had three shops and he wanted to get rid of one or two of them. He also mentioned that if things worked out with me, I could buy them from him and pay them off or something like that. Now that sort of offer half appealed to me, but in time, it would prove he just uttered meaningless words to impress me. There was another huge problem as we spoke, I knew nothing about retail business. I told him I had no experience in telephony or selling because my background was in the music industry.

He said, "Don't worry, start Monday and we will teach you as you go."

I told him I would come Monday and asked him, "What do you pay your staff?"

He said, "Seeing that you are not experienced, I will offer you $300 a week." Later, when you become my General Manager, we'll cut a deal to include a revised weekly salary of $500 - $600 per week, plus a small total percentage of all the sales made monthly from all my shops."

I calculated taking home about $1,000 each month as bonuses plus a weekly salary of $600 per week. Not bad I thought. The name of his shop was called 'Just Phones' and its address was No 1 Fitzgerald Street, Northbridge.

At dinner that evening, I explained everything discussed at the meeting to my wife Deirdre. She was very happy that I was trying out something new. She had already found herself a job she enjoyed.

MY JUST PHONES BUSINESS CARD

The retail outlet in Fitzgerald Street was also Tony Raj's head office. He had about nine staff there and the one thing I noticed from day one was, when Tony Raj appeared at work, he was always interviewing people. Amongst all those people was a lovely young guy by the name of Ben Stuckey. I think Ben was about 20 years old then. I had met him once or twice during his first week at Just Phones. I didn't speak to him for about two weeks after that. We both had things to do and learn. Tony Raj struck up a deal with Ben that went something like this; Ben had to go out to the suburbs door knocking and connect people to a mobile phone contract, either with Telstra or Optus.

Tony Raj offered Ben $100 a week in petrol money allowance. Sounds good but it wasn't. I think like me, he was a bit desperate to work and was a little blasé about the money side of things. He accepted the offer. Now I know why Tony Raj was always interviewing someone. It was people like Ben who only lasted four to six weeks and were replaced regularly. What about me, could I expect the same? I tried not to think about it.

Ben drove out to the suburbs daily, trying to sign up and connect 20 new customers per week as agreed, but it was a lot harder than he expected. Ben's incentive was, if he achieved his 20 weekly targets, Tony would give Ben an extra $300, which equates to $15 per connection for Ben. I asked Ben what if he only signed up 13 customers?

Ben said, "Nope, it must be 20 or more to collect the $300 bonus cash." Ben went on to say that after the first 20 connects, he was to be paid an extra $20 per connection. I thought it wasn't a very good deal because Ben had to pay parking fees and he had already got a parking infringement notice once. The most he ever connected was 13 customers. He told me later, in the week that he signed up the 13 new connections, most were either friends or family. He never got his $300 bonus in the six weeks he was there.

However, Tony Raj got paid $30 per connection Ben signed up, plus an 8% ongoing airtime usage commission from the customer's bill. Not bad, receiving eight cents in every dollar spent each month for at least two years. That's a lot of money for doing nothing, money for free. Plus, there was a great markup on the mobile phone handset sold. Sadly, all that has changed now, and I am happy I'm out of telecommunications too. What a great business it was to be in. Lots of 'Money Money Money' to be made back then and I was hungry for it.

As the weeks went by, I met a lot of people from the mobile phone industry. What I learned from everyone was that Tony Raj was making a heap of money from selling mobile phones. I just wished he paid his creditors on time and made my job easy.

Tony Raj was always a bit arrogant and had a bad habit of not paying his bills on time. It was me who had to deal with suppliers who rang up daily, asking to be paid or complaining that their cheques were not in the mail or had not arrived as promised. My way of doing business would have been totally different from his, especially if you were raking money in as he was. 'Pay your bills, receive your goods, service your customers, and keep them happy.' That sets a good standard of service, and a good business model to adopt, don't you think?

I covered for this guy as much as I could, losing my dignity at times. I would ring him up constantly wherever he was and say, "Tony, we need to pay this or that bill urgently." Normally his bills were three or four weeks overdue.

His typical answer was, "Wendell, they can wait. I have always paid my bills." He did, but never on time.

He'd say, "I'm in a meeting" and hang up.

I thought by now, something must give soon, I can't keep telling customers to come back tomorrow or the next day, or do I tell them the truth and say our supplier won't give us any more credit, we haven't paid our bill? I was getting sick of making excuses. I used to go home stressed out every day and mention all this to Deirdre.

Chapter 4

Meeting the Industry

During my 'Reign' at Just Phones, I met representatives from different suppliers and the area managers of Telstra and Optus quite often. They liked me because I came from a rock and roll background, where we pulled no punches. Both the Telco guys were very good to me because they understood my predicament. They had been dealing with Tony Raj for at least 12 months or more before I came on the scene.

They discretely told me, "Wendell, be careful he'll burn you out and replace you with somebody else, just as he has done to the last few so-called 'General Managers' before you."

It was a vibrant and new industry we were in. I loved it. Everyone was learning and teaching each other new things about the new telecommunications industry. The Telco boys taught me very well how to deal with Tony Raj, they certainly opened my eyes. That warning rather worried me, (the *burning you-out words*). I was working extremely hard at trying to learn something new and loving the business. Except I was getting stressed out daily and beginning to feel burnt out.

I'd get to work by 8.30 in the morning (normal opening hours were 9-5.30 pm) and probably leave there after 6 pm - after the last staff member had gone home. This was six days a week. By the weekend, I'd be tired but thought nothing of it. Keep doing that for six months and you would be burnt out, just as everyone had told me.

Now, this next episode usually happened about 3 days a week; I would wait for Tony Raj to show up in the morning to sign the cheques. On the mornings he showed up, not all the cheques that we needed to be signed were signed. He'd only sign a few, and of course, he'd interview some people then he'd rush off. You wouldn't see him for the rest of the day, sometimes the rest of the week, depending on whether he was in Australia, Singapore or somewhere else.

After about eight weeks working at Just Phones, I got to know the whole industry reasonably well, especially the smaller suppliers, people who sold batteries, accessories, leather cases, and the repairers etc. I was getting used to hearing the same story from them as I had from others.

They'd say, "Tony Raj always gives us some bullshit story about payment. I'll pay you next week or the cheque is in the mail."

It's not that he had no money, he just didn't like paying his bills on time. Believe me, I used to open his mail and the Telstra/Optus dividends were huge. I knew the income he got. Most times it ran into thousands of dollars a month just from airtime revenues alone, for doing nothing really. That was the nature of the beast back then.

I would go home each day and tell Deirdre all types of stories about the industry. I was starting to learn and understand that the mobile phone industry was beginning to boom. There was a lot of money to be made, something a musician never knew about or understood. But I learned quickly.

I kept saying to Deirdre, "After eight weeks of working at Just Phones, I know Tony Raj much better now. I do not believe a word he said, especially about selling me one or two of his shops. He's not even paying me the decent wage as he had promised. I should be earning a lot more instead of the lousy $300 a week I was getting."

Yes, I used to get an extra $50 or $60 commission from my weekly sales, but that was crappy money for the hours I worked. It was just an average wage that's all it was. The telecommunications business was exploding, someone was making a killing whilst we all got paid peanuts. She understood my frustrations and would simply say, "Well it's up to you, it's your choice. Stay or leave. But what else would you do instead?" I was now hooked on that industry. Should I stay or should I go?

Deirdre had her job with the Greek community in the nursing home division at Alexander Heights, Dianella. She applied for the job as an assistant to the accountant and got it. She was earning a decent wage about $400 a week compared to me. She was happy there and I wasn't happy where I was.

During the first weeks of learning how to sell mobile phones, an old adversary of mine from the music industry walked into Just Phones. It was Des Jose (RIP). He was a big name in the Perth music scene and managed most of the big bands here. He owned the "Rock Exchange" band booking agency, another big name in Perth. I quickly ducked out of sight and waited for him to leave. It was like a bad dream, it felt surreal, a very dreadful moment in my life. Remember, this was lunchtime, and we were busy.

Donna, our blonde bombshell typist, saleswoman, efficient phone programmer, stock controller, and chief bottle washer entered the back room where I was hiding and yelled at me to come out and serve. There were many customers waiting. I wasn't going to let Des Jose see me serving customers; it would have been too degrading for me. I was so embarrassed; I was going to walk out later and never come back to work as a day gig salesman. No, I didn't want to go through that scenario again. To my luck, Des Jose left the shop within 10 minutes of arriving and I was back on the floor, just another day gig salesman.

At Just Phones, Tony Raj had 8 different mobile phones we used as demonstration phones. Apparently, each wholesaler gave him one new model to use for demonstration purposes regularly. As I mentioned before, there was a beautiful young blonde lady by the name of Donna working there. She had been there for 18 months. She was sort of Tony

Raj's secretary and a salesperson. She used to program all the phones for us. Tony Raj also gave her the key to the large safe where all the mobile phones were kept. If you sold a mobile phone, she would get you a new one from the safe and program it for you. That's why I never learned to program mobile phones.

Now, after about two months of working for Tony Raj, I was not a happy man. I knew the guy backwards by now. He was full of promises and never meant a word he said about selling me some of his shops or becoming his General Manager. As soon as you reached the target he set for you for the month, he'd change them or get rid of you. That was one of the reasons why he was always interviewing people and changing staff. The warning bells were starting to ring aloud in my head. Danger, Danger! You could be next. I was not happy and what do you do when you're not happy? Well, you do something about it or shut up. It was a waiting game!

Chapter 5

Meeting Charles

One morning whilst driving to work, I saw a man on a small ladder doing some repairs to the front plate glass window on a building in Fitzgerald Street, and below him clearly was the lettering 'FOR LEASE'. I quickly turned the car around and went back to the building, pulled up, and introduced myself to the owner, Charles. I asked him how much he wanted for the building per week.

I nearly fell over backward when he said $600 per week. Now this building was at 281 Fitzgerald Street. Remember, Just Phones where I worked for Tony Raj, was at No 1 Fitzgerald Street. Red lights were flashing in my head, something was yelling out 'it's not a good idea'. Too close to Just Phones, too expensive, too dangerous, and too **Risky**. I had a small camera with me. I took a photo to show Deirdre the building.

Charles showed me around the building. It was twice as big as the Just Phones building. I immediately fell in love with the place. I suddenly felt an emotional attachment to the building. It just felt good.

I explained to Charles, I didn't need all this space. It is way too big for what I needed. The two small front rooms totalling about 45 square metres were all I needed. Even though there was not a door between the two rooms, it would be perfect. The back half of the building was about 180 square metres.

I said to Charles, "I could take the two small front rooms, but I don't need the rest of the building."

To my surprise, he said to me, "There were two other young artists looking at the building too." He was meeting them that afternoon. They also didn't need the two front rooms and were trying to negotiate a cheaper rent from him.

Charles said, "Let me talk to these guys this afternoon, and I will call you later with the outcome." I was quietly excited. Charles rang me at Just Phones that afternoon after speaking to those guys.

"The government grant did not come through for these guys, so they have pulled out of the lease agreement. I feel sorry for you as you sounded very keen about your new business venture. I also feel I'd like to help you. How about if I put a door block behind your two rooms and the rest of the building, and boarded it up properly? You could have that for $150 a week as discussed yesterday." I couldn't believe my ears.

This kind man added, "I'm sure there's somebody else out there who might want the back part of the building as it is." There was another entrance to the back area from the side laneway. There was also a roller door in the side laneway.

Charles said, "I am sure I can do this deal for you. Let me talk to my partner first, I mean my wife."

"Ok Charles, I'll be waiting for your call", I replied. Now that was music to my ears.

I said to him, "Please let me know urgently as I need to speak to my wife also. We might not be able to afford the rent even though she's got a good job. I'm trying to start a new business and I'm also worried about failure."

THE BUILDING FOR LEASE WHICH I SAW THAT MADE ME WANT TO START MY OWN BUSINESS.

He said, "Don't worry, go talk to your wife first, and we will have another chat tomorrow."

That evening I couldn't wait to give Deirdre the news. Ever the bean counter, she reminded me that one needs capital to open a business, especially a mobile phone retail shop. As usual, I pretended not to hear the "one needs capital bit" of her sentence. All that was in my head at that moment in time was, I wanted to open my own shop and show Tony Raj how business was meant to be operated. I meant well, but all this was with only two months of experience in the retail business. I was still a greenhorn, but all pumped up, ready to show my talent.

The next day I went back and met Charles. We struck up a deal, I could have the two front rooms for $150 a week. I negotiated the lease for 3 years with a + 3-year option.

And jokingly I said to him, "One day when I'm rich enough, I'd like to buy this building from you."

He smiled at me and said, "I hope so too."

We were now roughly in the middle of May. I thought, wouldn't it be good if we could maybe start a business in four weeks, in the middle of June? It all sounded good. I was on a high, so I went and spoke to an accountant.

My accountant said to me, "Mate, why don't you just leave it until 1st July to open your business? For accounting's sake, it would be easier to start a business on 1st July rather than in the middle of June, otherwise, you will have to put in your business tax papers for 1993/4. It does not make good business sense to open in the middle of June. Just leave it for two more weeks and open on 1st July." Which I agreed to.

I had made up my mind to leave Tony Raj, even though that was never my intention when I started there. This was not contrived; it was do or die for me on a personal basis. I felt uncomfortable leaving him, even though I was not happy there one little bit. I had to do it. My brain was twisted and my thoughts about loyalty started to kick in. What do I do?

I was having a "morals moment." I do have some morals. I also believe in gut feelings. My morals were saying it's ok, you have done nothing wrong. Resign or you'll probably get fired or die here. My gut feeling was saying, just do it, take that **risk**. All my stars were aligned. Demons were screaming in my ear, do it now or you may regret this for the rest of your life.

Chapter 6

Luck and Risks

With little time remaining at Just phones, I was hurriedly talking to all the representatives from Telstra, Optus and the other suppliers. I kept asking all of them if they would supply and do business with me if I opened my own retail shop? The short answer was yes.

"But be very careful," they all said. "Tony Raj has a lot of clout in the industry, and he won't be happy when he hears the 'Wendell is opening his own shop news."

Me: What would I have to do to become a successful retailer like Tony Raj?
Reps: Firstly; you must get a license from Telstra, and one from Optus.
Me: Naturally, my next question, how do you get a license from Telstra and Optus?
Reps: You must prove yourself to the Telco first.
Me: How do I do that, what do I have to do?
Reps: Show us how many phones you can sell and connect per month.
Me: How do I connect and sell phones without a license?
Reps: You need to go through a third-party.
Me: A third party?
Reps: There are other Telstra dealers and Optus dealers that you would have to put your connections through.
Me: And how do I do that? I don't know any other dealers!

Reps: The Telco representatives would consult with those third-party dealers for you. The third-party dealers would then update the Telco representatives on your connection status weekly and monthly.

The Telco representatives' short answer was yes, they were prepared to support me. It had to be transparent. They first needed to see how many customers I brought to the third-party dealers and so on. We also had to keep records of every transaction we did and show it to them weekly. I was so happy to hear they were prepared to support me. Another stroke of **luck** here.

On the other hand, we are talking about me opening a retail business, lacking capital, and not knowing everything about the telecommunications retail sales business. I understood my chances were not very good. However, being determined, I applied for, and opened an account with the big mobile phone wholesalers, Brightpoint, TelePacific, Roadhound, and accessory wholesalers Force and Cellnet.

Reps: You want us to give you credit knowing that Just Phones is less than 800 metres away from you?
Me: Yes, I would be so thankful if you did.
Reps: Do you think it's wise for you to open so close to the two other giants Meencomm Communications and Pocket Phones Communications who are also on the same street so close by?
Me: Wait and see. I have a good gut feeling I can break through their stranglehold.
Reps: Are you not worried about failure? You have only been around two months.
Me: Yes, of course, I'm worried. I have learned a lot in that time.
Reps: Why are you doing it then?
Me: Hey, do you think I'd put myself in a blatantly unrealistic situation, unlikely to succeed? No, I would never do that. I can be successful; I only need a chance to prove it.

I continued to talk to all the smaller accessory wholesalers, hoping they would deal with me. Nothing was easy because everyone in the industry knew, I'd only been a salesman at Just Phones for a lousy two months. Who is this guy Wendell Parnell, where did he come from? They all saw I was determined to succeed, no turning back from here now. It was all in for me. Everyone eventually opened an account for me with Talbora Pty Ltd, our parent company. Thank God for that.

It was mainly analogue phones in those days. You had to physically program the mobile phone so that the network would recognise your mobile number on that device, before you gave it to the customer. The program codes came from the supplier. Each mobile phone brand had its own codes. This was colloquially called 'hexing'. It was only much later the GSM network came into play. With the GSM network, they issued a sim card or chip to insert into the mobile phone, as they still do now.

My biggest challenge now was, who was going to be my third-party dealer for Telstra connections, and who would be my third-party dealer for my Optus connections?

In the first week of June, I gave Tony Raj my notice. I think he was aware something was going on but was not quite sure what. For the duration of the 10 weeks that I worked for him, he never took me out to a thank you lunch, never.

I don't believe he was a bad person, maybe just a little inconsiderate of other people's needs. I don't hate or dislike this man. He had his ways but did not see my talent. As a matter of fact, and to my luck, if he was a slightly different character, I might still be working there for him as General Manager or his Chief Executive Officer, making him millions and probably earning $50,000 a year. Thank you, Tony Raj, you're a good man as far as I'm concerned, I have no regrets. Thank you John.

Chapter 7

With A Little Help from my Friends

When I was working for Tony Raj, the Telstra area manager was Mark Langford. He helped me a lot by introducing me to Peter Langmead who owned a Telstra strip dealership called Pocket Phones Communications. Peter Langmead started his telecommunications business in 1988. He franchised his Pocket Phones enterprise and had four outlets. His flagship shop was also situated in Fitzgerald Street about one kilometre from where I was opening. Another big player was 200 metres up the road from me called Meencomm Communications. This company had a large database of Telstra customers. Their first impression of me was, "He's just another cowboy, won't last long, he'll be gone in three months," so they said.

(Mark Langford and Peter Langmead joined forces about four years later and started a new innovative company together which had nothing to do with Telstra. Their company was unique at that time. They sold devices that tracked vehicles, trucks, freighters, and semi-trailers for large trucking companies all around Australia, and I wished them good luck).

The Optus dealer manager was Michael Sealy. He introduced me to Horst, an Optus dealer who was prepared to put my connections through their Optus dealership in Main Street, Osborne Park. They would then report to the Optus dealer manager Mike Sealy on a weekly basis on how many customers they had put through their database that were from our new mobile phone shop.

The Optus connections through Horst were also noted daily by us. Michael Sealy eventually made recommendations to Optus that they should allow me to connect directly. Only then did Optus give me a license to connect directly with them. It was not a fully-fledged license as I would have preferred but a probationary license. I had what's called a 'minor license'. It was only time and determination that elevated my connections and got me a proper "licensed agent" status. Only then did I get a full dealer code from them. It was the most appropriate code, ETPH. Eventually, Telstra issued us a dealer code too, DVDC. It was a slow-going process, but I got dealer codes, sooner than expected.

For every connection made through Telstra or Optus, the dealership received a $30 connection fee. These dealers also received an 8% kickback on all calls made for the duration of that mobile number being used. So, the deal I had to strike up here with the third-party dealers went like this: For every connection I made through the third-party dealer, I received the connection fee of $30 which Telstra gave them. But they kept the monthly 8% ongoing airtime trailing commission. This could happen for up to two years, depending on the customer's contract. We were still liable to look after all the customers' future mobile phone service, repairs and problems. The customer remained on their database, not mine. Until I received a dealer code, I did not exist according to the Telcos. I was operating under the radar. This was the arrangement. However, we cut through the red tape rather quickly. Optus gave us a full dealership code to operate independently and, 'Boom!', we were in total control of our own customers in a hurried three months.

Everyone who knew about my new venture started to gossip and say I was opening a shop in competition with Just Phones. It spread like wildfire. That was not true at all. There were three big players nearby in Fitzgerald Street without me being a threat to anyone. The other two dealers were more of a threat to Tony Raj than I was. I was just starting up; it was a big risk I was taking. Call me the original "Mr. Naive Greenhorn" himself if you wish. I never poached any of Just Phones' customers either. They came to me. (Believe that and you would believe anything!)

By the Monday after my quitting Just Phones the previous Friday, word got out in the Telephony industry. Tony Raj hit the roof when he found out what I was doing. I got calls from many people in the industry telling me they have been warned that if they traded with me, he would take his business elsewhere. This put a lot of pressure and strain on them and me. I already knew Tony Raj had a big pull in the marketplace because of his buying power. He owned three very popular shops in the metropolitan area for years.

During that time, what nobody knew was, I had no spare capital to buy mobile phones or anything else for that matter. I only had my credit card and I had to start paying two weeks' rent to Charles from the second week of June as agreed. That was $300 from my last week's pay from Just Phones.

My next meeting was with the Optus dealer Horst in Main Street, Osborne Park. Thankfully, they were happy to sell me two mobile phones on credit card. Peter Langmead sold me two Nokias and two Motorolas, paid with my credit card. I also managed to buy two Telstra branded phones from a Telstra Shop, also on a credit card. One each for Ben and myself.

EXAMPLE OF TWO NOKIA MODELS WE USED TO SELL

We now had a premises with a stock of eight mobile phones, and an empty shop! Not even one cabinet in it, nothing. Just plain walls and linoleum on the floor. The second room had a sink and tap, which became my office.

During all this manoeuvring and my quitting Just Phones, I had already made friends with Ben Stuckey from day one. I asked him two weeks prior to me leaving Tony Raj, how was his commission structure panning out with his job.

He said his best week was last week when he got 13 new customer connections. Most were friends and family who connected to keep him in a job. This was after five weeks of slogging his guts out. Sometimes he averaged between 10 and 12 connects each week, I could see he was clearly miserable. He tried like hell, but never got paid that $300 bonus commission.

I seized the moment and explained to Ben my new venture and offered Ben a job; come and work for me. I offered him $300 a week.

I said, "You can start one week before we officially opened on the 1st of July." I needed help from someone else in establishing our shop.

He jumped at the opportunity and said yes. I was happy because Ben was more of a technical person than I was, and he knew how to program mobile phones which I didn't. Ben got special training from Donna because he was on the road working for Tony Raj. Ben joining me was now the icing on the cake I needed. But wait, there was more bad news to come. Ben advised me the following morning that Naomi (his girlfriend) was not happy. She objected big time and was upset that Ben wanted to leave Just Phones.

She told him, "Wendell has no experience, no money, and this job might only last three weeks.

Just Phones was a proven company. "Don't leave," were her words.

Prior to working for Just Phones, Ben had little experience in the workforce. He'd done odd jobs here and there but never had a steady job. I suppose you could see her reasoning.

I knew she had a stranglehold on Ben, but I was determined to convince Naomi to agree to Ben joining me. I planned and invited them both over for a Sunday afternoon tea at my place in Dianella. This was a wise move because it took about four hours of deliberating and guaranteeing that Ben would get paid $300 per week for the next three months guaranteed from sales or from Deirdre's wages. She was paid $400 a week by the Greek Community. We had crunched our numbers and agreed to the challenge. That was the guarantee Deirdre had to give Naomi. Nevertheless, there were tears, and lots of assurances had to be made. Naomi gave in, accepting Ben wanted to, and would come to come and work for me. There was no other way I could have done it, unless Ben joined me, and he did. Praise the Lord for that.

We still had no furnishings such as cabinets or stools, computers or a fridge, kettle and so on. That was not my concern. I was more worried about signage and a name. We had three weeks before opening. Trying to open a mobile phone shop on the smell of an oily rag was not what one termed 'good business practice'. Determination, desperation, and being a little naive probably helped.

The week before opening, I went to Ross's Auction House in Mount Lawley. I bought two cheap black cabinets that had a glass front and top, so you could look at the mobile phones from above. There was an opening door in front of the counter where we stood. The cabinets also had a lock and key for safety. I'm sure the cabinets were from an ex-jewellery store that went bust. I visualised we could present the mobile phones to look half decent with white cloth padding put under the mobile phones we displayed.

MY BLACK DISPLAY CABINETS

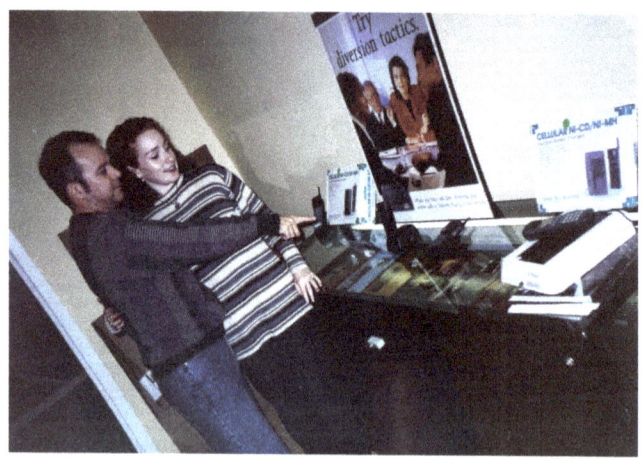

MY DAUGHTER CHARISSE AND ME PRE OPENING DAY

Chapter 8

Naming the shop 'E.T. Phone Home'

From the very start, the $64,000 question was: - What was I going to call our new mobile phone shop? For your information, in 1994, all the mobile phone shops in Perth had the word communications after whatever they called themselves. Here are some examples: Audiocomm Communications, Mobile Connections Communications, Meencomm Communications, Pocket Phones Communications, Eyelevel Communications, Mobi Communications, Nomad Communications, Let's Talk Communications, and Communique Communications. Too many communications for my liking. I wanted to be different.

Maybe I should call our shop 'Wij and Dij Communications' (Wij=Wendell and Dij=Deirdre, our nicknames) or 'Wendell's Mobile Communications'. Nothing attracted my attention by adding or ending in the word 'communications'. All these names looked and sounded too bland. I thought one needed to have a gimmick, just like in the music industry - something unique. I was looking for a highly original name, but I was struggling to come up with anything. All I needed was a name with some good gimmickry. Something the 'average Joe' could relate to. It was unimaginable that I could not come up with a name that would grab you by the throat when you saw it, or heard it mentioned. It had to say it all, something imaginative. I was wracking my brain for days without any success.

In the meantime, just before naming my shop and opening, there is another story that pumped my enthusiasm into another gear. There was this major player in the marketplace who had a unique story only dreams are made of. They were called In-Touch Communications. They had about four shops around the Perth metropolitan area I'm told. This company was owned by a gentleman by the name of Andy Cobb. From what I heard; Telstra had bought him out for a few million dollars and closed them all down. I dreamed of that situation and thought wow, that could be me one day.

Back to the name. How about 'Wendell.Comm'? No. No. No! I was frustrated and getting desperate. I thought of many names, but no, none were for me. All these names we threw around didn't have that original 'twang' to them. It had to be different. I was adamant. I didn't want a name sounding like the rest of them out there in the telecommunications world.

It finally hit me like a ton of bricks, I saw an ad for the movie, 'ET the Extra Terrestrial'. Yes! That was it! The name I'd been looking for. I was so excited. I decided to call our shop "E.T. Phone Home" with no communications behind it. Just plain old 'E.T. Phone Home'. It said it all. The Steven Spielberg movie had been such a huge hit. It was more commonly known than the words "mobile phone communications." I insisted I had to call my shop that name. I was told to be extremely careful by my lawyer Seng Fai Chan (Chan Galic and Associates) about using that name, but did I listen? A big NO, I didn't listen. But was I wrong in not listening to my lawyer? The answer is yes and no.

Yes, I was wrong for stealing and using a name that didn't belong to me, my apologies. **No**, because I took that **Risk,** and used it. By golly, it shot me into space and stardom very quickly, no pun intended.

THE BUILDING SIDE VIEW

Chapter 9

E.T. Phone Home Opening Day 1st July 1994

The 1st of July 1994 was the first day E.T. Phone Home opened for trading. It was the first day of the financial year, the first day of a new business venture, the first day of being excited as my own boss and the first day for me for everything that was going to happen in the unforeseeable future.

Both Ben and I arrived at the office at 8:00 am for a 9:00 am opening. We turned on the electric kettle as it was cold. Not forgetting it was July and winter. I bought some milk from the deli and had some tea, coffee, and sugar on hand. All the practical items came from my house because we didn't have money to go and buy a new kettle etc. I even brought the little bar fridge from home. It kept the milk nicely cooled and of course, we had a couple of bottles of water, beers and cool drinks in the fridge. I was very lucky that I had a facsimile machine and a printer that I brought back from Kuala Lumpur. Even though they weren't in the best of condition, they did the job for the time being.

Looking back at the photos, I didn't realise how empty and bare our shop looked. We had little signage in the shop, but it didn't matter. They were right, what a bunch of cowboys we must have seemed to be back then.

As you can imagine, we told all our friends, all our families, relatives, neighbours and everyone we knew, even strangers we had never met before, "Hey come and have a look at our new E.T. Phone Home shop in West Perth. We are selling mobile phones and all that type of stuff."

When you pushed open the front door at 281 Fitzgerald Street, you'd walk into a small room that was about 25 square metres. We called this room the showroom. On the right-hand side was a black jeweller's cabinet, and facing you was another black cabinet, both identical. You could open it only from behind the counter. The customer could see the mobile phones but could not touch them unless we open the cabinet with a key, from the other side where we stood behind the counter. The second room behind the first room was my office, a smaller room, roughly the same size or maybe slightly smaller, say 20 square metres. This room had a slide-up window, a tap, and a sink. There was no door between the two rooms.

Ben and I stood with a smile behind each counter, and exactly at 9 am we unlatched the front door lock. We stood behind one counter each, throwing high fives and the thumbs-up signs were happening. Schoolboys couldn't have acted any worse.

We were excited but no customers came in at 9 am. I guess that's how it was for the first hour or two then suddenly about 10.30 am, two customers came in to have a look. They saw the A-frame sign outside saying E.T. Phone Home mobile phones opening on 1st July. After wishing them good morning and telling them they were our first official customers.

I asked, "Are you in the market to buy a mobile phone?"

They said, "Yes, we are looking and saw your sign out there every day for the past two weeks. We don't work far from here."

We showed them our full range of six mobile phones. After about half an hour of hard salesmanship, we finally made the sale. One phone, our first sale, yippie, hooray! But we had to connect the mobile phone through a third-party dealer. So, after getting all his details and signing this guy up, Ben went into the back room and ever so quietly rang Pocket Phones to get a Telstra clearance on him. Once we got the OK, Ben would quickly and quietly, drive off in his car up to Pocket Phones, about one kilometre away. We didn't have a dealer code, or a license to put the contract through Telstra yet.

In the meantime, I would be entertaining these guys telling them a whole lot of bullshit just to keep them amused, without them being suspicious of what we had just done. Then Ben returned within minutes with the mobile phone as if nothing happened.

That's how we had to do business for the first three months. During the rest of the day, we made phone calls on our one-line landline handset from my office, trying to muzzle up some business. We'd be ringing up car dealers close by, or anyone we could think of. We rang up most businesses close to us. We looked in the West Australian newspaper to get most phone numbers. We'd let them know we were now open on Fitzgerald Street or just up the road from them. Why don't you come down and have a look?

Day one was a long and exciting day. We made two sales, the second one was an Optus connect, and again, Ben had to hop in his car and this time, he had to drive down to Osborne Park. We both played the same routine, I'd bullshit to the customer and Ben took the mobile phone to Osborne Park, get it connected, raced back, and pretend as if nothing happened. Don't forget it takes 10 minutes to drive each way, so I had to do a lot of entertaining, make cups of coffee, keeping the customer happy, hoping he's not going to walk out before paying. The last thing I wanted to hear was, "I'll come back tomorrow" from the customer. Usually, they don't come back.

All during the first day, we had a few suppliers drop in, also the Telco managers from Telstra and Optus popped in to say hello and wish us luck. We had a steady flow of people all day and boy, talk about running out of milk, we must've made 40 cups of coffee that day. As you can imagine, it was all part of the excitement, and it was a fabulous day.

Somehow it got much better at about 5.30 pm. A friend of mine, Joe Cipriani, walked in with a bottle of bubbly in his hand. I was surprised to see him.

"Are you going somewhere for dinner?" I asked.

"No, what do you mean, I've come here to celebrate the opening of your new business," he replied.

We quickly shut the front door. Then a couple of other friends arrived around the same time with a carton of beer. I raced next door and bought a bucket of Kentucky Fried Chicken and chips for us to nibble on. We celebrated all right.

At about 8.30 pm, the place was now a mess. We were tired and tipsy, and it was time to go home.

I said to Ben, "Turn off the lights, shut the door, and let's get the hell out of here."

Ben put the remaining four phones into the filing cabinet in my office and locked it. "We will come back early tomorrow morning to clean up and start again. "What do you think?" I asked Ben, and he agreed.

1st July 1994 was a Friday, the next day was a Saturday, a short day. I finally made it home at about 9 pm. Deirdre greeted me and asked, "How did you go?"

I said, "We've sold two phones, and we had some friends come round with some drinks to celebrate opening day." I told her we had visitors drop in all day. Some were customers and some were representatives from all the suppliers. We welcomed anyone who wanted to do business with us. We were happy to see anyone who dropped in. Everyone came to see how things were going. We were very happy with day one. I was a little bit tipsy, well maybe more drunk I'd say.

I went to bed and woke up at six the next morning all excited. I had a shave, showered, had breakfast, and went straight back to work. Ben and I both arrived at 8.00 am sharp. We both pulled into that little side laneway car park that we had at the side of the shop, which was ours. This would give us enough time to clean up the mess from the night before, or so we thought.

HOW E.T. PHONE HOME MADE ME A MILLIONAIRE, TWICE!

The parking space available for ETPH's customer are through the KFC restaurant

ETPH company's car with ET Phone on it. It is a way in advertising ETPH.

TWO PHOTOS SHOWING THE ORIGINAL BUILDING AND OUR ORIGINAL CAR

Chapter 10

First Break-in

Day two was Saturday, 2nd July. I walked behind Ben as he opened the front door. Oh my God, the place was in a mess. I turned the lights on, and we both looked at one another in shock. We saw a big gaping hole in that doorway wall, which the owner Charles blocked up, plastered, and painted the week before. This wall separated us from the rest of the building.

Someone had broken in through the back door of the building, smashed opened the plywood board, and opened all our cabinets with a crowbar. The filing cabinet was the only place that had a lock and key. We had nowhere else to lock and hide our phones at night. I was so grateful they didn't smash the two black cabinets' glass. We didn't have an alarm system, so the thieves were able to take their time looking around. They must have seen there were no phones in the black showcase cabinets. They robbed us of everything we ever owned, our complete stock. They even took the two beers we had left over from the night before. It looked like a mighty big disaster. More like a catastrophe. It was a dreadful, heartbreaking start to our opening.

I rang Deirdre straightaway and said, "Please come over and give us a hand to clean up, we have been burgled." At first, she thought I was joking. But she arrived within half an hour. I rang the police and explained what had happened. They said not to touch anything, and they finally showed up three hours later. We just couldn't believe what had happened, it was totally unbelievable. The place was in a mess, smelling of Kentucky Fried Chicken and beer cans overflowed in the bin. When I saw the cabinet split open, and saw the big hole in the plasterboard wall, it really broke my heart.

FIRST BREAKIN, GAPING HOLE PLUS FILING CABINET BROKEN OPEN

Then reality set in, and we had to clean up. The police finally arrived and did their job. There were some fingerprints on the filing cabinet but eventually, nothing came of it. Now at about 9 am when we opened the door, there was a couple standing outside waiting for us to open. There was a sign outside saying open from 9 am to 2 pm Saturdays.

I said to Ben, "Stay here inside, I'll go outside and have a talk to them."

I went outside and told them what had just happened. The couple felt so sorry for us and were sympathetic. They understood our predicament and they promised not to buy their phones anywhere else but from us. They would come back on Monday morning. They did come back later that week, thank God for that.

Throughout that morning, we must have had six or seven people who came to have a look, or maybe buy a mobile phone from E.T. Phone Home. Again, I had to face these customers with my tail between my legs and apologise for the inconvenience we may have caused them. After hearing our story, these people were so nice and decent, they simply said will be back next week so don't worry. We will come back and support you. That was so reassuring. Some came back, but not all of them. We couldn't touch anything before the police came, but we did manage to clean the mess up a little bit and get back to reality. I had to ring the owner Charles at home, who came immediately. He opened his station wagon, brought in some material, and repaired all the damage. He made it even stronger, put a steel frame over the damaged wall, and painted it again. He was so sorry for what had happened to us. This was the reality now. What do we do next?

At 2 pm we called it a day and shut the front door. I sat in the office with Ben trying to figure out what to do next.

I said, "Don't worry mate, all is not lost. You'll get paid as promised and we will open on Monday. I'll come up with some idea and we will trade somehow, we must. We've got the rest of today and all of Sunday to think about what to do. Just hang five, let's think about how to trade next week."

BACK VIEW OF GAPING HOLE

BACK VIEW OF GAPING HOLE NOW REINFORCED WITH STEEL BARS

Chapter 11

Damage Control via Media

I'm from a rock and roll musical background, and coming from that sort of background, you would do anything to get publicity, anything. First, I thought, I must inform the radio stations, the newspapers and TV stations about the burglary. I was thinking what can I do, what should I say? All Sunday afternoon I was at home thinking, and I finally wrote this long facsimile with a huge bold heading, which read something like "**E.T. Phone Home, Perth's newest mobile phone shop has been robbed on opening night**" blah blah blah. I was hoping somehow that it got the media's attention.

I spent all day Sunday looking up phone numbers and addresses for the media. I made a desperate effort to inform the television stations and every radio station, whether it was a commercial, private, or a community station. If I had an email address for them, they would have got my facsimile or email, the very next day.

Every local media outlet from Joondalup to Mandurah (north to south) got my facsimile or email. I think the only media I didn't send any emails to, was the media over in the Eastern States, and believe me, I was so tempted. I did manage to send one facsimile on Sunday night to Radio 6PR, a well-known and listened-to station in Perth. The rest were sent first thing Monday morning.

ET.PHONE HOME 328 3717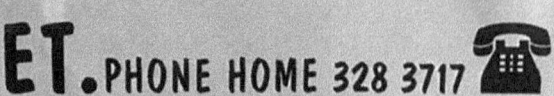

mobiles, pagers, faxes, cordless phones.
281 FITZGERALD ST. N/PERTH, WA 6006 ACN 009 125 428
FAX (09) 328 3713   PAGER (09) 324 9272

TO: CHANNEL NINE
ATTN: NEWS EDITOR
FAX: 345 1266
FROM: WENDELL PARNELL
DATE: 3RD JULY 94
PAGES: 1

Dear Sir,

The above store was opened on the 1st of July after months of hard work putting it all together. Well, the sad news is, ET. got burgled on the first day of trading. They took everything.

The point of this fax is to warn your readers not to buy mobile telephones from somebody you don't know. The average person is not aware that you cannot activate a stolen telephone. It is even worse for the burgler who doesn't realise that the stolen goods are of no use to him, once you report the phone stolen.

All dealers have a direct link to both Optus and Telecom, and within seconds of reporting the theft, these phones only have to be taken to any dealer be activated and bingo, we know it is stolen.

Please try and warn all your readers of this fast growing dishonest act.

Thanks,

WENDELL PARNELL

FAX ABOUT BREAKIN SENT TO ALL MEDIA

On Monday morning, believe it or not, as I woke up listening to the news, whacko, I couldn't believe my ears. On the morning news blurring out on radio 6PR, I heard them say (I only caught the end of it), "So please be aware of people who are trying to sell you a mobile phone because it is probably from E.T. Phone Home, a mobile phone shop who was broken into last Friday night."

When I got to work, the phone was running hot. We only had one line, so if you rang up, our phone was engaged most of the day. Everyone we knew called us. The media were in a frenzy. I was doing live crosses to radio stations; TV coverage came that day and showed the E.T. Phone Home name on the building. All the fuss was about the "E.T. Phone Home burglary." I couldn't have been happier. I hit the jackpot for once. All that damage control was paying off which I learnt from the good old Rock and Roll days.

In one interview I remember asking, "What do you mean by publicity stunt?"

I explained, "We just opened the business last Friday and we had a few drinks to celebrate the opening and went home. We came back the next morning only to find that we had been totally cleaned out. So yeah, that's what really happened, no publicity stunt here mate."

"So how much stock did you lose?" they asked.

I went on the defence, "I can't disclose it right now for insurance reasons (we had none). Anyway, we must do a stock take first to find out our total loss. I can assure you; they took everything."

Oh my god, if the media only knew we had four phones stolen, they might have not been so interested. Ben and I had one mobile each from the eight we initially bought, so technically we only lost four mobile phones. The other two of the six in stock were sold on Friday. So why would the media be so interested in four lousy mobile phones stolen? I'm sure my press release must have sounded like we had lost hundreds of mobile phones. Having said that, in those days, mobile phones cost heaps of money.

There, "You dragged it out of me." (Groucho Marx)

What started off being a tragedy, ended up being a triumph for my business. We ended up getting about $10,000 or more in publicity. That was a lot back in 1994. If you add it all up and if I had to pay for the same amount of publicity today, it would have cost me at least $50,000, probably more.

All these interviews on TV, radio, and in the newspapers only started on Monday, the day I sent most of the press release facsimiles. It intensified all day, culminating in the broadcast on most TV channel news Monday evening.

We were so occupied with media response and still coping with the loss, I forgot we had no stock. As an emergency fund, we were promised a $10,000 loan from Fay Ford, Deirdre's mum. That money would only arrive in our bank account three days later.

On Tuesday morning, it was hard to believe, there were about a dozen people lined up outside the front door to buy mobile phones from us. Yes, lined up outside the front door. I just could not believe what I was seeing. I should have taken a photo of that too, but sadly I didn't.

Boy, I was extremely happy about the burglary, but guess what? We had no mobile phones to sell. I quickly rang up Peter Langmead from Pocket Phones and Horst from the Optus dealership.

I said, "Look guys, you must have heard about the break-in at our shop over the weekend?" Yes, they were sick of hearing about it.

Speaking to other dealers later, most could not believe the publicity I was getting for free. I'm sure every mobile phone dealer spoke to the other on the way to work that Monday morning about our burglary.

I said to our third-party dealers, "We only have brochures of all the phones that you guys sold us."

I pleaded and said, "I'll pay you by Friday, but right now we have customers waiting for phones, can we facsimile you all the information and their driver's license details and come pick up the phones within 10 or 15 minutes of sending you the facsimile?"

They agreed to this because it was a sale on their dealer code, and it made their sales look good, even though the Telco representatives knew what was going on. They also made good money on the ongoing airtime commissions. We got a lousy $30 per customer for all that running around, but it covered our expenses in a small way. That was a win-win situation for all. That's how we traded that day and guess what? We ended up selling 11 mobile phones. Not bad for the third day of trade. Deirdre's mother's loan of $10,000 finally arrived and we continued trading.

I must say a big thank you to the Telco Reps, Peter Langmead and Horst. Without their help, my telecommunications business life would have been very tough to navigate in the first week of trade.

I'm 100% sure that the people who came to buy phones from E.T. Phone Home did not come because they liked me or Ben. They came purely for that name. The name not only paid dividends in the long run, but it also helped me to stall the customers from walking out of the shop whilst Ben was picking up their mobile phones from the third-party dealerships. As Ben left the front door, the first thing I would say to the customer was, "Can I offer you a tea or coffee, then go on to say, so I take it you have seen the **E.T.** movie?"

Most people said yep, I loved the movie, and my children have all the **E.T.** merchandise" etc.

Now, I knew I needed to keep talking for at least another 15 minutes or more before Ben returned. So, I added a little more question about the movie and ask them about all the good bits that they liked, and before you knew it, Ben was back. Ok, now for the serious part, how are you paying Sir/Madam? Here's your phone ready to use and thank you very much for shopping at E.T. Phone Home. Sign here. NEXT!

By the way, talking about signing here, we only had a cash receipt book to start with. Rather primitive but everything was done manually for the first few weeks, maybe months. We didn't have computers to print out a proper receipt, we didn't have all those modern gadgets that you have nowadays. No credit card machines, touch and go or easy pay. They had to pay by cheque or by cash and nothing else.

After another hectic day, I got home and said to Deirdre, "We now have sold 13 phones, all in three days. That represents $390 income, which means we can now afford to pay Ben $300 for his first week's wages. We can also pay $90 towards the rent, which was $150 a week. Hooray! I couldn't believe we were finally making money. We should have made more money by having add-ons like leather cases, batteries, or antennas, but we didn't have any because we didn't have the money to buy them. I guess that's how the cookie crumbles. It was all a good learning curve.

By the way, another stroke of good luck came my way about four weeks after the break-in. My credit card company refunded me all the money I paid the four stolen mobile phones. What can I say?!

Chapter 12

Ben and I Wore Cheap Suits

Ben and I bought $99 cheap suits to look different from the other strip dealers. Most dealers wore neat casual clothes at their shops. We were so enthusiastic about our business, we wanted to look like real professional salesmen. It also made Ben look important to his parents like he had an important office position somewhere. Both his parents were medical doctors.

Ben and his girlfriend Naomi had a rather strange relationship. She depended on Ben for everything, I mean everything.

On one quiet day, she rang him up and said, "My car won't start, will you come and help me?"

Obviously, he said, "Yes, sure just a minute", and he asked me if he could take an hour off to go and help her. Of course, I couldn't say no but I asked him what the problem was.

"She's got a flat battery" he said.

I asked Ben if she was in the RAC (Roadside Assistance Centre) and he said, "Yes."

I said, "Why doesn't she call the RAC and see what happens?" Fremantle from where we were situated was about 16 kilometres away.

So, Ben said to Naomi, "Wendell suggested you call the RAC."

I heard her from three feet away telling him off. Ben, good naturedly, finally called the RAC for her and got her car started. The next day he told me Naomi thinks I'm turning him against her. She claimed I didn't like her which we both knew was untrue. Anyway, from that day onwards I don't think she liked me anymore. They ended up marrying and had two lovely daughters Dominic and Madeleine. Like all good marriages, they are now divorced.

BEN AND I ON TOP OF THE WORLD AFTER SUCCESS FOLLOWING THE BREAKIN PUBLICITY

Our Patch

A little more about our building and the surrounding area. It was a single-story building with two frontages. Fitzgerald Street was the main road in the front of the building, and there was another narrow street called Eden Street, at the back of the building. We had a driveway between our building and the building next door. Our building was about 50 metres long and about 10 metres wide. There were toilets right out the back towards Eden Street. Right next door was Kentucky Fried Chicken, (now closed and demolished). Across the road from KFC was a very well-known hotel, The Hyde Park Hotel owned by Athol Higgins (RIP).

Athol was one of my first customers. A lovely man who sadly passed away about 18 months after we opened. There were also Torres Butchers around the corner at the traffic lights, diagonally opposite the Hyde Park Hotel. I'm telling you all this because they also patronised my business.

Frank Torres (RIP), like Athol Higgins, enjoyed leaving their businesses occasionally and coming over for a chat and to learn how to use their newly purchased mobile phones. These guys were the Godfathers of our area. Not in the 'mafia' sense, but both had been there a long time and were known by everyone in the surrounding suburbs. They certainly practiced the saying "support your local businesses" first. The true epitome of businessmen.

HYDE PARK HOTEL (CURRENT PHOTO)

Many a time, when our female staff were alone in the shop and if they felt threatened by creepy customers, they had a coded dial to Torres. The butchers would come running around the corner, wielding their butcher's knives, ready to help defend the girls. Upon seeing these burly Italian brutes, these creepy customers would soon depart our shop, empty-handed. Thank you to these lovely, kind butchers.

Poor Ben would be stuck with Athol and Frank asking him how to use their mobile phones. It was common knowledge that a few drug deals were being conducted in the Hyde Park Hotel car park daily. We were not privy to this information at that time.

When the wheels started to turn, our new business enterprise was all we were focused on, nothing else.

After the break-in, it was suggested by the Police we should invest in an alarm monitoring system. Great advice but that was going to set me back another $1000 or more, which I didn't have. But yes, I took their advice seriously and got one put in within a week after the first break-in.

Our area was not what you would call a "busy foot traffic strip for business". In fact, it was a very quiet area with a few specialist shops. There was a second-hand record shop (Bower Birds) diagonally across the road from us, and an expensive camera store five doors down which looked like a prison. It was fortified alright, we later found out why. They were also a victim of many break-ins. There was a chemist next to Torres Butchers on the corner. Some curtain fabric places and mostly offices all around our area. I forgot to mention the famous Italian Club, and the popular Northline Travel Agency were close by too.

We were at 281 Fitzgerald Street. One kilometre down the road to my right was Just Phones, at No 1 Fitzgerald Street. At the next set of lights, about 200 metres to my left was another mobile phone shop called Meencomm Communications. Another 700 metres past Meencomm Communications was Pocket Phones Communications.

So, here's little E.T. Phone Home, squeezed in between three well-established giants, all waiting to see when I would go under. They didn't think I would survive the first three months, especially with the strangle hold Tony Raj had on the big Telcos.

Knowing what I know today, I would never have opened a telecommunication store with all that competition around my area. As I mentioned before, we were plain 'Naive Green Horns.'

After the fanfare of the big break-in, getting all that publicity, and the razzamatazz, it was back to business as usual. We did get a damn good push start into the industry. One day, if I ever meet this person who broke into E.T. Phone Home that night on 1st July 1994, I will buy him a carton of beer. No, make it six cartons, LOL.

Back to the Story

Ben and I were always busy trying to come up with gimmicks to attract customers. At that time, we did not have a large advertising budget. We were cold calling all day unless there was a customer in the store. Someone gave me a desk and chair; they were throwing it out. I made a small office in the second room which housed the facsimile machine, kettle and the small bar fridge.

We used to spend hours in that room, brainstorming. In the first month, we were moving mobile phones alright. My daughter Charisse and I worked out a business plan to sell two mobile phones a day or 50 a month, which represented $1500 per month income. It paid Ben's wages and half the rent. By the end of July, we had 90 connections at $30 per connection. That was $2700 income, not bad I thought. It covered my wage, Ben's wage, and the rent, and I was delighted. This was all done through third-party Telcos.

Remember there's a trailing commission of 8% we were missing out on here. These connection figures were verified by the Telco Reps who kept an eye on how I was going. We had this large green logbook that the old accountants used to use. We recorded every customer there, line by line. Name, address, date purchased, make and model of the phone purchased, IMEI number (serial number), and mobile number. It was marked with a capitol 'T' for Telstra or an 'O' for Optus. Vodaphone was not on the scene yet. There was no way we were not going to get paid for that hard work. We knew every customer by first name. George Harding from Acton Real Estate Agency drove all the way from Claremont to buy his first mobile phone from us. I will go into details later. We also attracted some real nutters. I have set aside some pages for the 'Nutters and Con-Men stories' chapter. By the way, we were situated in a suburb called West Perth, a decent suburb really, but with many drug addicts loitering in the area. Something we found out in time.

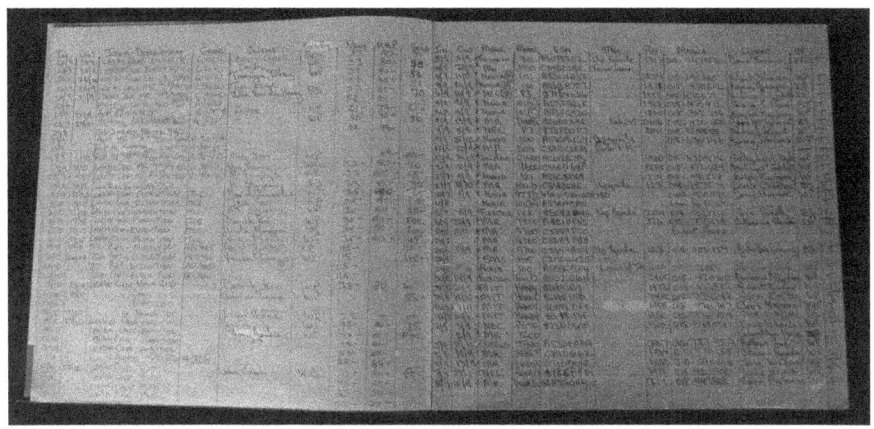

THE ORIGINAL ACCOUNTING BOOK

Our Lord and Masters

Mike Bryant and Geoff Ridgwell were two Englishman that looked after Telstra's interest in Western Australia. When we first started E.T. Phone Home in 1994, Mike Bryant was the State Manager, and Geoff Ridgwell was the area manager representative. Geoff took over from Mark Langford.

If you ever wanted a free lunch, all you had to do was ring Mike Bryant or tell Geoff Ridgwell you were not happy about something, and Mike would take you straight out to lunch. This could happen at the drop of a hat, no arguments. Generally, you'd come out with a happy result. However minute the problem you may have had, Mike would fix it, plus you'd have a beautiful lunch accompanied by the best wines. Yes indeed. Those were the days when Telstra spent money on us.

Chapter 13

These are two delightful stories:
The Beatles Dolls

Do you remember those days when there were door-to-door salespeople annoying you almost daily? We used to have a sign saying 'No Hawkers', but it did not stop them from trying their luck. You'd have to feel sorry for them. Just like us, they were new, and they were having a go at selling. Most sellers were either back packers or students that didn't speak English very well.

One sunny afternoon, who else, but an Irish man called Patrick McMahon walked into our shop carrying a large suitcase. He introduced himself and wanted to know if we liked The Beatles.

"Yes, of course." Everyone liked The Beatles. I jumped in before he said another word. "Are you here to buy a mobile phone from us?" Knowing all along he was going to try and sell us something.

He said he needed one but needed to sell some of his products first. Another "this is my first day in selling these new products story" coming up, I could tell. I'll never know why, but somehow, all these new startups would target us. If I had to guess, it was the name E.T. Phone Home that attracted them.

He opened his suitcase. Wrapped in plastic sleeves were four individually wrapped up 'Beatles' dolls wearing the 'Seargent Pepper's

Lonely Hearts Club Band' outfit. They were about 40 centimetres high. These dolls were made of good fabric and looked very attractive. We must have been showing signs of interest in buying. You couldn't help but love them.

He told us that the four Beatles, John, Paul, George and Ringo were sold as one set, and he was asking for $300 a set. I fell in love with them at first sight and I wanted a set. So how?

The 'Wendell bartering mode' kicked in and I went for it straight away. "Patrick, I won't give you some crappy story about it being too expensive, I don't think they are expensive at all, (he probably bought them for 50 bucks a set). As a matter of fact, I think they are worth much more. So, here's my offer. We have this beautiful, refurbished Motorola Micro Tac mobile phone which we are selling for $599. It is less than 3 months old, and I'll give you a warranty for another 12 months. I'm happy to make a fair swap, two sets of your Beatles Dolls for this mobile phone, what do you say?"

Typical Irishman, he had to give me a long sermon which went on for about five minutes, put up all the right arguments why the deal was not in his favour etc etc and finally said yes. Phew, we got him.

"One more thing Patrick, do you have your driver's license on you?"

He said, "Yes, as a matter of fact, I have." Bingo, we had another new connection. We traded-in that Motorola for $120 that very morning.

BEATLES DOLLS IN SGT PEPPERS' COSTUMES

Topolino and the Armani Leather Jackets

Two guys walked into our 281 Fitzgerald Street shop one day with about eight suit bags with Armani written all over it. Why they chose us, I'll never know, as we were just struggling to make ends meet.

One of them introduced himself as Topolino and the other as Andre. They said they just received their first shipment of leather goods from Singapore. They wanted us to see it and maybe purchase some. There was Ben, me and Deirdre, as she was visiting us on her day off. it was quiet and we had nothing to lose so I thought why not and agreed.

They opened the Armani bags one at a time and yes, the leather jackets not only smelt nice but were beautiful to touch. We were soon trying on the leather jackets and complimenting each other's looks. Now for the hard facts. We were told each one of those jackets was retailing in the shops for $1500 or more. That put a stop to all our excitement.

I explained to Topolino we were still new on the market and couldn't afford to buy any of his products, not at those prices anyway. He went on and explained to me that their cost price was nothing like the retail price.

"You should know that too, you yourself are a retailer" he said. Now we were mates.

So, after trying on the jackets, and getting the right sizes for each of us, Topolino said, "Wendell, it's your lucky day. Because it's our first day and I like you, how about if we did some trade-offs? You give me two mobile phones and you keep the jackets you have on." We looked at one another and before we said anything, he said, "Think about it, we'll go next door to Kentucky Fried Chicken and have some lunch, then come back."

"Okay" I said.

When they left, we were so excited about these jackets. I must admit, they looked smashing and felt soft and comfortable. Back to reality, these guys were returning soon, and we had to have a decision made.

Ben said, "Wendell, there are two Nokia mobiles we bought for $230 each at a fire sale from some poor dealer going broke recently." They were $299 to buy from the wholesaler and were on the market for $599 each. It meant we'd be paying roughly less than $150 each for these beautiful jackets. I could see both Ben and Deirdre were hooked, as was I.

When the two guys returned, I said, "Topolino, only because it's your first day selling these lovely jackets, let's do business."

I showed him the Nokia's and said, "You can have these two mobile phones worth $700 each, for the three jackets we are wearing. But only on one condition, you must connect these mobile phones with us here right now, today."

Topolino looked at Andre. They both shrugged their shoulders as Italians do and said "okay, It's ah alright ta. We make - a - the-deal. Maybe a some ah good dealer here." I hurriedly asked them for their driver's licenses and signed them up, the deal was done. Two new connections and an extra $60 coming from Telstra. Not sure about Ben, but Deirdre and I still have our jackets today.

THE ARMANI JACKETS

Chapter 14

Dirty Deeds, Done Dirt Cheap.

During the first two years of trading, my daughters Tasha and Charisse used to drop in and help us out. They were happy about their Papa owning a mobile phone shop, and of course, they had a mobile phone each bought for them by their Papa. Not forgetting their monthly bill attached to my business. They were at university studying, Charisse for some business degree, which I thought and hoped one day would be helpful for my business. Tasha was studying English and Theatre Studies, so she wasn't much help to me! Both helped us out where they could and did any and everything. Answering the phone, serving customers, mopping the floors, and making cups of tea. They were a great help.

Charisse frequently dropped in to learn about our business and was very much appreciated by both Ben and me. There's something else that she did which was very naughty and was encouraged, especially by Ben. We had done the same thing numerous times ourselves. I could say dozens of times, but that would be telling.

Ben would say to her, "Charisse, we need you to go to the Telstra Shops, buy some mobile phones and bring them back here."

She used her charms with the boys at these shops, and it worked. Telstra was selling certain mobile phones for $306. Telstra would run big ads in the newspaper. We couldn't compete with them. I used to argue about our disadvantage in the open marketplace with the State Managers of Telstra but got nowhere complaining.

Anyone off the street could walk into any of the Telstra Shops and buy that Telstra-stamped mobile phone for $306. You were then expected to connect it there. You didn't have to. We couldn't get hold of those mobile phones. They were exclusive to Telstra. As I've been telling you, Ben and I used to come up with all these scams.

Charisse would come back with six phones, and then we would on-sell them back in our shop. Now the thing with these phones was, you could not sell them for more than $306 because that was the price in the newspaper. If somebody drove to us in Fitzgerald Street to buy a mobile phone, we had to price match Telstra. When a customer walked into our shop with a newspaper under his arm, that was a dead giveaway sign they were shopping around. Part of our daily routine was, we'd buy the West Australian newspaper every morning, and write down every price that other Telcos were offering, this would be a heads up for us, especially when the customer walked in.

So why would you buy a phone for $306 and sell it for $306? There was no profit in it. But here's the answer; firstly, we get a connection fee of $30. Then we'd get their trailing airtime commission every month. The customer also went onto our database. We used a special Telstra code 'DVDC' upon connection. We would get 5% to 8% of all calls made during the life of the customer, only whilst the mobile phone was active on Telstra.

If we could have bought those mobile phones as Telstra did, we would have made an extra $56 profit, but only if we could buy these mobile phones at the price Telstra did. Obviously, we couldn't.

So yeah, that's what we had to do to survive. Technically, on-selling Telstra's mobile phones was against Telstra's principles. Buying phones from Telstra Shops and selling them back to the customer in our shop was a big no no. Telstra must have known this went on but did nothing about it. It just goes to show you how much they needed us, much more than we realised.

Think about It; if the customer made $100 worth of calls per month, which most businesspeople did, you got $8 a month from that customer for at least two years. $8 was a lot of money back then, I'll tell you why.

We used to calculate running our business on $4 per customer, for airtime trailing commission per month. Say you had 500 customers; you would receive $2000 a month in airtime trailing commissions. That was something we would have to work hard for. We did finally get there, sooner than expected.

We were there, at that level and beyond in our second year of trading. Our smaller airtime commission cheque compared to Tony Raj's, did pay wages, electricity, advertising, and the rent. I can tell you my first airtime trailing commission cheque, 18 months earlier, was $559 and growing rapidly. Yippieeeeee!

We'd also send different people to other different mobile phone dealers to buy some of their stock, just as we did Telstra's, at whatever price they were selling it at. There was a good markup on mobile phones too. A very good profit there, all the dealers did the same thing, I'm sure about that. That's why they called us strip dealers. Most of us were on some street or road. It was the strip dealer who was stripping Telstra of some of their millions in those days, lol! I'm sure their staff knew this went on, whether it was in Midland, Fremantle, or Joondalup. I'm sure they knew us from Telstra events we attended from time to time.

It was always preferred that the mobile phone you bought from the strip dealer shop, was connected at their shop. It meant the dealership would get the $30 connection fee, and you'd become one of their customers. The dealer would also receive the trailing airtime commission. That was what was supposed to happen.

In our case, that dealership would still make a profit on the handset by selling it outright to us. I would guess $50 to $100. However, we had to carefully instruct each person we sent out scamming. The instructions were when buying a mobile phone for us, use the same spiel each time.

Remember, always say, "I'm giving this to my daughter/son or wife for their birthday, it's a surprise." Plus, always ask the salesperson you are talking to, "Give me your business card. I'll ask my daughter to come here, you can then connect her, as we only live up the road." Yeah, bullshit!

Of course, that never happened. I'm sure, it has also happened to us, from time to time. It was all part of the fun and games we all played.

There you go, I'm giving away some trade secrets. I'm not proud of what we did one little bit, but believe you me, if you were in my position with my finances, you'd do any and everything to stay afloat, otherwise you'd go bust.

Most of the dealers in the industry swore that I would probably only last three to six months at best.

Chapter 15

Customer Service

In our early days, we did any and everything to stay afloat. One of our top priorities was providing excellent service. That meant sometimes, if a business customer came in with a problem, you gave them your full attention. They just paid good money for their mobile phone, and if they said their mobile phone is not working, you listened carefully. We didn't have any second-hand phones to lend them, not in those early days. We knew that it could take one day, one week, or maybe longer to repair the customer's mobile phone problem. So, either Ben or I would have to take our sim card out of our mobile phone and put their sim card in. Thus, lending them our personal mobile phone. Most times the customer had names and numbers stored in their phones and on their sim cards. Ben would have to download some of the names and numbers stored on their phone, onto their sim card.

Poor Ben would be stuck with that job. I was no good at it. He was the man. Back then, you could store names and numbers on the mobile phone or on the sim card. Nowadays it's all on the sim card or up in the sky with iCloud. We did whatever they needed and sent them on their way as soon as possible. Sometimes it took an hour and sometimes it took more. It was called 'exquisite' service back then; I hope they still do the same today. We strived so hard to deliver extraordinary service. Credibility was important to us. Also upholding the good name of E.T. Phone Home.

Now, these happy customers were so impressed with our service, they used to bring their friends along to give us more business, all because of how we operated. Can you imagine lending your iPhone to someone you didn't really know or had just met? All your passwords, banking, secrets, and not to mention those photos and videos (oops) you don't want anyone else to see. Let's not go there!

Business was good because we gave people satisfaction by helping them out when they needed their mobile phone the most. That's something that is probably much easier to do today. There are thousands of mobiles available for loan nowadays. Back in those days, we only had a stock of maybe 8 or 10 mobile phones, especially when they were all brand-new. It was a bit hard to comprehend opening a brand-new box. If we took one of those new mobiles from the box, it would automatically be deemed second hand, and that would be another scandal or catastrophe we didn't need. As I said, we gave them our personal mobile phone as a loan phone. That helped us build our business customer confidence, and it sure worked. Well almost, until you read about Amy next.

Amy, the Bikie's Girlfriend

I vividly remember this one occasion when this stunningly beautiful Chinese girl walked into our shop. She must have been about 25 years old. She was gorgeous and a very good-looking woman at that. Both Ben and I were drooling over her like schoolboys. We were infatuated with her. She was so pretty and asked a lot of questions. We didn't mind how long she took or how many questions she asked. We were hoping she'd never leave. Finally, we convinced her into buying a Nokia mobile phone which was the most popular name and brand at that time. Amy was her name and she ended up buying it. Everything went well with her Telstra application, and she left very happy.

About two months later, she called me and said, "Wendell my phone stopped working."

I went through all the preliminary checks like, have you checked the charger, turned the phone off and on, and does the red light come on when charging? All those minor things you try before you send a phone away to be looked at. She tried those things but to no avail.

"Come over, let's see if we can help you out here this afternoon". I suggested.

She came late that afternoon, and we tried all the tricks in the book to revive her phone, but no, it was dead. She needed a phone because of her work situation.

"You can borrow my phone" I said as there were no loan phones available. We had a very good friend at a place called Alltech. They were the official Telstra mobile phone repairer. I asked my friend, Jason Crane, if could he help me out and have a quick look at her phone and tell me what he thought was wrong. Otherwise, we would have to send it over East, and I'd just lent this customer my personal mobile phone. I was very lucky my friend was able to help me out straight away.

"Bring it over immediately, I'll have a quick look at it for you," Jason said.

I took it over straight away. He met me as soon as I arrived, took the phone into the back room, and he came back out to me within five minutes. The phone was in three pieces, and he said to me, pointing to the middle piece, "See this on the motherboard. It's had a lot of dampness, commonly known as water ingression." That's the general term for any phone that's got moisture or water in it.

He said, "Mate that's it, sorry we can't do a thing to help you. The motherboard is destroyed, you might as well throw this telephone into the bin and give your customer the bad news."

I rang Amy up on Ben's mobile phone. She said she couldn't come in until tomorrow morning.

I asked, "Can you please make sure you drop in and bring my mobile phone back because I need mine too? I'll explain to you what's wrong with your mobile phone when you come in."

She was quite okay about that, and the next morning she showed up at opening time. She returned my phone and thanked me for lending it to her.

"I have some bad news for you. Your phone has been for a swim," I said.

"What do you mean by that?" she asked.

"It's been water ingressed."

She got really upset and couldn't accept my word for it. She accused us of fabricating the story and called us liars. She stormed out of the shop, yelling out to us, "My boyfriend is a bikie and I'm going to send him over to deal with you."

It was disappointing to hear her say those words, but what could we do?

I just replied, "Sure not a problem, and sorry." This was a slap in the face for us in the early days. We wanted all our customers to be happy.

About two hours later, three motorbikes pull up outside the shop. Now, I must describe to you that the front door and the footpath were inseparable. They were next to one another. From the front door, if you walk out two metres further, you'll end up being hit by a bus on the main road.

We were on a busy street with buses and cars, whilst remembering we were a very narrow little shop or shopfront. Typically, as all bikie's do, they drove their bikes onto the footpath. These bikies had to make a hell of a racket and rev their engines up to intimidate us, which almost sent us crazy and deaf. Finally, they turned their motorbikes off, parked their bikes on the footpath and came into the shop.

Let me tell you it was scary. I was so stressed out; my knees were trembling.

"How can I help you?" I asked them nervously.

"You know why we are here," said one of them.

"Oh, about your girlfriend Amy's phone." I had to stay calm and handle the situation with empathy. Ben was looking a bit white.

This guy that looked like the devil said, "Now what's this I hear about Amy's mobile phone going for a swim? She hates the water, hates the beach, what's the real problem?"

I explained the situation to him about what happened the day before, how I took her mobile phone down to the repairer in Osborne Park, who then showed me the problem. "I showed it to your girlfriend, but she wouldn't accept it. She accused us of doing something to the phone and walked out. We haven't done anything to the phone."

This bikie wasn't looking very friendly at all, and that worried me. I had no choice but to explain the problem. Ben was standing there, hoping he'd still have a pair of arms and legs to meet his family when he got home that night.

"Wait, I'll bring you the phone and show it to you," I said.

When he looked at it and showed it to his mates, these were his exact words. "I told the fucking slut not to take her phone to work and leave it beside the wok she cooks on." Turns out she was a Chinese cook, and steam was in the air, which settled on her phone. She didn't have a leather case on it either. He shook his head and threw the phone back on the table and said, "Sorry mate about all this. "I'll have a talk to her and it's up to her, but I can't get involved here. This is not your fault."

"Mate I'm so happy you said that because you know we don't need to get into trouble with you guys. Especially when it's not our fault. Your girlfriend will hate me regardless, but I'm prepared to give her a big discount on a new phone," I said.

After they left, Ben and I looked at one another and Ben said, "Thank God, they did not beat us up first, then ask questions later."

Mobile Phone Disappearing in Shop.

One day I heard the front doorbell go off about 3 pm. I was on the phone with someone as usual, haggling some poor supplier for a better price. Ben was taking care of business out the front and we had an understanding if another customer walked in, Ben would poke his head around the corner, and I would go and help the new customer.

On this occasion, Ben poked his head around the corner but had a worried look. I went to see what the problem was. There was only one guy there about six foot tall, probably 120 kilograms, and wearing baggy clothes.

"Good day" I said to the guy and asked Ben what was wrong. Ben said he showed the guy four mobile phones but now there's only three left. I thought that was strange and asked the customer where the fourth phone was.

The guy answered, "I only looked at three."

I asked Ben again, "Are you sure?"

Ben said, "Yes, I'm sure." He gave me that look to say this guy was lying.

I explained to the guy that stealing was an offence. "Please give back the phone if you have it, and we will forget all about it."

The customer again claimed he didn't have the phone. I quickly went behind the counter and picked up the hammer we had hidden for times like these. I then walked to the front door, closed and locked it. I stood in front of it and asked Ben to call the police, which he did. I said to this guy to take a seat as he was going nowhere. I was trembling because this guy could have knocked both of us over with very little effort. I held the large hammer in my right hand and hoped he'd sit down. He kept insisting he had done nothing wrong and hadn't stolen any phones and wanted to leave. I stood my ground, stood in front of the locked door behind me, and blocked the doorway. He finally sat down and within a few minutes started crying. What was I supposed to do?

After about half an hour, the cops arrived. They asked him the same questions I did. Finally, they searched him and found a mobile phone in his underwear. They also found two syringes in his pockets. One of the policemen later spoke to me and said I was lucky not to search him as the syringes had contaminated drops of blood in them. They took him away and reported to us the next day they charged him with stealing. He was a heroin addict and stole from other premises nearby. Was the drama becoming just another day at work? I guess so.

Chapter 16

Second Break-In

We had peace for about six months, well alarmed, and a sign saying; "These premises are monitored 24/7." It was about 3 am in the morning when I get a phone call from the alarm monitoring company. "Mr. Parnell, at your shop in Fitzgerald Street, sections one and three are flashing a red light which tells us you've had a break-in. Could you please go over as soon as you can? We have sent a patrol car into the neighbourhood to assist you."

I quickly hopped in my car and raced over there and saw the blue light flashing away above the front door of the shop. The original brown colour varnished front door was slammed into and broken down by a car ramming into it (the new replacement door was painted fire engine red). The thieves must have run into the shop, smashed the Telstra cabinets, grabbed what they could, and taken off. This probably took less than five minutes. When I arrived at the shop 15 minutes later, the patrol car from the alarm monitoring company was already there waiting for me to enter.

Apparently, they are not allowed to enter the premises in case the thieves were still inside. So, they waited for someone to come and turn the alarm off and turn the blue flashing lights off. Two minutes after I arrived, Ben arrived in his pyjamas and jumper. He too got a call about the break-in from the alarm monitoring people. He looked rather disturbed and tired. It was our second break-in, but the first one with an alarm system. We shared our disappointment again. We had to get used to it. There was more to come. On this break-in we lost 14 mobile phones and a few accessories.

I immediately rang the police, and they arrived about 10 minutes later. They did their usual checks to see if there was anything familiar, they could keep as evidence. Sadly, there was nothing that they could do.

We cleaned up and one of us went home, got showered, changed, and came back. Then the other did the same thing two hours later. We couldn't leave the premises unattended, as we had no front door left.

Later that morning a second wave of policemen arrived. These were from the scientific squad that took fingerprints and did a lot of photographing of the premises. They hoped to find some evidence like other cases they were investigating, but sadly they found nothing. The cops can only do so much. Unless they catch the criminals in the act. It is almost a waste of their time.

To our luck, fortunately this time, we were fully insured. The next day we had to get in touch with the insurance people to explain what had happened. They wanted to know all the details, so we had to get the police report to them. We photographed evidence of the break-in together with the claim forms. We sent everything they asked for, the following day. Then we had to wait to see if they would pay us or not.

Were we going to be told; "Sorry you are not entitled to any insurance because of blah blah blah?" This was my very first insurance claim and from what others told me insurance companies do everything not to pay you. I waited and was stressed but we did get paid eventually.

I did my usual thing and informed the press and media about our second break-in. We got a mention, but nothing like the first break-in. The very first break-in was the one that I needed without understanding why. The second break-in I suppose was just a little extra free advertising, and why not!

Third Break-In

THIRD BREAK IN SMASHED FRONT GLASS PANE

About two months after the second break-in whilst I was having a wonderful sleep at about 4 am in the morning, the alarm monitoring company rang me to tell me they suspected there had been another break-in. I hopped in the car and raced towards the shop; except this time, I had a gun with me. I used to own a .22 semi-automatic rifle made by Givarm. I was so angry because in such a short space of time, I'd had three break-ins and of course, you worry not knowing if this is going to be a regular thing.

How about the insurance company? Would they ever insure me again? How were we going to deal with it? I had all these questions running through my head. In less than 15 minutes I pulled up and noticed that Ben's car was already there. I hopped out with my rifle loaded and raced into the shop. Ben had the lights turned on and the siren turned off by now.

He looked at me and said, "Oh my god you are angry."

This break-in was most unusual, and I'll tell you why. These thieves succeeded in breaking into the shop, but this time from the front of the shop. They had to break in through a very thick plate glass window which was about two metres in height and three metres in length. You needed a very large sledgehammer or a pickaxe to break in through that plate glass.

That is exactly what the police told us after they arrived and examined the scene.

"Wow, somebody was very keen to get in. If you stood in front of the shop, the road was only two metres from the front door" they said.

This was a very busy street during the day. When I say very busy, there was a lot of traffic passing. It was the main route of many buses from the suburbs. And even at about 4 am in the morning, if you were driving past, somebody would have seen these guys smashing the plate glass window. At least one car would have come past there every 30 seconds. You would think somebody must have seen them smashing down the front plate glass, but nobody bothered to call the police. It wasn't a large hole, but they got in somehow.

Ben and I had to clean up as we always did. By that time of the morning, one of us had to stay in the shop while the other went home, got showered, changed, and came back so that the other person could go home and do the same. It was becoming common practice for us.

It was very disheartening when two young guys are trying to make a business successful, and all the criminals did was make it impossible for us. I mentioned to Ben, maybe this is not the right business for us. "I don't have the capital to keep topping up mobile phones. I'm starting to get worn down by these break-ins."

Then, we looked at each other and said, "We're not going to let them beat us."

We opened that very morning, explaining to the customers what happened a few hours ago. So, the routine was the same; clean up, call the police, and ring up the insurance company. It wasn't necessary to let everybody else know what had happened. Those who came saw the smashed glass frontage. We couldn't possibly serve them because the shop was in a mess. It took two days to replace that glass. One of us had to stay there overnight in the shop. So, I stayed alone in the shop both nights. It didn't worry me in the least. I was angry and had my friend Givarm with me. I'm glad no one came in to surprise me on those nights, or I'd be writing this from my jail cell.

Chapter 17

Charles my Landlord

After the first year of trading, Deirdre and I were on a short break in Singapore for four nights. Charisse, my daughter, stepped in to help Ben. Apparently, Charles my landlord came to see me. Ben told him I was in Singapore and will be back in three days.

"Shall I tell him you came to see him?" Ben asked.

"Ben, tell Wendell I want to sell him this building, I can't wait any longer," Charles said.

Ben sent me a facsimile. Charles's asking price was $185,000. I read Ben's facsimile out to Deirdre.

You may recall earlier in the book I mentioned that Charles and I hit it off right from day one. I said to Charles maybe one day, when business improves, I'd like to buy this building from you. I absolutely loved how the building felt. It felt like an E.T. Phone Home building.

The problem we had at that time was we were negotiating to buy another business and didn't have the finances to buy both. It was one or the other.

Deirdre said I should call him and ask for more time. So, I rang Charles from Singapore and asked him to wait until our return. You can read the letter he faxed back. Charles returned a few days later and gave Ben a letter for me.

Ben had three days off upon my return, so I gave Charles a ring on his mobile phone. No answer. I rang again two or three times. Still no answer. When Ben returned from his short break, I went out to where Charles lived in Nedlands. I thought if I could talk to him face-to-face, we could come to some arrangement about financing me a little. I knew his address, so I went there, and I knocked on the door, his wife opened the door. She looked very bereaved and sad. I'd met her once or twice when they inspected the building from time to time. She knew who I was. She broke down and cried and she said, "Wendell, it's obvious you haven't heard but Charles has taken his life."

Oh my god! I couldn't believe what I was hearing. Reality soon set in. I did my best to console her, gave her our condolences, and left. I felt shocked and sick in the stomach whilst driving back to West Perth. I gave Deirdre and Ben the news. Deirdre was so upset as Charles usually picked up the weekly rent cheque from her, and they had a happy rapport between them.

What was I going to do? Maybe the offer fell through, but I couldn't talk to his wife about buying the building during those weeks. Was it too early to ask what she intended to do with the building? I thought I'd wait three or four weeks and approach her.

After this initial horrible shock, Ben said to me, "Oh I forgot to mention that Charles left a letter for you." Upon reading his letter, it all made sense.

Remember, this was after me seeing his wife. I opened the letter which read, *"Hi Wendell, I didn't know you were on holiday. You mentioned you might want to buy this property one day. Unfortunately, I could not wait for you to return, therefore I have sold it to a Vietnamese fellow who sells fabrics and clothing in Brisbane Street Northbridge. He knows about our agreement and lease. He is willing to honour it, Charles."*

In that letter, which to my regret, I don't have anymore, Charles went on to say that in his heart he believed that the building was meant to be mine. He was sad that he could not wait for my return but wished me good luck in the future. That letter was sad to read. To this day, I still get choked up thinking about Charles and the kindness and belief he gave to me, and I'll never know why he decided to end his life. REST IN PEACE my dear friend and thank you for believing in me.

Eventually, I met the new owner who told me he would probably store some of his fabrics in the back part of the large building sometime later. He already had premises in Northbridge. By this time, we were growing rapidly, so I asked the new owner for the third larger room adjoining our two small rooms. This was done successfully and made space more abundant. This new space became my office, leaving the second room to become Bens' office, the front room remained as our showroom.

CHARLES

ASSOCIATES

```
Wendell Parnell      LOGISTICS:
ET Phone Home  SURVEYORS OF COMMON SENSE
281 Fitzgerald St
WEST PERTH

Dear Wendell,

By the time you phoned me last evening Licia
and I had signed the offer and acceptance.

Apparently it was not possible for me to slow
the process as I had thought until 10am Wed.

After our discussion I thought it unresonable
for me to expect you to come up with an
unconditional offer - and I am sure you will
agree after thinking about it over night.

So at this point there is a conditional offer
and acceptance in place. Although it would be
expected to proceed, it could fall though.

You can be assured that if the offer falls thru
you will be the first to know and given the fi
opportunity to come up with an acceptable offe

Wendell, over the past few months I believe
George and I have encouraged you to purchase
the building but an offer has not been possible

I genuinely belive we have been as open and fai
as possible throughout.

        Regards
                  Charles -
```

LETTER FROM CHARLES MY LANDLORD

Theevin - My Security Guru

My brother Les had a friend by the name of Theevin. This guy was not very well educated, but he was a brilliant handyman. A 'handyman's handyman' so to speak. He was very inventive and resourceful. He could build you anything, I mean anything. I'm sure if you asked him to build you an airplane, he probably could have. Thank God he never did. His mother always complained to Les, that Theevin was a lazy son of a bitch.

My brother was a tree lopper back then, who employed Theevin on a part-time basis as an offsider. Les would tell me how brilliant this guy was with his hands. Theevin, with little effort, built Les a huge shed in his backyard. Also took care of all the maintenance jobs in his house. He could fix anything. He welded Les's trailer, replaced his engine, and kept all the tree-lopping equipment in top condition. This guy was Les's biggest asset at a very small cost. My brother was very happy with Theevin.

Well, after the third break-in, and now we had expanded somewhat into the third room, my insurance company, understandably, demanded I install more security for the building. I asked Theevin if he would be kind enough to come and have a look. I was desperate for some advice quickly, especially after the insurance company threatened to cancel my policy. I asked him, can he help me secure the building asap, as I needed more security according to the insurance company.

Theevin came to our building and had a look. He was an expert in undoing security, he understood this line of business well, according to my brother. Theevin said he could build me a solid iron gate for the laneway, front and rear. He then suggested cell-like bars blocking the front door, the small windows at the rear of the building, the second entrance or side door, the window above the sink in Ben's office, on the side of the building and the full front of the shop plate glass. Not forgetting there was also a back door entrance in Eden Street, we would then look more like a prison than a retail shop.

You may recall me saying earlier, our very first break-in took place from the back door entrance. They came into the building from there, kicked the plasterboard wall down, situated between the large empty back space of the building and our two rooms, and ransacked our little E.T. Phone Home shop.

After Theevin explained his idea about the prison look, I agreed with him. He knew best. He said he would build us an internal cage to store all our mobile phones. The cell-like cage would be built opposite me in my new office. I couldn't believe what I was hearing. A cage for our stock! I was dumbfounded but happy. Yes please!

Now for the costs. I was expecting it to be at least $5000 plus. Theevin said the material would cost me about $1800 to buy. He would charge me $900 to build it. I jumped at it.

"Yes, let's do it, when can you start?" I asked.

"How about tomorrow?" he said. I gave him $1100 towards the material required. I was a bit worried because Theevin also liked a drink. To my luck, he bought the material we needed and not the booze he desired.

I rang the insurance company and informed them of my plans regarding security. They agreed and gave me two weeks to complete the job. They wanted to see all plans and photographs in detail. I was so relieved that we still had insurance.

Within days, Theevin was out on the footpath outside the shop, welding and hammering away. I found it fascinating, watching him work. He was not trained in anything but could accomplish anything he put his mind to. He had some of the best welding equipment and tools money could buy. Forgive me for saying this Theevin, but I'm sure that his tools came from one of his previous jobs. Theevin was a naughty boy in his younger days.

He built two iron gates for the laneway, a prison-looking iron gate for the front door, and the same for the side windows and the back door. It was all built to fit outside our normal doors, windows and entrances.

The doors had huge anti-theft locks on them too. One thing's for sure, nobody would ever try to break in again and nobody did for a long time because it was very well made. He also built a two-metre high, by two-metre-long square cage that resembled a prison cell in my office. He bolted this cage deep into the concrete wall, which housed our stocks of mobile phones. This cage was a beauty. This guy was a professional. He knew what he was doing and believe me, he did a great job to keep the thieves out.

(I have a photo of Theevin's work. They are all in the photo gallery in this book. The current owner has since removed the iron bars which covered the front thick plate glass wall on Fitzgerald Street.)

We now had Monitored Alarms, insurance, and all our entrances were very secured by these iron gates. Before Theevin's protective masterpiece, we had had four break-ins. We did have a fifth break-in, the last one ever. They came in from the side roller doors, the only place we could not prison bar up.

But try as they did, they could not get into that cage Theevin built for us. They even brought a steel grinder (and left it behind), other power tools, and a long extension cord (also left behind). It would have taken them 30 minutes of their time to look for the PowerPoint. Theevin advised us to disarm the power points, which we disarmed nightly. You'd have to be an accomplished burglar to beat our fortress. And remember, we were always there within 10 to 15 minutes of the break-in call. They just didn't have the time. Bad luck.

It was a big concern for us as we were storing more phones in West Perth, more than ever before. Just like the big boys, we were now buying mobile phones by the pallets. This handyman was a genius. The insurance company was happy with the new security arrangements. Thank you, Theevin.

SIDE ROLLER DOOR ENTRANCE (CURRENT PHOTO)

THEEVINS' CAST IRON BARS (CURRENT PHOTO)

Chapter 18

Adelaide Grand Prix 1995

One of the many highlights I experience working with Telstra was a prize I never expected to win. The prize was a trip to the Grand Prix in Adelaide, the last ever Grand-Prix race to be held there before it shifted to Melbourne.

We had now been operating for 16 months, and our monthly connections were looking pretty good. The race was held in November 1995. Telstra held a competition to include all their dealers nationally.

Naturally, there was a catch. It always had to do with connections. They give you targets that are impossible or beyond your normal capacity of connecting.

Geoff Ridgwell and I got on extremely well. He was my Telstra local area manager and was an Englishman. I think he was the best Telstra dealer manager we ever had. He liked the way I did business, as I called a spade a spade.

It was the middle of July 1995.

Geoff walks in and says, "Wendell there's a national competition that I think you should enter." He opened his briefcase and showed me the terms and conditions required to win.

He said, "Look, you must have a go, I know you can do it."

I accepted the challenge and went into the competition. The main object was to get more connections than normal, what else! By doing so and reaching your target set by Telstra, you could win yourself a seat at the Australian Grand Prix.

Geoff helped me with the paperwork and set my connections target. It was 101 new connects a month for three months. What a friend! Back then, we were lucky to connect 100 new customers a month.

Surprisingly, we connected 400 new customers over the next three months. It meant we connected 25% more than our target. Mind you, I did manage to convince some of my family and friends to help here. In my wildest dreams, I never thought it was possible to have made this many connections in three months.

Lo and behold, in the middle of October 1995, Geoff Ridgwell walks into my office with a large envelope saying, "Mr Parnell you are one of only two winners from Western Australia going to the Grand Prix." I'd never been to any motor racing like that before and I was delighted, totally thrilled. But wait, there were more surprises in store.

Before the main event in the Grand Prix race, they held a Celebrity Challenge car race. I think these drivers probably only drove 8 to 10 laps. A Telstra-sponsored race before the main event. There were 24 Holden cars racing. If you won your nominated target set for you (which I did by 25%), your dealership was also given a car and driver to represent your business. They displayed your dealership name on the car and gave you a driver drawn from a hat. Our driver was Natalie Avellino, a champion basketball player from the Commonwealth Games team. She was big news at that time. There were 24 well-known celebrities driving. Look at the photos provided.

WITH OUR CELEBRITY DRIVER NATALIE AVELINO

THE GRAND PRIX TRACK IN ACTION

MY ORIGINAL GRAND PRIX T-SHIRT

CELEBRITY DRIVERS

I was in total shock. Less than 18 months ago, I was a mere salesman earning $300 a week. Now I was off to the Grand Prix and getting **E.T. Phone Home** splashed on a car watched by 100,000 people at the track, millions more watching all around Australia, and tens of millions watching around the world. Maybe it was there that Steven Spielberg's lawyers saw the E.T. Phone Home car in the celebrity race. I'm sure I carried a packet of Valium around with me. It was all too much in a short time for the little drummer boy, but it was a wonderful experience.

"What else did the prize include?" I asked Geoff.

"You get picked up at the airport in Adelaide and taken to your hotel, The Intercontinental. They will provide you three meals a day including drinks, whatever else you want, just ask."

I think we stayed there for four nights. Every day, we were chauffeured, treated to delicious lunches, and taken to the Grand Prix circuit for the warmup sessions. During the main race, we were fortunate enough to be in the Telstra tent, which was a luxurious experience Telstra could afford. Our evenings were spent dining at the finest restaurants in Adelaide, where money was no object. These were truly extravagant times. The whole Telecommunications industry was in its infancy. Telstra spent big money on their dealers, and they knew how to spend their budget. That's where I learned how to consume expensive wines, thanks to Telstra.

During my stay at the hotel, I had the pleasure of meeting a kind-hearted man named Gary Gould who happened to be of Jewish descent and hailed from Melbourne. Gary was the proud owner of Telefax and had several mobile phone stores in Melbourne. He specialized in selling and installing telephone systems and facsimile machines for big corporations. I later learned that he was responsible for installing the phone system and handsets in every room at the Melbourne Crown Casino, making him a prominent figure in the industry.

Gary and I became fast friends after striking up a conversation on the day of my arrival. He was patient in answering all my naive questions about Telstra's futuristic plans and how to scale up a business. He took me under his wing, and I am grateful for his guidance. Gary introduced me to other Telstra dealers from around Australia he knew from attending other conferences, fairs and events like that. He always introduced me as 'Mr. E.T. Phone Home' from Perth, then he would mention my name, Wendell. I suppose my nickname in the industry was E.T. for a while. That all soon changed.

Because I was from Perth, Western Australia, most of the eastern states' dealers had never heard of E.T. Phone Home.

The first question the big boys asked was, "How many shops have you got now?"

My stock standard answer was, "I've got one at the moment but I'm planning to open six more very soon" (which was a load of crap).

Their next famous question was, "How many connections do you do a month?" On this one, you could not bullshit. You would be caught out quickly. Without losing face, I told them the truth. They would then tell you their stories about how well their businesses were going and so on. Some less affluent dealers like me, would tell me to be careful because expanding too quickly could bring you down very quickly too. Good advice.

I had the pleasure of attending the Grand Prix in Adelaide and had a great time. I was lucky enough to also have access to the Telstra stand, which provided an excellent view of the cars changing tyres and refuelling.

The Celebrity Race was great fun. I met most of the celebrities. I've included a few photos. See if you can guess who they are. I'm not sure, but I don't think they have the Celebrity Race anymore. Or should I say because Telstra is not sponsoring it anymore, who knows? I have since only been to one other Grand Prix and that was in Monaco.

Throughout the event of the Grand Prix and my stay in Adelaide, I was able to observe, listen, and learn from my peers. Did I return home any the wiser? No, just hung over.

During lunchtime, I witnessed a man carrying a platter of 20 large crayfish halves up the stairs towards our Telstra stand. Each crayfish half must have weighed around half a kilogram or more, and they were placed on a long buffet table. I couldn't resist telling Gary that I would love to try at least two halves of the delicious-looking lobsters. I asked him how I could get my hands on them.

He said, "You aren't allowed two." He saw my disappointment and quickly said, "You can have as many as you wish, there are hundreds being served."

Guess what? I had no less than four halves. I was full, happy, and on top of the world, life could not have been better. Gary and I have maintained our friendship ever since the first meeting and he is now my personal and best friend in Melbourne. We regularly meet each time I visit Melbourne and we have had several overseas trips together over the years. I have met his whole family, and they now treat me as one of them. Thank you, Gary, and Telstra, for the Adelaide Grand Prix adventure.

ME WITH MY FRIEND GARY IN MELBOURNE (CURRENT PHOTO)

Chapter 19

Spielberg shuts down E.T. Phone Home

Just when business was running smoothly, an unexpected shock to my system landed.

I received a long letter from Steven Spielberg's lawyers in Sydney. The letter went something like this; "*Dear Mr. Parnell, it has been brought to our attention that you are using our trademark name E.T. Phone Home as your business name, and you are also using our logos in your advertising.*" Ben had come up with the brilliant idea of placing a mobile phone in the hand of E.T. in our newspaper ads. They pointed out laws that I was breaking and went on with legal jargon I won't bore you with.

E.T. PHONE HOME NEWSPAPER AD. (ORIGINAL PAPER AD)

The long and short of it was, they were saying, I was a naughty boy. I shouldn't be using E.T. Phone Home in any of my business because the name does not belong to me, it belongs to them. If I want to use their name, I should have applied for permission. I should have sent them a business proposal and if they so agreed, they might charge me $50,000 for the naming rights fee, plus an ongoing 10% of my annual revenue profits, etc. I found it rude and disgusting. I was shocked and stressed out because things were going so well for us, and now this! I registered the business name and thought as the name was not rejected, it was ok to use it.

I asked myself, "Why does somebody have to come along and screw it all up?" There wasn't much choice in the matter now, these were the facts, and now I had to deal with the facts. I explained this to Ben and Deirdre.

"Look, we're in the shit here because we are using a name that's copyrighted and we can get sued. Who wants to fight Steven Spielberg in court? We don't have that type of money." I kept it quiet and did not mention it to anyone immediately. I was afraid, especially if Telstra found out, they might see us as amateurs, (which we were). I kept it a secret for about a week.

Now this was way beyond my comprehension. The following week, I rang up my lawyer, made an appointment, and rushed over to show him the letter to get some legal advice. My lawyer's name is Seng Fai Chan. He is a Chinese Malaysian, now an Australian citizen. We met about 15 years earlier on a Qantas flight to Singapore. We've now been friends for maybe 40 years.

We met at his office, and I showed him the letter. He had a big smile on his face as he read.

He then looked at me and said, "I told you this might happen. I told you it was their intellectual property." He did tell me that before I first opened the shop.

"It's only three words out of a two-hour movie, no-one is going to miss them," I said.

"You can't use that name E.T. Phone Home," he reminded me. Did I listen? No, I did not. Instead, I convinced myself; that by using three words from the whole movie couldn't possibly get me into trouble. Well, I was wrong.

"So, what can we do now?" I asked?

"Wendell, let me think about it, come back tomorrow, and let's have another chat." More lawyers' fees I thought.

The following day, I went back to his office, and he said, "Wendell, I've been speaking to other barristers and people who are more in tune with Trademark and Copyright affairs than myself. You know that these are specialist cases. I have a good friend who gave me some good advice which is not going to cost you anything, yet. That guy owes me a favour, so he's giving me all this advice for free."

"Okay, what's the advice?" I asked intrigued.

"You are going to have to change the name of your shop."

Those words were painful to my ears, and I felt nauseated. My blood pressure must've gone up or down because I certainly felt like throwing up. Wow, here I am riding high on this name and they're telling me I can't use it anymore.

He said, "If you keep using it, they're going to sue you for every cent you've got. Wendell, I'm telling you, the best thing you can do, is to change the name."

I was now thinking fast, but stupidly, I was desperate to find a resolution.

"We could change the name to Elvis Telecommunication Phones Home. E.T. Phones Home instead of E.T. Phone Home."

That was another way of getting around the legalities of a trade name I thought. I uttered this loudly to my lawyer, feeling so big and tough, not realising how terribly naïve I was back then.

I thought it was worth a chance to try that, maybe engage in some dialogue by writing a long letter back to the Sydney lawyers explaining that E.T. (Elvis Telecommunication) Phones Home wasn't their name, it was ours, and there was nothing they could do about it.

My lawyer, under my instructions, sent their lawyers a letter outlining that Elvis Telecommunication Phones Home, (E.T. Phones Home) wasn't their name, either. We were just testing the waters, pushing my luck. We waited for about two weeks and sure enough, a letter came back.

They basically replied, "Sure, there's nothing stopping you from using the words Elvis Telecommunication, but the E.T. Phones Home implications, will cause you a lot of headaches. We will take you to the highest court and any logical-thinking judge will see what you are trying to do. Especially since you have been trading as E.T. Phone Home for the past 18 months." Their lawyers said that whatever I was trying to do was against the copyright laws.

Okay, after reading their letter, we both sat there and scratched our heads, trying to figure out how to get around this confusion. Seng Fai said I could win this case using the new name. He also said, by the time the case ended, I possibly would be dead! They had the money to drag this out for years.

The Spielberg lawyers said, "We strongly recommend you give up our name and we will put this whole affair to rest." They gave me four weeks to stop.

Eventually, Seng Fai said, "You won't stand a chance."

"What about all the money I've spent on advertising and promoting their good name E.T. Phone Home? I've spent money on T-shirts, sweatshirts, pens, pencils, letterheads, signage, and business cards?" I came up with a ridiculous list of things that I hate to admit were totally exaggerated. If you added up all my expenses for the E.T. Phone Home branding to date, including the signage outside the shop (not professionally done, only hand-painted), I think it was no more than $3000.

THE BUILDING SIDE VIEW

But I was angry and wanted compensation for my investment.

"Why don't we just write back to them and give them a list of things we spent money on and ask them if they could help us recover some of that cost?" I was sure from all the publicity we got from the break-ins; Steven Spielberg would have benefited financially in some way.

We both agreed it was a good idea and we had nothing to lose but try it on them. In the end if our attempts fail, we might have to accept defeat; and must stop using their name. But lets' just wait and see.

So, we sent them a list of all my expenses. I have no idea now what was on the list we sent them. All I can say today is that I still have one sweatshirt (sloppyJoe) left with the words E.T. Phone Home and the original phone number of E.T. Phone Home 9328 3717 on the front. My daughters also have one each. Only five sweatshirts (sloppyJoes) were ever made, one for Deirdre, Ben, my daughters and me. They cost about $30 each. Expensive in those days. It is a black sweatshirt with white lettering on it. That's all we could afford back then.

RUSSELL GILBERT AT T HE GRAND PRIX

MY DAUGHTERS WEARING THEIR ORIGINAL SLOPPY JOES

I tried to name many more expenses but could only name less than a dozen items, with a total bill of about $12,000. No way did I print 1000 business cards each for Ben, Deirdre, and myself. And maybe only 50 T-shirts as giveaways were ever printed. I won't mention the rest, it is too embarrassing.

I was young and cocky in those days and asked Seng Fai to draft a nice long letter. I detailed all the costs, and he sent it to the lawyers of Steven Spielberg. We waited for weeks before we receive a letter back from these lawyers.

In the meantime, did I mention to you we were negotiating to buy another business in the Garden City Shopping Centre Booragoon? Which is why we didn't buy the building from Charles. To my luck, about four weeks before all this 'Spielberg E.T. Phone Home name stealing' case took place, I bought a business named Phone Shop in Garden City. Luckily, that happened just before this Spielberg's business name upheaval took place. We were going to change 'Phone Shop' Garden City name to 'E.T. Phone Home'. Making that our second branch. That was my plan. Except we ended up having to trade by swapping business names the other way around. Keeping 'Phone Shop' name and cease using 'E.T. Phone Home'.

Continuing the Spielberg saga, now I was in a great position, even though I did not want to give up the E.T. Phone Home name, I had no choice, I at least had another name we could use that had some sort of mobile phone telecommunication credibility to it. I knew that we had a good clientele by now, and people knew us, so we could keep them posted about the name change and they had to come back to us eventually for service and warranty purposes. It did not matter what we called ourselves from now on. We can always put in our advertising.........

**Newspaper Ads read:
Phone Shop ex E.T. Phone Home**
(had to change names as demanded by Steven Spielberg)

We again received more public sympathy from these ads. What a win. Yep, that was a great stunt we pulled. So, we ran with that sort of advertising whilst waiting for a reply.

A letter from Spielberg's lawyers arrived at Seng Fai's office a few weeks later. Seng Fai called me unexpectedly one afternoon and said, "You better come over quickly; we have had a reply from them."

Of course, I got stressed out and worried by this alarming phone call.

All he said was, "I can't discuss the contents of the letter over the phone, I prefer a face-to-face discussion." Demons in my head suggested more bad news. I assumed that these guys were not interested in doing any deals with me. As a matter of fact, I was convinced this letter was proceedings to go to court. I hopped in my car and raced over to Seng Fai's office.

At his office, I'm rather perturbed and said, "Okay, what's the bad news?"

Seng Fai gave me the letter and said, "You better read the letter yourself."

I opened the letter, and in the letter was a cheque for 'an undisclosed sum of money'. Sorry about that, but I signed a confidentiality clause not to mention the amount that was paid. I get goosebumps even now thinking about it.

You have no idea how thrilled and delighted I felt. Mind you, the lawyer's costs were half as much as I received, but he was worth every cent. I still came out way in front.

Here I was, high in orbit, living off a name that didn't belong to me. Now they're helping me recover some of my costs to stop me from using their name. That is something I will never forget. Something I will eternally be happy about, and I'm thankful to my lawyer Seng Fai Chan, and the Spielberg Organisation.

I'm not big-noting myself here, nor am I saying what a smart businessman I was. I'm just saying that I took some foolish risks back then, and luckily, of all the risks I took, this one certainly paid off.

Chapter 20

Buying Phone Shop Garden City 1996

1996 was my second year with Telstra. Our new State Manager's name was Alan Sharpe. He was a nice and easy-going chap. At every meeting I had with Alan regarding Telstra business or even if I had a minor complaint, we'd end up talking about fishing, which was a good diversion. He loved fishing. These guys were there to put out fires, not start them.

From time to time, we managed to overcome some of the frustrations the dealers had with Telstra, and vice versa. We got on well, and at different times he would put me onto different ideas in business, which generally I wouldn't listen to. I never used to listen to anything, but I enjoyed working with him, and Geoff Ridgwell.

This is one story that changed the course of my business.

One morning I had an unexpected visit from Alan, together with our Area Manager Geoff Ridgwell. Usually, the area manager would warn me in advance saying he's bringing his State Manager along for the weekly visit.

I was surprised to see Alan that day. We sat down in my new office at the back of the shop for a meeting. After making them a coffee, of course,

I was curious to know why the hell was he dropping in and seeing me like this. Normally the protocol was, I would get a call from Alan's office inviting me for a meeting. I would go to head office and see him there. But him coming to see me! What's the catch, I wondered?

On this occasion, Alan said, "Wendell, isn't it time that you expanded your business?"

Now here I am, thinking I was just making ends meet, but business was going well, to be honest; it was going remarkably well. I didn't know it at the time, but Telstra was carefully monitoring my sales figures.

"Congratulations, E.T. Phone Home is going extremely well," Alan said.

By this time, we were at the 'Premium Dealer' level of Telstra's commission rate of 8%. As a Telstra dealer, 8% was the highest they paid to any dealer. Unless of course, if you had twenty or more stores nationally, then you negotiated a higher commission rate; the big boys were getting 10% plus. When we first got our License, we started off receiving 5% for the first six months. You would have read that earlier.

Alan said to me, "There's a guy by the name of Donald Black who has a shop in the Garden City Shopping Centre, and he is looking for a buyer. I'm going to recommend you have a chat with him. The name of the business is called 'Phone Shop'. They are only selling facsimile machines, photocopiers, home phone systems, cordless phones, novelty phones, and accessories of all sorts. Everything except mobile phones."

He continued, "There is a big demand for mobile phones in that shopping centre." He said Telstra wanted someone to jump in there at Garden City and sell Telstra products. The nearest mobile phone dealer was Audiocomm Communications situated in Fremantle, about five kilometres away!

Complimenting me, he said, "We believe you are the man to do it." A little ego booster here if I ever needed one.

The story he gave me was, Donald Black wanted to get out of business badly. He had had enough.

"Wendell over the past two months I've sent at least 3 different Telstra dealers to see Donald, to buy him out," Alan said.

The three dealers Alan spoke of were the bigger boys of the industry. They were not small fries like me who only had one small shop in West Perth. Alan explained that Donald was asking for around $150,000. That included the goodwill and included the stock. He estimated the stock was worth around $60,000, give or take depending on the time of sale. The rest was goodwill. Gulp!

I appreciated the advice and tip he was giving me but couldn't figure out why the bigger players didn't buy Donald's business if the demand was so high for mobile phones in Garden City, Booragoon. People like the big boys wouldn't have knocked it back. They knew the market much better than me.

So, one of the few questions I asked Alan was, "What's the rent at the shopping centre?"

He said, "It's only a 60 square metre shop, I think it's $5,000 a month." I nearly had a heart attack when I heard the words $5,000. Remember I was running a small business and now only paying $200 a week. Telstra wanted me to go and stitch myself up to premises that I had to pay $5,000 a month. Phew! Notwithstanding there was a $15,000 rent deposit in advance. It shook my foundations big time.

I thought, should I even contemplate talking to this Donald Black? But on the other hand, I was in business and had to take **risks**. My current business was doing well; I had to meet this Donald Black fellow to find out about this 'appealing new business' according to Telstra. They gave me his telephone number.

When these guys left around midday, I picked up the phone, rang Donald and introduced myself. I told him Alan Sharpe asked me to call him and asked if we could have a coffee to discuss the sale of his business.

He chuckled a little and said, "Sure why not?" I think he chuckled a little because I was the fourth Telstra dealer sent by Alan Sharpe to see him. He explained to me that this business of his was only a one-man show.

"Generally, my wife comes here for a couple of hours to help me out with other chores like ordering stock, getting change from the bank, etc.

I don't leave the shop even to have a bite to eat. I can't leave the shop and have a coffee with you," he explained.

"I understand, I'll come over anyway around 3 pm." I said.

He agreed and said fine.

I explained to Ben later that afternoon, I was going to the Garden City Shopping Centre to see Donald Black about the sale of his shop, Phone Shop. By the way, in those days, Garden City, Booragoon was the number one shopping centre in Perth and still is. They were the newest and most modern, with the highest rents nestled in a high-income suburb.

That afternoon I went there and introduced myself to Donald. I was dressed in a suit and tie expecting to meet another businessman dressed alike. He was dressed neatly and casually. Before I went into Phone Shop to meet Donald, I spent a few minutes standing outside looking at his display. It was totally unfamiliar to me. We all knew what a facsimile machine looked like, especially home phones, small business four-line systems, walkie-talkies, and all that type of telecommunication stuff. Then something caught my eye in the window. I later learned they were novelty phones.

Still, it was all foreign to me. We did not sell all those products at E.T. Phone Home in West Perth. We were basically a mobile phone shop. We had a few odds and ends of accessories, but in general, we stuck to the core product, mobile phones what we understood and were in tune with.

I walked into Donald's shop, introduced myself and struck up a conversation. In the beginning, I was asking all silly questions about his products in general. I was trying to get a feel for this guy. He was lovely and friendly. He told me he also installed telephone systems for medium and large businesses. If you need a phone system installed with sixteen or twenty handsets, you will ask Donald to install it for you. He was the man!

I'm telling you this now, because later, in our business relationship which lasted quite a long time, Donald would install phone systems for me. He would subcontract for me, but that's to come later.

Now this is the most surprising part of the story. Whilst we were having a meeting at his shop counter, I stood there looking like a customer talking to Donald. People would walk in and browse around looking at different products. Some people would come and stand near me to try to get a word in.

Donald would excuse himself for a minute and speak to the customer. He'd come back and say, "They were looking for a mobile phone. I don't sell mobile phones." He told me this with passion, shaking his head.

Now that struck me as being very odd because mobile phones were the happening thing at that time. I mean, anyone would have easily picked up on that. This little upstart me, picked that up quickly, and fast. Donald kept attending to people during our meeting. He'd come back and talk to me again.

During our meeting, yet another person or persons would walk in and ask, "Do you sell mobile phones?"

His stock standard answer was, "No, but if you go down to Fremantle which was about five kilometres away, there's a mobile phone shop there called Audiocomm."

Now Audiocomm was one of the big dealers in Perth at the time. They had about eight outlets and their core business was selling and installing car radios.

As we continued talking, another person walked in and said, "I see you don't have mobile phones in your window display. Do you have any in the back room?"

Again, Donald explained, "Sorry mate we don't sell mobiles, the nearest shop is Audiocomm in Fremantle." I was frustrated, almost tempted to jump in and say, 'try E.T. Phone Home in West Perth, about seven kilometres away!', or give them Ben's number. But I had to hold my peace and say nothing.

Here I was, a prospective buyer of his business, being interrupted by customers every five minutes. It was a little annoying, but I understood. I spent two hours there talking to him. We spoke about the industry in general. I swear to you, at least five people came in and asked to buy a mobile phone. Can you imagine my frustration?

At first, I thought I had been set up by Donald. I really did not believe what had happened. I said to myself, this is a clever trick. A good one at that. He's managed to get all these people, maybe some of his relatives and other shopkeepers to help him out, or whatever, to ask for mobile phones. I was trying to figure it out. All I knew was, while I was there, five people came in and asked for a mobile phone. I could not understand why this guy was not selling mobile phones. Was I in a dream here?

I asked why he was against selling mobile phones. He was not interested in buying mobile phones from a wholesaler, then connecting them to the Telco of their choice. Only after you had connected the customer, Telstra or Optus would give you a code reference number which you sent in together with a copy of their contract with an invoice to Telstra or Optus. With a bit of luck, 28 to 35 days later, you would be refunded your original handset purchase price, plus a connection fee of $30, plus the ongoing airtime commissions. This was a long and tedious process, but that was the business. Donald was dead against it. Not for him. No way. Too much hassle.

I went through the rent and lease with him.

"Donald, how much is the rent per month?" I asked.

"$60,000 a year, divide that by 12 and its $5,000 a month, plus outgoings."

I started thinking, Oh my God, $60,000 a year! Wendell, what are you getting yourself into? We were used to paying only $200 a week.

Finally, I asked Donald, "What's the asking price for your business?"

His immediate reply was, "I want $150,000, but I'm happy to let it go for $140,000 if you are serious. If you move on it quickly, in the next week, I'll take $10.000 off."

I said I found that price intriguing because my State Manager Alan Sharpe said to me you only wanted $120,000 (I was playing dumb here).

Donald said, "No no no, that is what the other three dealers have based my business to be worth. It's always been $150,000. I suppose if you offered me cash today, I'd even take an extra $5,000 off."

"Okay, well, I'll consult my partner and think about it and let you know very soon." I thanked Donald, shook his hand, and left.

Whilst driving back to West Perth I was trying to crunch numbers. As you know, I'm not a number cruncher, yet. I didn't quite understand that type of retail business. In those days, everything had to be done on a business plan. I had to number crunch, come up with a business plan and forecast sales for the future. Then you present it to Telstra hoping they think you can do the business there, only then they would grant you a license. It was Telstra who sent me there in the first place, remember?

When I got back to our shop, Ben was keenly waiting to find out what happened. I explain to him in detail everything discussed between Donald and me. Ben is a sharp guy, he's not silly, even though he had no previous experience in business, just like me. I think Ben was only 21 years old back then and he listened to me keenly.

"I smell a rat here," I said.

Ben being funny said, "Rat! What rat" as his eyes quickly swept the corners of the room.

I said, "Mate you won't believe this, but whilst I was there for two hours, I counted five people walking in and asking for a mobile phone. Therefore, it must be one of two things. One, either people were genuinely looking for a mobile phone, or two, he was so desperate to get rid of his shop, he hired people to come in the shop and approach him for a mobile phone while I was there."

I went on, "Ben, but my gut feeling is good. Common sense tells me, he couldn't have had time to organise these people, because I only spoke to him about 12 pm that same day, and I was there three hours later. Think about it. It's just not possible for the man to hire so many people to drop in on our conversation and ask for a mobile phone. All that to sell his business or to impress me!"

I continued, "I think those customers were legitimate. I'm going to have to talk to Deirdre. Now, we don't have that type of money."

Wow, it was exciting, believe me, very exciting. Just the thought of a shop in Garden City without competition, can you imagine!

Remember, we were stuck out in Fitzgerald Street, West Perth surrounded by three other large Telstra dealers, and as you already know, you wouldn't have counted 20 people walking past our shopping area in one day. They either came to buy Kentucky Fried Chicken next door or look at the records across the road in Bowerbirds. Some came to look in the camera shop or go into the butchers or chemist.

Nobody came to that area for shopping there. It wasn't that type of a street, a busy street for cars and buses, but not for foot traffic shoppers, like in other areas.

While I was walking out of Donald's shop, I realised what a great position he had in the shopping centre. The Phone Shop was right in the middle of the mall where everybody crossed paths. It was right on the corner of a large junction where people had to go past. I thought Oh God, how exciting this is going to be if we take up this great opportunity.

When I was standing outside looking at his goods, dozens of people walked past the shop. We're not used to seeing dozens of people. The Garden City Shopping Centre was a huge plus that came with a huge rent too. That bit really frightened me, and I had to deal with it. Okay, we will have to build it up and sell many phones to cover our costs, otherwise a big bust, but hopefully a big boom instead.

That evening I shared my excitement and discussed with Deirdre there was a great business opportunity to expand to. I knew the risks; we hadn't done much else in 18 months except grow steadily and we did show a decent profit. We only had one shop and maybe, only maybe, it was time to take another risk because I could see the opportunity that was there.

I explained to her about the other dealers who had approached Donald to buy the Phone Shop business and none of them were successful because they all probably thought the same as one another; he was desperate to sell. So, they all offered him well below the market worth. The money they offered him was under $100,000, which was a slap in his face. I explained to Deirdre that Donald said he was not budging from $150,000. If we could do a deal quickly, he would take $10,000 off, but for a quick sale only.

I wanted Phone Shop badly. During our first meeting, whilst I was talking to Donald, I think I had already made up my mind about buying

Phone Shop. One side of me was saying don't rush into it, it's a con job, you might get burnt here, and you'll be stuck paying $5000 a month rent for the next five years. His lease had two years left with a three-year option.

I rang Donald the following day and asked him when his wife was coming in to relieve him. He said she was supposed to be there at 2 pm. I asked him if we could meet at The Coffee Shop and have a chat.

"I have an offer to make to you," I said.

"Yeah sure, why not?"

At The Coffee Shop, I said, "Donald, by now you must have heard about E.T. Phone Home in West Perth. I want to expand, and I do want to buy your business. I have got permission from the bank (white lies at that moment) and my biggest problem is the limit my bank will give me. I cannot squeeze another cent out of them. Now, what I can offer you is $130,000 in total. That is for goodwill and stock. So that's my offer." I said, "If you want it, shake my hand right now, because once I shake your hand, I'm in all the way, end of story. I'll never back out from this deal."

He sipped his coffee, looked at me, smiled, and said, "You know Wendell, I'm going to take your offer because you're the first Telstra dealer whom I've spoken to, who is not a crook or trying to rape me."

Of course, I took that as a compliment and said, "Well, I'm not sure if these other dealers were crooks, but these guys are just shrewd businessmen that want to get a good deal. Knowing that you were desperate to get out of your business, they'll try anything, they're trying to screw you for every cent they could get."

I said, "I'm so happy that you didn't do business with them and you're going to do business with me instead." We finished our coffee and shook hands. Done deal.

I rushed to talk with my lawyer and accountant. Donald had to do the same. We were going to meet again in three or four days and start finalising the fine print and negotiating stock take checks, all that stuff you must do. We both agreed everything looked good and if we could clean this whole thing up in the next fortnight, we might be able to have a handover at the end of the next month.

Donald had to talk to the shopping centre and give them the news. The shopping centre had to then interview me to make sure that I could pay my bills, especially their rent. They were not interested in who I was. It's how much I have got. I didn't have money like the other big boys, so I met with the shopping centre and explained my situation. I think they accepted my story and were pleased because they too were desperate to get a mobile telephone shop in their shopping centre, especially a Telstra shop.

Now, because I was so keen, desperate, and inexperienced, I didn't think to squeeze the shopping centre for any compensation or to ask for an exclusive contract to not allow another Telstra dealer to open a shop in opposition for the next five years as I should have. I didn't know this was possible at the time. I found out later as I got friendly with some of the Garden City office staff. They told me confidentially of course, that if I'd hung out just a little longer and put a bit of pressure on them, they would have contributed $20,000 towards refurbishing my shop, which was coming up in two years.

There you go, I've never been a retailer in a large shopping centre before. It was a lesson I'll always remember. Disappointing, but you know, it was a lesson.

I made the deal with Donald Black for $130,000 which included stock and goodwill. But where was the money coming from? We had no money.

So, Deirdre and I decided to offer our dear friend and loyal employee Ben Stuckey to become a business partner. The next day we offered him a 50% share for $130,000. That would cover the cost of buying Phone Shop Booragoon. He was so happy especially because the 50% share was not just for Phone Shop Garden City, the 50% share included our company Talbora Pty Ltd, which owned E.T. Phone Home.

Both of Ben's parents were medical practitioners with their own private practices. His mother was an endocrinologist running a successful research clinic and his dad was an immunologist. Both were wealthy, according to Ben, with many properties in Perth. He was going to approach them that evening and was excited about finally becoming a partner with us. He was going to tell his parents the good news that night.

But the next day Ben came to work looking rather gloomy. I thought he was unwell, but he was well alright; he was just annoyed with his parents. They were not interested in backing him in an unproven industry and his dreams of becoming a partner were shattered.

At that time, the business had not taken off yet for E.T. Phone Home. We needed Phone Shop Garden City to give us that lift. I'm sure anyone reading this book might not have agreed to invest $130,000 in our business back then either. Everything was so unpredictable. No one knew what Telstra's future plans were. Especially us.

Anyway, we went to the bank and talked to our bank manager. He worked out that our property in Dianella still had $70,000 owing and it was worth around $220,000.

The bank manager said, "Okay, I've looked at all your figures and records, you've done well in business. It looks like you should be able to manage this new business without too much trouble. I will bankroll you. In other words, give you an overdraft. Go for it and buy the business, you'll be fine."

Day one was exciting at our new shop. Unlike in West Perth, this place was buzzing from eight am until close. I was hoping we would get three sales of mobile phone but was surprised by the sale of eight mobile phones. Ben and I spent a whole week figuring out what to take to the new shop. Yes, Mobile phones, and what else? We only had mobile phones in West Perth. I started to order stock for Garden City weeks before we took over. Being practical and not knowing what to expect, I ordered twice as much as I ordered normally for West Perth. That was a big mistake. We were not ready for the onslaught.

We employed two new staff and trained them two weeks before we took over Garden City. In those days, there was a huge shortage of mobile phone salespeople. Everyone you employed was a greenhorn. And to make things worse, we were struggling, not having much knowledge of the new products sold in Garden City. Somehow, we pulled through. Did

I mention that I would have been lost without my dodgy partner Ben? Phone Shop Garden City changed the course of my telecommunications gamble.

We had phenomenal success at Garden City and doubled our turnover in twelve months. After we bought Phone Shop from Donald, he continued with us as a sub-contractor. He was installing phone systems for us when requested. We were advertising multi handset phone systems which we knew very little about. We used to pass it on to Donald. He negotiated and worked out what the customer needed and install it for them. We would get a small kickback from the deal. We had a good business partnership with Donald for a very long time. Thanks, Donald.

BUILDING NOW RE-BRANDED AS PHONE SHOP WITH E.T. PHONE HOME PAINTED OVER

Chapter 21

The Dudes from One-Tel

Ben poked his head around the corner into my office and signalled me to come and join him in the front room. I was in the next room in my office having an argument with a ten-dollar customer who wore thongs and had bad breath. I excused myself from this guy and went to see what was so important that made Ben look so concerned. Ben introduced me to Mark K, Jodee and Brad. They came in unannounced and wanted to have a meeting with me. I had no idea who they were at the time, so I went back to dog breath, refunded him his ten dollars, and kicked him out of my office.

Ben brought in my guests, and I asked them, "What brings you here?" Mark K introduced himself as the Managing Director, and Jodee Rich and Brad Keeling as the two owners of One-Tel. Oops! OMG. I was so embarrassed not knowing who they were by name.

Of course, I had heard of One-Tel, everyone had. They were the new kids on the Telco block. They created a 'youth-oriented' image and challenged Telstra's market share. They held hands with Optus, the second-biggest Telco in Australia. They were also backed by the Murdoch and Packer families. James Packer and Lachlan Murdoch sat on the One-Tel board.

Now these were some very high-profile people here in my office.

Jodee asked, "Do you have an exclusive contract with Telstra?"

"No, not that I was aware of. We were recently given a premium dealer status, that's all I know." I was hedging my bets.

"Was I aware the telecommunications industry was opening up and there was to be no more monopoly in the industry?" he asked.

I answered, "Yes, I went to that ATCA conference at Darling Harbour Sydney just last month (Australian Telecommunications Conference Association). The conference was fronted by Bob Mansfield for Optus, Frank Blunt for Telstra, the CEO from Vodafone, and a few other speakers whom I can't remember."

Jodee went on, "Therefore, all mobile phone dealers nationally had the choice to connect to any Telco they choose."

I agreed, "I'm sure that's what I heard. I was very encouraged by what I heard at that conference."

I was now curious to find out what these two wanted from me. About a month before, we had signed a contract to only connect Telstra customers in our shops. We were established with Telstra; we had huge Telstra display cabinets and lots of Telstra signage in our Garden City and West Perth shops.

Apart from their youth-oriented image to sell their mobile phones and internet services to, they also became Australia's fourth-largest telecommunications company. These guys went on to tell us about their plans for the future and we were drawn in by each word uttered.

Jodee was enticing. "Here's the deal. If you come on board with us, we put similar cabinets and signage as Telstra has in your Garden City and West Perth shops. For every new connection you get us, we will pay you 50% more than Telstra does."

Telstra was paying us $30 per connection. One-Tel now offering us $45 per connection.

Jodee continued, "Plus, we will pay you 12% in airtime revenue commissions (Telstra was paying 8%). That's not all, we'll pay you within 14 days of connecting."

Wow, I'm thinking to myself, keep talking Jodee, all those wonderful offers on the table and we only just met. What more was he going to offer us? Keep talking, please!

That was music to my ears. I mention to Jodee that at present, we were connecting to Optus through a third party in Main Street Osborne Park.

He said, "You won't have to do that anymore. You will have your own dealer code like you have with Telstra, and you can ring the connection straight to us. You will have a dedicated operator, a direct line to us. We already have 100 staff in our St George's Terrace office." That was true alright, I did hear something like that from our Optus dealer manager.

Jodee concluded, "We are expanding in a big way over here in Perth and would love to have you aboard. Think about it, I'm in Perth until tomorrow night. I'd like to meet you and show you our head office first thing tomorrow morning."

I was flabbergasted. We shook hands and they left.

Ben heard everything as he sat in on the conversation. There was only Ben and me to serve at West Perth, so thank God no customers came in during this meeting. Ben was blown out. He was listening and liked their image. It was very modern. Their advertising was headed by a cartoon mascot known as "The Dude." The Dude was a cartoon-like depiction of a man in his late twenties; unshaven, groovy-looking and very hip.

PHOTO OF 'THE DUDE'

How exciting. The owners of One-Tel coming to me, to our small headquarters in West Perth. What a boost to my ego.

The next morning, I went to their head office on the 31st floor in St Georges Terrace. The reception area looked rather fancy, and modern with many artworks hanging on the walls, mostly green which was their colour. Mark W came to greet me and I followed him through another door that opened out into a huge area of about 300 square metres. There were scores of young people connecting customers from dealers all around Australia.

I was shown around the office area and introduced to the key people and finally met with Jodee for a meeting. I explained to Jodee that his offer was too good to refuse, and I would dearly like to take up his offer.

"What if Telstra objected to my new venture and sacked me. They might even take me to court for breach of contract." I asked.

Jodee immediately replied, "Should Telstra take you to court, we will cover whatever cost you incur for your court costs and lawyers' fees."

This was very reassuring as these guys were serious about helping me with their company cheque book and with all my lawyers' fees. Wow, they were very serious. We had coffee and went on to talk about contracts etc. All the while, I was wondering secretly, should I have talked to Telstra first?

We did not sign any contracts on that day with One-Tel but agreed to meet in a week to finalise our agreements. They guaranteed me, that within forty-eight hours, they would have my shop decked out with the best-looking One-Tel cabinets to display their products.

I left the meeting on a high. I told Ben all about their offices and staffing. Somehow, my gut instincts were not feeling good. Was it a wise move? I'm asking myself.

True to their word, first thing Friday morning this beautiful large cabinet arrived and was set up on the opposite side of the showroom to Telstra. They hung some banners that looked much better than what the Telstra banners did. They were funkier by a mile!

That Friday, we connected half a dozen One-Tel (Optus) connections which we pushed like hell, and about four Telstra connections. The last Telstra connection we put through from Garden City was about 4 pm on Friday afternoon. It got rejected. Our system was dead. We thought our network was down as it sometimes happens. I phoned around a few other dealers who told me that they were putting through connects without any problems. That was very odd and strange, so I picked up the phone and called the Telstra dealer helpline and asked them what was going on. The operator told me that my dealer code DVDC had been suspended.

I couldn't believe it. I asked the operator many more questions, but the poor operator was limited in the information they could give me. I rang my state manager, who informed me bluntly that I had been sacked. He told me if I wanted to take the matter up further, wait until Monday morning and speak to his boss, Chris Cheri. This man was the National dealer manager for Telstra.

I was disturbed and freaked out by this occurrence. Telstra was not on our side anymore, only One-Tel now. I rang Ben and told him what happened. Ben and I were bewildered, both speechless for once.

I rang my lawyer and went to see him straight away. We spent two hours trying to figure out what we should do next. Being a little green and not expecting Telstra's response in that manner, I was at a loss. They had the right to do what they did.

I was so upset, I said to my lawyer "We should sue Telstra for sacking me." This was late Friday night. We continued connecting One-Tel customers on Saturday morning and again on Monday. Not having Telstra connects was a real bummer. We missed the potential to connect six or more connects on Saturday.

I had to wait till Monday morning to talk to Chris Cheri. I did not mention the Telstra sacking to One-Tel because I thought it best to find out what Telstra's intention was first, rather than to have everybody panicking. I thought I'd do all the panicking. Monday morning didn't come soon enough.

It was 7 am Perth time and 9 am in Melbourne. On the phone, Chris Cheri explained to me very patiently, that Telstra's license agreement did not allow us to connect any other telco through any of our outlets. I explained to Chris about the telecommunications conference that I had attended in Sydney recently. I must admit, I had a late night at the casino the night before and was half asleep at the conference.

Chris simply replied "Wendell, there's no agreement in place yet about anything that you heard at that conference. It was just a proposal to see if all the telcos could join one network and save costs. They haven't decided yet. They are still in discussions about it."

Therefore, my suspended license stood as far as Telstra was concerned. I could not put any more connections through their network. They were coming to take away all their cabinets and signage as soon as possible.

I decided to inform Mark K about the suspension I had received. One-Tel were curious to see what Telstra was prepared to do ongoing. They were 100% behind me. They were going to support me financially and they were going to give me all the publicity I could get which would also give them a lot of publicity. Don't forget, One-Tel was still the new kid on the block and was taking away market share from Telstra. Understandably, Telstra was not happy with my association or my allowing One-Tel into our Phone Shops.

I spoke to a couple of journalists I'd made friends with during the E.T. Phone Home break-ins. I told them what had happened on Friday with Telstra. I said it was against the Fair-Trading Act. They didn't have the right to do that. I wanted to ring up every TV station, newspaper, and radio station with the news. I was going to take an injunction out against Telstra and challenge them in court.

In desperation, I wasn't thinking clearly and made an impulsive choice. I was reluctant, but I gave these reporters Chris Cheri's direct line and said, "Ask him about the sacking." They did. Chris Cheri did not want this thing to be made public. I think Telstra didn't want One-Tel to get any more publicity than they were already getting. So, he promised a journalist the story next Friday.

Back to my lawyer's office for more crisis discussions. My lawyer advised me to inform Jodee personally about the drama taking place. After all, they were paying my lawyer's costs.

That same afternoon I got a call back from Chris Cheri.

"Wendell you are the first Telstra dealer who has signed up with One-Tel (I had not signed any contract with One-Tel, yet). We only found out about the One-Tel signage on Friday and the first thing we did was to suspend you from trading." That was a big relief to hear the word suspend and not sacked.

He continued, "I've spoken to my bosses, and it has also been brought to the attention of our new CEO. Telstra has given me permission to put an end to this minor hiccup, one way or another."

Chris went on to say, "I'm flying in early Thursday morning, and I've booked a room at Mallesons to have a meeting (they are Telstra's big gun lawyers nationally). Can you and your lawyer be present at 10 am that morning?"

"Sure, I'll ring up my lawyer and make sure that we're both there 10 am, see you then." I replied.

Before we hung up, I asked him, "What am I going to do for trade, what about my Telstra connections?"

"Wendell, we cannot do anything about your connections until we resolve this matter and that's why I am taking this emergency step to come and meet with you on Thursday morning. In the meantime, we suggest you get rid of all One-Tel cabinets and signage."

Embarrassingly, I had to ring and mention all this to Jodee Rich, keeping him in the loop.

So, all day Monday, Tuesday, Wednesday, and Thursday, we were almost out of business without Telstra connections. We lost about 30 Telstra customers who came to connect or buy a mobile phone, and probably ten One-Tel customers. We couldn't do a thing about selling Telstra or One-Tel. Quietly, we did some connections through Optus as before with Horst in Osborne Park. It was risky but I was satisfied Telstra knew about this arrangement from before. My main worry was some spy from Telstra might come for a One-Tel connection and trap me.

We told customers, "Sorry but our dealer code with One-Tel had not been activated yet. Come back next week." We knew there was little chance of anyone coming back.

No one in the industry knew about my predicament except Jodee Rich. I explained to him we were having a meeting with Chris Cheri from Telstra on Thursday morning, and that I had halted all trading until then. We told no one, not one other person knew about it.

It wasn't easy explaining this to customers, but we just used the "our computers are down" storyline, day after day.

I realised at that moment; I had made a big mistake doing business with One-Tel. Most people still preferred to connect with Telstra rather than One-Tel or Optus. I had to take this one on the chin. I felt terrible being in this position at that time.

I informed my lawyer of the meeting I set up for us at Mallesons' on Thursday morning at 10 am. To my luck, he agreed and said he was available.

Monday, Tuesday and Wednesday were very anxious and difficult days for me. I was rather depressed but more worried about my future. I didn't have a Telstra dealer code anymore. I'd been suspended. Not a good position to be in.

First thing Thursday morning, I picked up my lawyer and headed for Mallesons' offices in St George's Terrace. When we arrived, the receptionist asked us to take a seat. A few minutes later, she picked up the phone and informed someone that we had arrived. She then led us into this boardroom. The table was big enough to seat twenty people. My lawyer Seng Fai and I sat on one side of the table and waited nervously.

Within minutes, four men entered followed by Chris Cheri and took the seats opposite us. Very politely introductions were made all around the table. To Chris' right was a Queen's Council, a senior partner from Mallesons, and two other Barristers or maybe just lawyers; I don't really know, my head was so clouded. All I could think of was that I was going to sue them. I was going to take them to the highest court. I was going on 60 Minutes. This was all in my head. I was so hyped up. There was small talk at the beginning, the conversation was light-hearted. Business cards were exchanged between the lawyers. Which matter was going to be dealt with first?

For me, there was only one matter. That matter was getting my dealer code back from Telstra. I didn't realise it at the time, but my lawyer kept asking me to sit. I kept standing up and arguing my point. My lawyer did warn me on the way between his office and Mallesons, that this is a very delicate and important matter, otherwise, Chris Cheri would not have flown to Perth to resolve this problem.

"Whatever you do, let me do the talking," he warned. He knows me, I can fly off the handle at any given opportunity. My lawyer was intensively arguing on my behalf against all the legal matters that arose. By my instructions, he did mention, if necessary, we intended to take this matter to the highest court in Australia. Whilst they were debating legal issues, I stood up once more and started mouthing off again, and this time my lawyer grabbed me by the hand, hissed at me and forced me to sit down.

He asked Chris if we could have a 15-minute recess which they agreed to. They gave us a small office to discuss the terms and conditions that they spoke about with my lawyer which I didn't fully understand. When we got into this smaller room, my lawyer said "Wendell, did you understand what just happened and what was said?"

"No, not really."

Seng Fai explained, "These guys are trying to make peace with you and want to forget this whole thing ever happened, but only on one condition. Stop dealing with One-Tel immediately. You must get their cabinet and signage out of your shop pronto. Do that by the end of today because your dealer manager will come by and check."

"So, do you still want to sue Telstra?" asked Seng Fai. I was in shock but thrilled to hear this news.

"No, come on lah, I was only joking." We both had a laugh and shook hands.

Seng Fai warned me again, "Wendell when we walk back into that room, please don't say a word, let me do the talking." I agreed.

We went back to the meeting and my lawyer said to them, "My client has agreed to your terms and conditions. He will carry out your request by the end of today."

Chris put his hand out and agreed that we should kiss and make up and pretend nothing ever happened. Amen. We all shook hands and we left. What a relief that was.

On the way home I said to Seng Fai, "I wonder if I should have asked Telstra, would they give me $45 per connection and raise my trailing commission to 12% like I was receiving from One-Tel?"

He said, "Wendell, you're lucky that they didn't turn around and say, by the way, and add on some other conditions that you don't really need. Like dropping your 8% airtime commission to 5%. I'm glad you didn't push your luck too far this time."

As they promised, my Telstra code DVDC was reinstated, no later than 4 pm that Friday afternoon. I was so relieved and emotionally so drained. Thank God it was over.

I was so relieved because we already had a good database clientele with Telstra, and we were earning good money from the airtime commissions, business was good and going well. I think the choice I made was good because in time, as we all know, One-Tel went into liquidation. That took the whole telecommunications industry by surprise.

The first thing I did when I got back from Mallesons was to ring up Mark W from One-Tel and explain to him what had just happened.

He wasn't overly happy but said, "Let me first talk to Jodee and I'll get back to you."

I got a call back from One-Tel that same day. They were unhappy about the result but were decent about their commitment to cover my lawyers' fees. They did cover all my fees and removed everything they installed in both of our shops. What gentlemen!

The Packer and Murdoch families were embarrassed by the failure of the company One-Tel, especially after it was reported that both James Packer and Lachlan Murdoch had persuaded their fathers to back the company and invest hundreds of millions of dollars, which they did and lost it all.

I was back being a Telstra Premium dealer. Hooray!

Chapter 22

Deirdre Comes Aboard

After our purchase of Phone Shop Garden City, business was getting a little hectic. We had to employ and train many new staff. We also had to learn all about Panasonic cordless phones, Sony facsimile machines, NEC printers, Uniden phone systems, Ericsson two-way radios, and much more than our current E.T. Phone Home was handling. It was a huge learning curve for both Ben and me. We were learning and trying hard to get accustomed to all these new products. Even though Ben and I trained at Phone Shop under Donald's guidance for two weeks, it wasn't long enough. We needed more, probably eight weeks.

I mentioned to Deirdre it was about time she joined us at West Perth headquarters because of workload increases, after all, she was a director in the company. She refused initially. Deirdre was busy working at the Greek Community retirement village based in Alexander Heights as their accountants' secretary.

Very generously, she was looking after our books and accounts in her spare time for free. The company did buy her a traded-in Red Datsun 120y for $150. She was happy in her current job, but finally and luckily for me she saw the light. Our business was growing fast. She was needed as our accountant, receptionist, salesperson, and chief bottle washer.

I jokingly said, "It's an important role we have for you here." I offered her $420 a week and she accepted. Deirdre was immensely talented for the job. She knew she would be paid weekly as she handled all our banking and saw our sales figures daily.

The airtime commission cheque was growing faster than anticipated. It was very timely when she joined us. Phone Shop Garden city had unwittingly taken off like a rocket. We were not prepared for the demand. For the very first time, people could buy a Telstra product at Phone Shop Garden City and get connected there. The race was on. I would send Ben some stock in the morning and by lunch time he'd be asking me for more stock. We hired an extra six staff. I was making two trips or more a day to Garden City from West Perth HQ. I was ordering more stock daily, not weekly. Garden City was selling ten times more than West Perth was. We were on a big winner here.

Ben and I thought of all sorts of creative ways to make an extra buck. In those days, the average price for a leather case was about $49 to $59 each.

As a bargain hunter myself, I had an inkling of what would sell.

I said to Ben, "In our next large newspaper advertisement, let's sell all leather cases for all models of mobile phones for $29 each."

That was almost less than half the price. Ben agreed and we did just that. In three months, we sold over 600 leather cases. Now that's nearly a $10,000 clear profit. Not bad for the new kid on the block. People came from everywhere to buy a leather case. Some even bought a new mobile phone and other accessories from us. A La Mc Donald's (any coke and fries sir?). What a killing we made!

Understandably, everyone in the industry had to follow suit and we killed that $49 to $59 monopoly leather case price tag forever. The cases did finally go back up to $39. A big win for the customers. There was still a good mark up for all dealers selling leather cases. I'm sure my name was not on the top ten list amongst the dealers for a few months after that.

Director Deirdre

Telstra had not once included Deirdre in any of the meetings, correspondence, or outings that I went to. Since 1983, Deirdre and I were co-directors of Talbora Pty Ltd, who in turn was the Licensee of the agreement with which we had with Telstra. There were only two directors in this company, Deirdre, and me.

One day at our lawyer's office, while reading through the renewal of our contract with Telstra, our lawyer pointed out to Deirdre that 'Talbora Pty Ltd' was the Licensee for Telstra in our contract agreement. Meaning both of us should be recognised equally.

Our lawyer questioned me, "Why was Deirdre not attending the annual conference of Telstra in Melbourne that you go to?"

Yes, that was strange, so we asked our state manager what their rationale was.

Apparently, there were another married couple who ran a Telstra Licensed Shop, and this couple had marital problems. It disrupted the daily operations of Telstra's business. And the husband sometimes wouldn't open the shop as required at 9 am and sometimes refused to sign cheques to pay bills. They co-signed and because his signature was required, this made things complicated, and suppliers and customers rang Telstra and complained. Telstra used this couple as an example. In this case, Telstra nominated the wife as the Licensee from then on. From thereon in, all partners were ignored and not recognised or included in any of Telstra's meetings. Telstra had decided to nominate only one person to be the Licensee per shop, and that was me.

Now, from time to time, Telstra introduced new plans for customer connections. We had to sign off and agree to all Letters of Agreement. Sometimes I was interstate or overseas and Telstra wouldn't accept Deirdre's signature, which interrupted the daily operating of our business. Poor old Deirdre had to be across the legal and accounting side of the whole business, too.

What Telstra wanted was for us to change the structure of our Company Shareholding to suit them, which we refused. Finally, they recognised and accepted Deirdre as co-Licensee.

Deirdre Robbed and Bashed

It's true, this happened once at E.T. Phone Home, West Perth, late one Tuesday afternoon in July 1997. I had to deliver a mobile phone to an important client about three kilometres away. Ben was out servicing another client.

I said to Deirdre, "It will only take me 20 minutes in this rush hour traffic to deliver this phone, will you be alright here by yourself?" She was fine about me going, so I went.

Upon my return, the traffic was backed up quite a bit. It was Tuesday so I expected some delays. The traffic was always heavier at that hour. I was driving along Bulwer Street towards Fitzgerald Street. When I finally got to the lights, I looked towards my building and saw an ambulance parked outside our shop with lights flashing. As soon as the traffic lights turned green, I slammed my foot on the pedal and flew into Fitzgerald Street. I parked my car in the driveway and raced into the shop.

There were three people in the front room, I thought they were customers. I was wrong. In the second room, I saw an ambulance officer attending to Deirdre. He had given Deirdre a green tube to suck on which calmed her down a bit, a quick sedative. He was examining her side. I saw a lady also nursing Deirdre, holding her hand. "What happened?" I screamed in fear. Deirdre had been robbed and bashed. I was astounded by what I heard. The story went something like this from the nurse.

Nurses' Version of Bashing

'X' MARKS THE SPOT

I was sitting near the front on the left-hand side of the bus as it slowly moved forward along Fitzgerald Street, when suddenly I saw the shop door open and two people struggling. They poured out into the street only a few feet from the bus.

The bus was at a standstill in traffic, so I ran up to the driver and demanded that the driver open the door.

"A woman's been bashed on the footpath and needs help. I'm a nurse, open the door quickly," I said.

I asked the lady (on the ground) if she was ok, and she murmured she was, but I could see she was gasping for air. I examined her the best I could and waited a few minutes. With help from another passenger, we helped her into the shop and sat her on a chair in the back room. The lady was crying and was in shock. She was absorbing the pain without medication. The bus had left by then. The lady said her husband (me) was due back at any moment. The ambulance arrived without delay, and they took over.

Ambulance Officer

According to the ambulance report, they received an emergency 000 call reporting a woman had been bashed and was lying hurt on the footpath. They gave the address as 281 Fitzgerald Street, next door to the Kentucky Fried Chicken shop. There is a large number 281 plastered on the front wall.

"When we arrived, the victim was in the back room of the shop. We saw she was in terrible pain, so we immediately gave her a green lollipop stick to suck. It has a strong relaxing sedative mixture in it. This calmed her down, we examined her and found possible broken ribs. We drove her to Royal Perth Hospital immediately."

Deirdre's Version

A man came into the shop to look at some phones.(Deirdre by now knew the language on how to explain the various Telstra plans. She also knew a bit about the product since she has been listening to Ben and me for the past three months in the shop. She felt she knew a bit about mobile phones, so she answered a few questions at first). The customer was happy to look down at the mobile phone from above the see-through glass cabinet. The customer then said he wanted to touch and feel the Motorola Micro-Tac. They were new on the market.

He apparently wanted to hold it, so Deirdre opened the cabinet door from behind the counter and held it in her hand at first, opening the flip top, and closing it. That model was the latest on the market. The mobile phone was in her right hand. He jumped at her hand and grabbed it. Her response was to grab onto the mobile phone as tight as her hand would allow. She used her left hand, trying to remove his right hand from the mobile phone. The man was too strong for her. She managed to get her body around the counter and was now on the opposite side next to the robber, not letting go. They somehow struggled, pulled, and finally ended up on the footpath outside. He then kneed Deirdre on her right side, and she fell to the ground. He got away from her with the Motorola MicroTac and ran towards the service station on Vincent Street and disappeared. This took place ten minutes before I arrived.

The Police came within minutes after I arrived and took statements from the nurse and Deirdre. Deirdre was still in some pain and the ambulance attendants advised they were taking her to the Hospital for further examinations. There, she was sent off for X-Rays. I was sitting next to her when the Doctor came in with the results. "You have two broken ribs and one cracked rib." Say no more, welcome to the telecommunications business. Poor Deirdre.

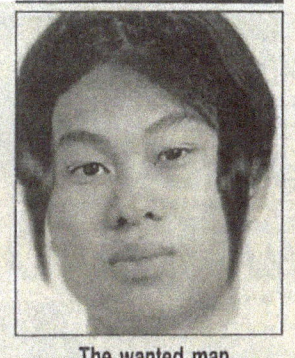

The wanted man.

Bandit sought

POLICE are looking for a man who held up a city telephone shop on Tuesday, July 29 about 4.15pm.

The bandit entered the shop and asked a woman assistant to show him some mobile phones.

After he agreed to buy one of the phones, he hit the assistant with his elbow and ran out.

The woman chased the man, who turned around and kneed her, leaving her with a broken rib.

He jumped into a red Ford Laser sedan being driven by an Asian male aged about 25.

The other man was Asian, between 18 and 25, of medium build, 178cm tall, with long

BANDIT SOUGHT (ORIGINAL ARTICLE)

Hello Darling Novelty Phones

A small portion of the products we sold at Phone Shop; Garden City were novelty phones. Yes, these designer novelty handsets could be plugged into your normal, wall-mounted Telstra sockets. They were purchased as novelty gifts, especially for birthdays, sometimes at Christmas. They were not a big selling item, but very profitable. More importantly, they looked good in the window to attract customers. We had a special display area for all our novelty phones. It really made you stop and look. Their price range was from $129 to $399 each.

Just imagine seeing and hearing an Elvis Presley statue handset that played 'Jailhouse Rock' when a call came in. R2D2 was the same, those squiggling noises. Barbie, Motorboat, Buzz Lightyear, Micky Mouse and Garfield all had their own ring sound. Very popular was the very old-fashioned 'wall phone' too.

When we bought Phone Shop from Donald Black, he gave us all his supplier's contacts. 'Hello Darling' was an importer of all these products from China. They were based in Sydney in the Queen Victoria Building (commonly known as the famous QVB building on Pitt Street). It was a tiny shop but the way they displayed their novelty phones was dazzling.

I rang them and said, "I'm coming to Sydney for a Telstra conference soon." I set up a meeting and met with the owner who seemed a little apprehensive towards me. We had a long chat and I found out he wanted to get out of that business and building. The rents there were unfeasible.

Upon my return, I spoke to Deirdre about Hello Darling wanting to get out of business and sell their stock. Deirdre being smart with numbers, reminded me that if we sold all the items listed, and we sold 60 per year, it would take five years to clear the stock. My argument was, we'd get all our investment back in the first two years. Not bad profit I thought.

We agreed to buy all the stock from Hello Darling. But the price was going to be the difference between buying or not. Their asking price was $35,000. I made an offer of $18,000 which he accepted. We had them all shipped to Perth by road which cost us another $2,000. Everything arrived, every single item was counted and inspected, and all goods were correct as per our agreement.

No sooner after we got hold of our stock from Sydney, we received a letter from the EDS, Electrical Department of Safety. We were advised that the new regulations for any overseas electrical products had to now carry a government-approved 'C tick' sticker, otherwise, you were not allowed to sell it. I should have guessed it, no wonder Hello Darling didn't argue about the price I offered them, darn.

This is the part I want you to read carefully. Apparently, the wiring, soldering, casing and other components may not comply with our Australian standards and regulations.

ORIGINAL AD IN A MAGAZINE

Consequently, you had to take one of each novelty phone model to their workshop somewhere in a suburb called Welshpool. Here's the best part, they charged $375 per model to be checked, to be deemed safe for use in Australia. Only then, you would get an approved 'C tick' which had to be affixed under the phones. If an inspector came around one day and you didn't have that sticker, there was an $8,500 fine, and all your stock would be confiscated. This was a very scary new venture for us.

Part of the reasoning for all these safety issues was that during an electrical thunderstorm, it is said, you may get electrocuted using one of these devices. Sounds reasonable, doesn't it? Well, it wasn't.

There were thousands of these phones and other similar products being used all around Australia for years and not once was anyone electrocuted during any electrical storms. This was just another money-raising, job-justification government project, instigated by some bored government official, at our cost.

Finally, we got all the approved 'C tick' stickers for the cost of $4,000. And guess what? We did not have to modify any one of the products. They were all certified good and safe. Praise the Lord. The lesson here; read and double-check everything when buying electrical products, especially if it is made overseas. However, we made a few dollars with these novelty phones. Got all our money back in the first year plus a huge profit. How? We sold all of them at half price. Well done.

ORIGINAL ELVIS NOVELTY PHONE HELD BY THE 'ELVIS' GUY

Fair Work case with the Twins.

Like all smart retail shop owners, we employed mostly young people because they were the ones playing with these new gadgets on the market. The computer, mobile phone, and IT world were for the young, not the old. Having said that, we did employ some Baby Boomers and Gen X.

On this occasion, I advertised for retail staff and had quite a few replies. After the first interview over the phone, I planned to interview the good ones face-to-face.

I was quite surprised when Andy and Pandy came to our headquarters in West Perth for the second interview. They both walked in and I asked, "Who's Andy?"

"Me," Andy said.

I then asked what Pandy was doing there too. Well, Andy introduced Pandy as his twin brother who was also seeking work. We didn't really need two new staff, I'd already put three new staff on that week, but I thought what the hell, we were growing and sooner or later we'd be looking for more staff, so I decided to give them both a job.

They presented well in appearance and came from a nice family, so it seemed. I gave Andy a position as a salesperson and Pandy delivered stock to our shops. Pandy also learned to sell mobile phones. As I said, young people were very quick at learning new technology and mobile phones were the thing to know.

One day, our service manager, Ian, had a chat with me about the twins. He said they were always up to something he didn't like, and he overheard them discussing lifting some phones to resell to their friends. Ian also mentioned that they often smoked in the laneway and threw their cigarette butts in the laneway which Ian use to sweep every second day. Before he mentioned this to me, I also heard that Ian and Andy had words a few days ago about some delivery cock up Pandy had made. I ignored what I heard because young people do have strong opinions in life and I thought it would blow over, just a misunderstanding, they'll sort it out.

Ian saw me again with a concern which attracted my attention. He said that he had three refurbished mobiles for sale and now one was missing. I called the twins in my office and asked them if they knew anything about the missing handset. Both said they knew nothing, which I accepted.

The following week, Ian approached me again and this time, Ian had nailed them. He told me he saw something suspicious being done by the twins. He said he watched them wrap a brand-new phone in a McDonald's bag and throw it into the rubbish bin. We went to the bin and yep, there was a mobile phone wrapped in a McDonalds take-away bag.

I summonsed the twins to my office together with Ian. I asked for an explanation. They denied doing any of it and accused Ian of making it all up. I'd had enough by then with these two and fired them on the spot.

It didn't take long before I got a call from Fair Work. They asked me questions about unfair dismissal laws. I was close to telling them to F off but held my cool.

I told them point blank, "Take me to court!" I refused to talk to them. It was only a matter of time before we ended up before a judge. Unfortunately, this all took about eight weeks of stress that I didn't need.

The day before I appeared in court, out of nowhere, one of my staff Alan, came to me and confessed the twins did conspire to steal from us. Alan was a young nineteen-year-old, blue-eyed blond surfie. I lent him money to buy a new surfboard four months earlier. He offered to testify against the twins. He said he knew the truth and Ian was right. I was disappointed he let me know so late in the piece but was overjoyed when he offered to testify against the twins in court the following day.

In court, the twins brought their mother along for moral support, I think. You should have seen the look on their faces when they saw Alan. I won't drag this out too long, just to say the case was kicked out of court and the twins had to repay me for two stolen phones. Their mother did not look so happy. Case dismissed.

Coloured Girl's Big Breasts

One day this eloquently dressed lady walked into my shop in West Perth. She was a stunner. I just happened to be walking out for a meeting when she asked a staff member, who was the boss and if he was in. The staff member pointed me out to her and said, "That's him."

I immediately introduced myself and asked, "How can I help you?" She said she was looking for a job and was currently working for Harvey Norman. I was bewitched by this mystical, good looking, coloured girl and so was my staff. I explained I had a meeting at 1 pm and would be back in an hour or so.

She said, "She had the day off and would return at 3 pm."

I acknowledged the time and said, "3 pm is good."

When I arrived back at 2.30 pm, she was waiting. I walked into the shop whilst she was telling two male staff members some stories all about Africa.

"You're on time," I said.

"I never left," she explained. Very impressive I thought.

I invited her into my office, which everyone could see into, but not hear the conversation. She introduced herself as Lo-Anne and was from South Africa but born in Mozambique. I was keen to find out why she dropped in when we weren't advertising for staff. She said she saw our advertising on TV and thought I might be able to use some of her talents. I asked her what she was proposing. She asked if we need a specialised person in corporate marketing.

"We do have a representative that talks to large businesses but no, no one yet, at least for now." I said.

We chatted for an hour about different ideas on how to market the corporate sector, including direct marketing which sounded interesting. I was impressed. I agreed to put her on a trial basis for four weeks, starting the following Monday.

I explained to Deirdre what I had in mind and Deirdre agreed there was a market out there that we didn't quite have our hands on. Deirdre also commented on her dress saying it was a little risqué and not appropriate for an office or retail environment. I forgot to mention that Deirdre's office was behind mine, so she could also see whoever I spoke to.

The first-day Lo-Anne entered the shop, jaws dropped by all the male staff, including mine. She wore this tight skirt and a shirt two sizes too small. She showed 60% of her breast. She shocked the females working there, especially Deirdre. It was hard to hold a decent conversation with her when her breasts were half popping out. I tried to keep cool and gave her my thoughts on where to begin. She said she'd try ringing the manager of the buying department at each corporation. I agreed and let her go do her work. We gave her the fifth spare office; I suppose it was wait and see what happened next.

Lo-Anne came to work daily showing the same amount of flesh as she did on day one. She met some potential clients daily and I was hoping she would get us a few new clients. She did manage to get a couple, but her strike rate was poor. As a matter of fact, our Subiaco representative, Tim Guest, was beating her hands down by selling many more products to these major clients than Lo-Anne was. By the third week, Deirdre had had enough of her half-naked body.

She asked me to please ask Lo-Anne to dress properly at work. I had to agree with Deirdre as even I was having trouble concentrating!

At our next day's meeting, I said, "Lo-Anne, I don't know how to put this to you, but could you kindly show less of your breast at work? I don't mind it, but you know, there are others who whisper things about your dress, you know that."

She replied, "I get that all the time. People always comment about my dress code. I don't mean to offend anyone, that's how I've always dressed. I'm a model."

"I understand what you're saying" I commented, "But can you at least try?"

She agreed and left rather abruptly. Deirdre was happy I listened to her and gave Lo-Anne that nudge about her dress.

The following morning, everyone was waiting with anticipation for Lo-Anne to show up. At 8.55 am she walked in. We all pretended to be too busy to look, but we were dying to cast our eyes upon Lo-Anne.

Lo-Anne came for the morning meeting. Don't get me wrong here, but from the 60% she was showing on day one, it was now 40%. I knew Deirdre would not approve of this either. Lo-Anne did make an effort. But how do you tell someone who looks so pretty, not to look so pretty at work?

At lunchtime Lo-Anne left the office and in came Deirdre.

"You haven't given her my message," she said. "You might as well ask her to go back to the 60% she was showing yesterday, this new look is just as bad!" I must agree with Deirdre; it was still too tantalizing no matter what Lo-Anne did!

"Okay, I'll talk to her when she comes back from lunch," I sighed.

I summoned Lo-Anne to my office after lunch. Before I could say anything, Lo-Anne was so excited and said not to worry about her dress anymore, and that she was resigning. The modelling agency had offered her a leading role in a fashion parade in Sydney and she apologised for having to leave in such a hurry. I was in disbelief; she didn't know how relieved I was. Deirdre would be delighted. I knew that she wasn't going to listen or compromise her dress standard for anyone; why should she? She was gorgeous, and stunning, and wanted to be noticed every minute of the day. Here Here!

My last words to her were, "I'll miss seeing you daily, and our morning chats too." I really wanted to say or should have said, I'll miss seeing them daily, they used to wake me up and brighten my day, oops sorry, you know what I mean." LOL.

Chapter 23

TV Radio and Newspaper Advertising 1997

ORIGINAL GEL FROM OUR VAL MORGAN ADVERTISING
CAMPAIGN AT THE MOVIES

By 1997, we were fully operational in the telephony business at Phone Shop in Garden City which was now our flagship. We sold so many mobile phones there and made so much money it was unbelievable. Telstra realised by then that I was ready to expand my wings and open more shops and maybe take over more businesses.

Telstra started to support me by contributing 50% towards all my advertising. This was a huge boost to sales. As you can imagine, who wants to or can afford to pay thousands of extra dollars more per month in advertising? Why not let them pay the other half? We were now advertising in the newspaper, on the radio, and finally on television. Our business was booming.

For the TV advertisement, I'd have to write the script and submit it to Telstra for approval. Then submit it to the TV station and meet the producer of the advertising and promotion department at Channel 9 (our first TV station). They in turn hired a voice-over actor. We would then make a time slot for recording the advertisement and spent two to three hours getting the voice-over correct. The 108 commercial slots also required the products Telstra wanted in the advertisement, and the TV commercial had to sound and look professional.

The Phone Shop advertisement on TV appeared to be well made, but it only featured still images of the products and a polished voiceover, no moving pictures. I personally felt that it lacked something. While the content and products were great, I thought the advertisement itself seemed remarkably dull. Every time I watched it, I couldn't help but think that it was just another generic TV ad. It needed something more. Me!

By the way, I always wanted to front our TV ads but never pushed for it. There's a famous car dealer here in Perth by the name of John Hughes who owns the biggest car yards in Western Australia. He fronts all his TV, radio, and newspaper ads. He is extremely successful in Perth. There were a few other businesspeople in Perth who fronted their own television advertisements too, like Brian Gardner, Rick Hart, and the Spud Shed man.

I thought, maybe I should do the same. I spoke to Geoff Ridgwell, my area manager.

"Geoff, I think we can do better TV advertising by me appearing as frontman. I should front the television ad which might put more personality into the commercials. Don't forget, I was a drummer and musician in my first career and appeared on TV many times. It was my idea on the name E.T. Phone Home that had worked."

Telstra finally agreed and I got in touch with a small advertising film studio and struck a deal with them. I proposed to make at least four ads a year through their company, but they had to give me a special deal for the first twelve months. They agree to my offer.

I proposed it to Telstra who agreed. Telstra now raised their contributions towards the television advertisement to 75% of the whole cost. I was on television now and only paid 25% of the total bill. Anyone would have been happy with that deal, I was. I didn't do anything special except wear nice suits. By this stage, both Ben and I stopped wearing cheap suits, we were the big boys now and could afford more expensive suits.

I always ended the commercial with the words, "And that's not all we sell." And it worked. I was a star overnight. Well, in Perth anyway!

During my days in business, I must have appeared on TV hundreds of times. I was starting to get recognised. Sadly today, I'm totally forgotten LOL.

It was an experience fronting a television camera when you are not used to it. Especially making a television ad. I'd go to the recording studio with the script in hand but could not remember all the words for the 30 seconds duration I needed to keep talking. We finally agreed to do the recording line by line, meaning, all I had to remember was one line and then cut, then start again. Then record the next sentence until we had it right. We got it done alright. It had to be my way, or we'd be there for a long-time recording. I could never understand how newsreaders handled it. I'm a drummer, not an actor.

So, there you have it; Mr. Wendell Parnell was on Channel 9 almost every day of the week at least twice, sometimes six times. The name Phone Shop was getting noticed around Perth. Mind you, the big boys would always offer something better the following day in the media. It was tough competition out there. The TV ads with 'yours truly' as the frontman was taking effect. We were getting a new audience from all the ads. Most of the people who were customers from the E.T. Phone Home era were notified about our name change ages ago.

The old customers, and there were about 2,000 of them, were okay with the name change as they still had a warranty on their mobile phones with us. We informed them that we'd changed our name only; our office was still in Fitzgerald Street and now we had a new shop in Garden City as well. We captured a new audience; I was the Phone Shop face on the television ads like it or not.

People throughout the industry talked about my appearances on TV and some thought it was crappy. Was I worried? NO! No publicity is bad publicity. Most Telstra strip dealers got a bit jealous I'm sure because there I was, backed by Telstra, spending all their money, and reaping all the rewards.

Chapter 24

Nutters and Con Men Stories Electro Magnetic BOX

Being on TV a lot must have caught the attention of many people, and many different nutters and con men seemed to seek me out. This is another one of those stories I want to tell you about.

I got an unexpected call from Mr. Albert Longmuir. "Hello Wendell, this is Albert Longmuir, you don't know me, but I have seen you on TV and I'd like to do some business with you, buy you out of working forever."

I replied jokingly, "Oh really, buy me out? Yes, well err, I'm always ready to sell, maybe even sell you a mobile phone."

He said, "I'm serious, can I come and see you?"

"Sure, I'm in West Perth and you can drop in anytime and have a coffee here," I replied.

About two hours later, Ben poked his head around the doorway and said, "There is a Mr. Longmuir here to see you." So soon, I thought. Just spoke to him a few hours ago.

"Okay, bring him into my office."

He was well dressed but in an old suit. I'd say about 65 years old and wore thick-rimmed glasses.

I introduced myself and offered him a seat. "So how can I help you?"

"How would you like to stop working for the rest of your life? I want to share something that will make both of us rich overnight."

"Overnight, really?" I mused.

"Yes," was his answer.

Ben made us a coffee and went back outside to the front room, our showcase area.

"Okay shoot, what's this million-dollar deal you have for me?" I asked.

His brother-in-law worked for the CSIRO and had invented this Electro Magnetic??????????BOX. Even though I didn't understand what the hell he was talking about, I acted as if I knew what he was saying. Nodding my head listening. I interrupted him, asking him to please explain it more simply, so I can follow this high-tech invention a little better.

He said his brother-in-law, Indie, invented this contraption that would revolutionise and solve all the world's electricity problems.

Now I'm talking to someone appearing to be well educated and well dressed, yet I'm wondering why he has come to me; I'm a musician and mobile phone salesman. Why me?

"How does it work?" I asked, I was curious.

He explained that this battery pack Indie invented would cut your electricity bill by 95%. There was an initial cost of buying the (I'll call it a BOX) BOX for around $1200. The BOX and its components were top secret, and he couldn't tell me any more about it until we got acquainted with one another a little bit better.

He said, "What do you think?"

I was stuck for words, so I asked, "Tell me how it works."

"You first need to have a three-phase power outlet in the house (most households don't have one). The box was about one square metre in size. This unit had to be mounted on the roof cavity, inside the rooftop of your house. You had to use your current electricity to power this BOX, only for one hour per day. After that, you get all your electrical power delivered by this BOX, by remote control to anywhere in your house."

Too good to be true? This was in 1997 and it reminded me of the solar-powered panel systems being used at that time. I took the opportunity and mentioned this similarity to him.

"It' not the same. Indie's invention is a thousand times cheaper to run. Indie has invented this energy Electro Magnetic???????BOX no one has ever thought of. He's a brilliant scientist," said Mr Longmuir.

"Okay, so tell me Mr Longmuir, how do I get involved in this top-secret multi-million-dollar project?" I asked.

"We are looking for some capital. We need $600,000 to finish the prototype model he is working on."

Aha, so that's the catch! My gut instinct kicked in quickly. It sounded too good to be true: Lessons one, two, and three. If it's too good to be true, be very careful.

I said I was interested and happy to outlay the capital needed on one condition, we become partners and go 50/50 in the venture.

I had to ask, "Do you own your house?" (I didn't have that kind of money but if it was true, boy, forget millions, I was seeing billions).

He said, "Yes."

"Where do you live?" I asked.

"In the Manning area."

"Good, then mortgage your house, raise $300,000 and I will raise the same. Another thing, I must first meet your brother-in-law, Indie. He needs to explain his invention to me, he must convince me first, okay?"

Surprisingly, he agreed and left. We agreed to meet in a few days' time so Indie could get time off from work because it would take hours to discuss everything in detail.

I'm going to digress a little and mention that today in 2023 (26 years later), you can get a power pack that delivers power to your iPhone without using any cables. Just as he explained about Indie's invention. Was Mr Longmuir well before his time in thinking?

When he left, I said to Ben, "I wish it was all true what this guy has told me." I had street-level instincts telling me otherwise. Ben made a movement with his right hand, indicating masturbation. I agreed.

A few days later a woman came into our shop half hysterical demanding to see me. I came out and greeted her and asked her to calm down and tell me what her problem was. She accused me of encouraging her husband to mortgage their house. She then went on to say I must also be insane. (Me, insane?) She said her husband had been released from the mental asylum just four weeks ago.

After listening to her explanation and account of his condition, I could see the full story in his imagination. But what a shame, billions could have been made if it was true!

I said "Madam, my apologies to you, I also had a bad feeling there was something wrong with him. Now you have cleared my suspicions, thank you very much." End of story.

His brother-in-law, Indie, was a scientist and did work for the CSIRO. As for the rest of the story laid on me by Mr. Longmuir, was it worth mentioning? Yes, it was, as I did attract some nutters. Wait there's more in the next story.

The Lebanese Connection

Another phone call from an eastern-sounding man. "Hello Sir, I'm Ali from Lebanon but I live here in Perth."

"Pleased to meet you Ali, how can I help you?" I asked.

"I want to meet with you, can I?"

"Sure," I said. "When?"

"How about tomorrow?"

I answered, "Sure, 10 am ok?"

"Yes."

People always wanted to see me, and yes, I loved seeing people because I needed to sell mobile phones to them, what else?!

The next morning around 10 am Ali arrived. I invited him into my office, made a coffee for both of us and commenced with: - "How can I help you?"

His immediate answer was, "Do you have knowledge of what's happening in Lebanon?"

"Yes, it's been on the news for years now. How's the war going?"

He answered. "Praise be to Allah; it has finally ended. The problem is, the country needs help, and urgently."

"Yes, the country looked pretty beaten up with all that shelling into buildings. I've been seeing it on the nightly news. So why are you here seeing me, I'm only a small businessman with two shops. What can I do to help?"

At first, I thought he was going to ask for a donation or something. He explained, it is now vital to get their communication systems restarted. All their mobile networks are in tatters, they need to rebuild their transmitting towers and infrastructures and the like.

Yes, I agreed that the war went on for a long time and they bombed the shit out of each other. The place looked wrecked on TV.

"What can I do?" was my question.

He told me his distant cousin was married to the Minister of Communications. She asked him to find someone in Australia to help rebuild their network. It could be worth millions to a smart entrepreneur like me. You are on TV and must be in cahoots with Telstra big time. I was impressed that he had that opinion of me. But little did he know, I was still finding my feet financially too.

"Why are you not talking to Alan Bond (RIP) and men of that calibre?" I enquired.

"They are all crooks. I'd rather see someone like you reap all the rewards. They don't need any more money; they are too rich already," he explained.

My head was spinning. It's way out of my league. But I was in business and I liked taking **risks**.

I continued "Tell me more and what's in it for you?"

If I find someone to help Lebanon, the Minister could meet you next week. But you must go to Lebanon and talk business there. If you do strike up a deal, my commission is $15,000." He could get me an appointment to meet the Minister. I was excited but cautious.

"Okay, I'll think about this, you come back tomorrow. Talk to your cousin, tell him I'm interested and can fly out next Friday to meet him." Today was Saturday, so I had six days to get my act together.

I said to Ben, "You might have to go to Lebanon and work from there if this deal comes through. You know more about mobile phones than me. He was confused but said he was ready for any challenge I put to him. I went home and explained everything to Deirdre, and she was happy for us but threw a wet blanket over the situation. Are you sure about this? Deirdre was not just a pretty face. She can tell when it's fake or not.

I promised her I would check it out and make sure everything was true and correct. All it was going to cost me was an airfare and $15,000. But I had to hear that the deal was genuine. Ali was going to speak to the Minister from my office, and so was I. He spoke English well, so I was told.

Around 4 pm the next day, Ali came to my office. It was about 10 am in Lebanon. I rang Telstra and got the number for the Minister of Communications office in Lebanon. I made the call and a woman answered in Arabic. I gave the phone to Ali, and they spoke in Arabic for about three minutes. He was half yelling at her. I thought they were having a fight, but Ali explained later, it was how they talked. Ali said The Minister was in Germany, called away unexpectedly. We should try Tuesday. At least I witnessed the call made from my office, I dialled the number, and the phone number was given to me by Telstra, all legitimate. I told Deirdre all this, later at dinner.

We planned to meet Tuesday, same time at 4 pm. In the meantime, I booked a fully refundable flight to Beirut Thursday morning at 11 am arriving that evening for an early morning meeting on Friday.

On Tuesday at 4 pm, we rang the Minister's office, and again he was in another urgent meeting. This time more questions were asked like my full name, occupation, address, passport details, and where I was staying in Lebanon. Ali looked at me and repeated the meeting date and time twice to confirm I understood. I felt comfortable that I had a meeting with the Minister of Communications.

Now for the commission, I agreed to pay him $7,500 before I left, only if I got the appointment, and the other half after I got back. This was a big **risk** and yes, nothing might come of it, but it was an experience of a lifetime trying to strike up a deal like that, for me at least. I could just see the headlines "Budding Perth businessman Wendell Parnell from Phone Shop going to rescue Lebanon." At least the imaginative headlines seemed to be real in my head.

Ali was going to drive me to the airport Thursday morning, and I would pay him then. Everything was set and I was ready. Deirdre, however, was not in favour of my meeting anyone, especially in Lebanon.

On Wednesday about lunchtime, I rang the Embassy of Lebanon in Canberra because I forgot the address of the Minister's office. It was close to my hotel apparently, but best to be sure. This time, the lady who answered the phone spoke English fluently, named Cynthia. I asked for the address of the Minister's office in Beirut. I was so excited, I told her why I was asking for the address, I had a meeting with the Minister tomorrow.

She interrupted me and said, "Excuse me, you said you had a meeting with the Minister of Communications in Beirut?"

"Yes," I said, "My friend Ali's cousin was married to the Minister, and we fixed the meeting from my office on Tuesday." She asked me for my phone number and said she would call me back soon.

Ten minutes later I got a call from Cynthia. "Mr. Parnell, I was suspicious about this meeting, so I called the Minister's office in Beirut, and yes, you are booked to meet him at 10 am tomorrow. But we know he is in London for four days. This Ali is a fraudulent man and you're the second person he has made an appointment to see the Minister. I must tell you that it is a custom and an obligation for our government to meet with businesspeople. Anyone can make an appointment to see any Minister, but only if he's in town, then he might see them."

Cynthia went on to say, "I would advise you to cancel your trip, and try to speak to the Minister in Beirut before leaving Australia."

Point taken, thank you very much. I rang the fraud squad and explained the whole story to them but there was nothing they could do.

"He has not committed any crime. Ali said he'd get you an appointment and he did. You had not given him any money, so we can't charge him for fraudulently taking money from you" they said. Case closed. I went home to see Deirdre with my tail between my legs.

Black Dollars

Being seen on TV daily made me a target for crazy people. One day, I get a call from a man who sounded South African. He said he was from Zimbabwe and his name was George. He wanted to make an appointment to see me, as he had a surprise business package that would make me a rich man.

Isn't it wonderful that there are people in this world who want to make you rich, without even knowing you? How marvellous!

I agreed to meet George the following day at 1 pm. I was eager to find out what the 'surprise business package' he had to offer. The next day at about 1 pm, a rather large African man walked into our shop with a small suitcase that looked like it was heavy. He laid it on my desk, put his right hand forward to shake my hand and introduced himself.

"In this suitcase, is my surprise for you. It is going to make you a very rich man" he said.

I was very curious and dying to see what was in the suitcase. He picked up the suitcase and placed it beside the chair he was sitting down on. He put his hand into his pocket and brought out a small rectangular piece of paper, which looked exactly like currency. It looked like an old American one-dollar bill, or about that size, except it was totally black in colour.

George asked me if I had heard of Robert Mugabe.

"Of course, he's the President of Zimbabwe, am I right?"

George replied, "Yes." He continued to tell me that Robert Mugabe was married to his second cousin's sister-in-law's daughter. I tried to piece that bit together, but it was too complicated.

"Oh yeah, okay whatever, so he's your relative, fine." I said.

"Yes, we are related in some form somehow" George clarified.

He continued, "As you must already know, there are some very corrupt officials in that Mugabe government."

"That's nothing new," I said.

He told me, to smuggle this suitcase out of Zimbabwe, he paid a US $5,000 bribe.

He pulled out from his coat pocket, a small nail polish bottle, plus a packet of cotton wool buds, sometimes referred to as earbuds.

"Watch me," he said as he dipped the bud into the bottle and started to clean this black note ever so carefully and slowly. He kept rubbing the note with the tips of the cotton wool buds dipped in the bottle of solution and finally, a bit of white started to appear. It was rather suspenseful watching him. The more he rubbed, the more I saw what I thought looked like an American $100 bill Yep, it sure was a $100 bill amazing!

Whilst he was cleaning the note, he explained to me that the process usually took no more than one minute, and yes, that's probably how long it took until I saw the whole American one-hundred-dollar bill appear.

The solution was very expensive, but he would throw in two litres, more than enough to clean what he had in the suitcase, but only if we struck a deal.

The $100 bill wasn't what you would call; totally clean, but I bet, if you got a whole bag of these notes, and threw it all in the washing machine for five minutes on a gentle slow spin wash, they would come out perfectly new.

He presented me the $100 bill to inspect and said, "If you wish to see more, I have a suitcase full of these suckers."

I wanted to see more all right.

"Yeah, open the suitcase please."

When he opened it, there were all these neatly folded notes. All black, tied together in bundles. You've seen these many times in briefcases, in spy movies.

"I've counted these twice, and so far, each time I count them, I get a different result. Yesterday, I counted 10,009 notes, and the second count was 10,020 notes" George said.

Trying to be funny, I responded, "There's some discrepancy here, but who cares? Let's call it $1m in dirty dollars or 10,000 dirty notes which need cleaning." I thought I was funny, but he didn't laugh.

George explained he had it all worked out. "If you employed somebody at $500 a week and give them 400 notes to clean a day, he said, you'd have them all clean in about five weeks."

All along I'm calculating the profit margin and getting carried away in this la la land deal. When you do the maths and add it all up, after wages of $2,500, plus say another $1,000 for the costs of cotton buds and buying some extra solution to clean the notes, it was chicken feed to what I was going to make.

There was so much money to be made here, but what was the deal? There must be a catch! I asked him to tell me the business deal. It went like this.

He said, "Wendell, I'm in a bit of a jam at present, I need $10,000 Australian dollars urgently upfront. After you clean all these notes, and when you are happy with the outcome, I'll expect to receive another $200,000 Australian dollars as a final payment. That can be transferred to my overseas bank account. I'm happy for you to keep the rest of the money. That money is the last lot we managed to bring out of the country. I'll be flying back to South Africa by the end of this month."

"I thought you were from Zimbabwe?"

"I can't go back there, I'm a wanted man for taking all these US dollars that belong to Robert Mugabe. That's why it's coloured black" George explained.

Hmmmm!! I smelt a rat here, but I let him go on.

I said, "I get your business deal, but here's mine. I want a second test tomorrow. We clean another ten notes picked at random by me. If they all come out kosher, then I hand you the $10,000 Australian dollars in cash. If one out of the ten fails, we don't have a deal, the deals off, okay?" He agreed.

Before he left, he said he didn't have any Aussie dollars for the cab fare, would I swap an Aussie $100 bill for the American $100 bill he had just cleaned?

"Of course," I said, "We're doing big business tomorrow, aren't we?"

"Indeed, we are."

"Here, take two of mine, 2 x $100 Australian dollar bills for your clean $100 American dollar bill." He was very grateful for my generosity.

As he left, I said, "George, I think we might have a deal here. It's not too late to order $10,000 in cash from the bank, but it probably won't be ready until tomorrow morning." I rang the bank immediately and they agreed to deliver it by 10 am tomorrow.

"I also need to talk to my wife about this, as she co-signs all company cheques. I thank you for offering me this very good deal and I shall call you a little later. I will confirm what time the bank will have the money here."

He gave me his mobile number and I gave him mine and said, "Let's talk either late today or early tomorrow morning."

George left my office carrying that heavy suitcase. I was a little apprehensive at first, especially after hearing about African conmen. There were some stories out there. I thought, from time to time, you must take some **risks**.

Ben, who was listening to everything in the next room, was sort of waiting to speak to me.

"Ben, you must've heard most of the conversation?" I asked him.

Ben was about eight feet away from us all the time, but with his back to us pretending to read the newspaper.

"Yeah, I heard everything you guys said." Ben was rubbing his hands together and asked me if he could buy a twenty percent share in it.

"Ben, I'm happy for you to buy into this but, I don't think I liked what I saw. However, we still have tomorrow for the real test. Don't forget, we are going to randomly pick out ten notes to be cleaned, Ben. You pick five and I'll pick five."

Deirdre rang me for something after George had left.

I said, "Deirdre, wait until I get home, I have to tell you about this secret deal I just agreed to."

"What secret deal?" She sounded apprehensive. I had to explain to her everything that took place that afternoon.

"Even Ben wants to buy a 20% stake in this deal, that's how good this deal is." She was not happy at all.

"That $10,000 in the bank is there to pay our end-of-month bills. Are you crazy?" she retorted.

"Wait dear, when I tell you how many black $100 bills there were in his suitcase, for a lousy $10,000 from us, you will soon change your mind," I tried to reason. Those words didn't help either; we ended up having a tiff and she hung up.

That day, I had an appointment with my doctor in Dianella at 6.30 pm. I left the shop at 5.45 pm and arrived home just as the news was starting on TV. Deirdre was watching and had the volume turned down low. She still had the shits with me. Lo and behold, I recognised the image of the African man on the TV news.

"Quick, turn up the TV volume," I blurted out. She did. The newsreader went on to say, "the Police raided his hotel room at 4 pm today." And went on to say, "This man was charged with possession of a firearm and a quantity of drugs. The police had him under surveillance prior to his arrest."

"Oh shit, guess who that man was. Yes, it was George, that African man." I screamed out to Deirdre. I was in disbelief! Surely it couldn't be him? He was at my office at only 1 pm. He had the same clothes on. It couldn't be. I was in denial and rang Ben. He had not seen any news yet. I told him what I saw. I then asked Deirdre to watch the other news channel programs and let me know if she learned anything more.

I arrived home about 7.30 pm and sure enough, it was him, according to Deirdre. It was that African man who nearly conned me. Deirdre and I were so relieved.

The next morning while Ben and I talked about George, there was a knock on the door. We had not opened the shop yet; It was 8.30 am. We open at 9 am. Talk about a raid, everyone came in: the Police Dog Squad, Special Armed Squad, Drug Squad, Federal Police, and local Detectives. All in the one hit. We had about a dozen cops in our little shop. Ben and I were questioned.

Police: Mr. Parnell, your business acquaintance George Oosthuizen is safely locked up in prison. What was the nature of your business with him?

Me: I hardly know the guy. I had a meeting with him yesterday and that was the first time I've ever seen him. He came to buy a mobile phone.

I couldn't tell them the truth just in case they implicated me in some money laundering scheme. They asked all types of questions but couldn't get anywhere with my answers. Within fifteen minutes most had left. We only had three small rooms and the dogs couldn't do their job because there were no jobs for them to do. I was clean as, and the cops must have recognised that.

Police: So, tell me, Mr. Parnell, did you see what he carried in the suitcase?

Me: As a matter of fact, yes, I did. There were bundles of what looked like money, all in black bundles.

Police: Yes, it did look like money. But why would he show you those bundles?

Me: He opened his suitcase to get a large bottle of water. Was it real money?

Police: No, just blank paper dipped in black ink. We have no idea why anyone would carry around worthless black paper bundles.

Me: I agree.

Police: Did you see any guns or drugs in that suitcase?

Me: No, nothing like that, no guns, no drugs, just bundles of paper.

Ben looked at me and I looked at Ben.

Me: We couldn't work it out either. Why would someone carry around lots of black paper bundles in a suitcase?
Police: (To his offsider) I wonder who George was going to hold up with that gun?
Me: (Smiling at Ben) "Maybe someone holding $10,000 in cash?"
Police: Why did you say that?
Me: We ordered………..
Ben (Jumping in quickly, interrupting me), and said, "We ordered KFC from next door for this guy as he was hungry."
Me: (Smiling at Ben) Yes, it was part of the deal if he bought a mobile phone.

We both laughed at that little joke which baffled the cops. The police looked a little suspicious at our statement, and even more disappointed with all our answers. They then left empty-handed. Never heard from them again.

Ten minutes after the cops left, an armoured van pulled up right in front of our shop's front door. Out jumped two security guards with a bag and entered our shop. They asked to see Mr. Parnell, and I introduced myself. They then opened the bag, produced $10,000 in cash, and said it was from my bank. Please sign here.

Halleluiah, we were very lucky on that occasion, not to have been heard on the news about being held up for $10,000. Looked like that was his plan. Another lesson: one, two, and three. When it's too good to be true, usually it's not true.

Chapter 25

Meencomm Takeover 1998

You read about them earlier, remember? They harmlessly insinuated that we would last no more than three to six months in the industry. They were a situated in 318 Fitzgerald Street, about 200 metres up the road from us in West Perth. They were a telecommunications giant in our area. Their West Perth headquarters had a huge sign saying 'Ultimate/Meencomm Communications'. They operated from a large building with a huge antenna on the roof. When you drove past them, they looked bigger than Ben-Hur. They also owned a mobile phone shop in the very popular Karrinyup Shopping Centre. It was a very low-key affair over there. They hardly advertised it and were not showing good numbers like Phone Shop in Garden City were.

Alan Sharpe our State Manager once again tipped me off that Meencomm Communications wanted to get out of the industry. He told me Michael Meeney was more interested in computer software, computer solutions, solving computer problems, and writing computer programs. They had an office in Walter Road Morley, for that division.

I got in touch with Michael Meeney immediately after Alan Sharpe's tip-off. I rang Michael and went over to his office. It was roughly two hundred square metres in size. We had some meetings there at first. After about four weeks of negotiations, we struck up a deal and I announced to the industry that I was buying Ultimate Solutions/Meencomm

Communications in West Perth, and their Meencomm Communications Shop in Karrinyup Shopping Centre. Telstra was delighted.

They were quite happy to sell all their stock, and their customer database, subject to Telstra's approval. They had an ongoing monthly airtime commission cheque around $4,000. I quickly did the sums and worked out that we could afford to buy this business and turn it into a profit in about two years. Because we were so close to them, I did not want to take over their premises and staff. I did not need all their West Perth staff except for one guy but kept their Karrinyup staff.

There was this young man by the name of Tim Guest at their West Perth office who was their representative on the road. I needed this guy because he had been handling all their larger clients, like all the Shire Councils in and around Perth for the Meeney's for years. Tim had a good portfolio of government contacts in his books. If he went to work for another Telstra dealer, all these customers would have followed him. I couldn't have that, so I made him an offer to join us and offered him a little more money. We also paid him a commission for every new connect he made. So roughly, he got an extra $600 as a bonus each month, besides his weekly pay.

We now had to turn our little three-room E.T. Phone Home shop into our large headquarters, but how?

Remember back when we couldn't afford the $600 per week rent for the whole building at 281 Fitzgerald Street? By buying Meencomm Communications, everything changed dramatically.

I rang my new Vietnamese landlord and asked him if I could lease the rest of the building from him. We were still only paying $200 per week. All he had were some fabrics stored in the larger back part of our building. He was willing and very happy to remove all his fabrics, for an extra $450 a week. He also owned a large fabric shop in the Northbridge area.

We finally took over the whole building. Memories came flooding back. I remembered the conversation with Charles about buying this building from him one day. I also remembered many people commenting, "This

Wendell guy who's only worked at Just Phones for two months wants to open a small telecommunications shop next to three major players? He knows nothing about the business." Everyone believed that I would last three months and go bust for sure.

Well, I've got news for you buddy, not only did we not go bust, but we also bought out three more Telstra dealerships within three years of operations.

I did not want to take over the Meencomm Communications building and lease, as it was huge, very well decked out with lots of offices, all apparently built by Colin Richmond. I didn't want to move there either. It was perfect in every way except it didn't feel right, even though it had a large readymade office for me. I was quite happy where I was.

"I'll buy your business, equipment, all your stock and furniture on one condition, I do not want to take over your building or your lease," I informed Michael.

Michael agreed and came back with one other condition. If we were serious, we had to put a deposit down of $28,850 in two weeks. I agreed and we shook hands. We deposited the money into Poli and Associates Trust Account, their accountant's bank account, on Collier Road, Morley. I wrote to Telstra about the takeover, and they agreed to the sale almost immediately. I wonder why?

My dreams were now coming true, except for the building that I always wanted to own one day. That dream didn't come true. I sadly missed out on that one. But at least now, I was going to lease the whole building as first offered to me four years ago by Charles. We were still operating from only three rooms in West Perth all this time. We now had the Phone Shop in Garden City, where we stored most of our mobile phones. They were safer there with security guards with dogs inside patrolling the shopping centre all night.

Through Michael Meeney, I met this lovely man by the name of Colin Richmond. Colin was a teetotaller. A Scottish man that lived in the hills at Kalamunda, an outer suburb of Perth. Colin was an extremely good handyman who built all the offices for the Meaney's. I asked him if he could disassemble those offices at the Meeney's and reassemble them at our new premises. And could he also move all the office furniture and equipment we bought from the Meeney's. Move everything down to 281 Fitzgerald Street and re-erect it all down the road. He was so helpful and said yes. He had to dismantle and erect five offices to my premises just like he did in their building. Most of their offices were put up at different stages as they expanded. You could see each other through the top glass panels. They were your typical 'grey slapped together' offices you see in most buildings nowadays.

Colin did his research and measured out every inch of our building, working out how many offices we could build in there. He said he could fit all five offices down the road. Then we started the process of our transition into 281 Fitzgerald St West Perth. There was a lot of furniture, stock, tools, bits and pieces we had to transport down from Meencomm. Colin did all this with my help. This man was a genius with his hands and know-how. Within two weeks, we had a fully functional head office with seven offices. The five offices Colin built, my new third room office, and my old second room office, which is now Ben's office. He tore down the wooden panels that Charles had erected to separate the three-front rooms from the rest of the building. That gave us a straight walk-through from the front door to the back door in Eden Street. Wow, now we were starting to look like the big boys, hooray and thank you, Colin.

FINALLY EXPANDING DOWN IN TO THE BACK OF THE BUILDING. YOU CAN SEE THE GREY WALLS OF THE OFFICES COLIN INSTALLED FOR US

Michael and Catherina Meeney were a delightful couple to do business with and we wished them well in the future.

As we expanded, having taken over the whole building, our three small-room operations turned into a major headquarters. We now had five times more space to establish ourselves.

Our first move was to give Ben my office which delighted him. At last, Ben could invite customers into his office, rather than talk to them standing up in the front showroom. After Colin pulled down the plywood which Charles used to border up to separate the building, my new office was three times as big as my old one. This space was directly behind the original two rooms. Behind me was a glass panel in which you could see the other five offices. Deirdre occupied one, and later we had to employ an in-house accountant to help Deirdre. Then Deirdre needed a secretary, so another office was taken up by her secretary. We then employed another person to do our marketing, and another to do phone sales. So, all offices were taken up and we were flying high.

I forgot to mention, we then hired a technician to do our repairs; his name was Derek. We got so busy we hired a second technician; his name was Ian. We were the only strip dealer in Perth who had their own service centre. Can you imagine that?

I will now tell you a little story about our second technician, Ian.

He had an identical twin who looked 100% like him, (so I am told). How do I know his twin looked 100% like Ian? I didn't. Here's the answer.

Ian worked for us for about three years. Some days he would call in sick, as all staff do. Here's the irony of this story which I was only told about, one month after Ian left: on some days, unbeknown to us, his twin would substitute for him without us even knowing.

I never met his twin brother. But one of our ex-staff told me this when they had one too many drinks at a Telstra function. I thought it was funny, outside of the improvement his twin might have made, no one knew the difference.

He said it did not happen often, but it did happen. Ian's brother was also a technician. According to my ex-staff member, because he was friends with Ian, he could not rat on his friend. Typical Aussie attitude. But also like a typical Aussie, his tongue got loose after a couple of beers.

The technicians had their own workshop out the back of 281 Fitzgerald Street towards the back street. I hardly saw them because I was concentrating on the well-being of our Phone Shops in the shopping centres. In the beginning we were a two-man operation. Now we had grown to having ten staff working out of 281 Fitzgerald Street and eight more in the shopping centre stores. We were on fire.

We were going extremely well in Garden City, even though we lost our name E.T. Phone Home. We were now called Phone Shop in three suburbs and growing. The Karrinyup shopping centre shop was doing average business at first, but when we changed their name to Phone Shop and when our TV advertising kicked in, it made a huge difference to our whole business. Karrinyup started to make money as I predicted.

Yours truly was fronting the TV ads campaign and as I said before, some people didn't like me, but I'm sure a lot more liked me because they certainly came and bought mobile phones from us.

Eyelevel Communications Takeover 1998

Fred Pascoe was a gentle giant. A real Aussie bloke. Enjoyed a beer and was down to earth. He was a Telstra strip dealer at Erindale Road Balcatta. I met him at a few Telstra events, and we got to be good friends, so to speak. My good friend Geoff Ridgwell at Telstra tipped me off about Fred having personal problems and losing interest in the Telstra business. His business wasn't performing that well and he wanted to get out of the telecommunications industry.

Immediately I was on the case. I rang up Fred and invited him out to lunch. I questioned him about the reasons why he was quitting Telstra. He gave me many, but I won't disclose what they were. We met a few more times after that and I made him an offer. I didn't want to take over his shop. It was in a lousy spot I thought. To my luck, his lease was about to end anyway, and he wasn't going to renew it. The best way out for Fred was for him to sell his stock and the ongoing airtime commission cheques to another Telstra Premium dealer (guess who?) as soon as possible.

We agreed to a price for all his stock and airtime commission cheques. I had to honour his current customer's warranty on their mobile phones and had to send every one of his customers a letter explaining our takeover. I advised them that our Karrinyup Phone Shop was only three kilometres away and that we would serve their needs in the future. We also mentioned our West Perth head office was another point of call in an emergency. I submitted a long letter to Telstra outlining my proposal to buy Eyelevel Communications and showed them our letter being sent to all of Fred's client base.

Telstra as usual, acted surprised and pretended they knew nothing about my takeover. Within two weeks, Telstra approved the purchase and eventually continued to send me all Eyelevel Communications' airtime commission cheques. I promised Fred I would not disclose the buyout figure deal to anyone except Telstra, it was part of the due diligence process. Fred was happy about that.

It didn't take long for word to get out. 'Wendell is at it again; he's bought out Fred Pascoe's Eyelevel Communications business.' I wasn't aware of it at that time, but I was causing a few dealers to get the jitters. Nobody wanted to be axed by Telstra because they weren't performing well. I was just buying up when a good opportunity came along and kept opening new shops. That's all I was doing. Unbeknown to me, our enterprise had grown to become and recognised as: 1/ the first Telstra strip Dealership in Western Australia to have a string of stores in all major shopping centres, 2/ Have their own repair centre, and 3/ was the only dealership expanding. No other strip dealer had opened another shop anywhere in ten years.

Chapter 26

Subiaco Business Central 1997

Subiaco was the last Phone Shop we built from scratch. Being an affluent area, Telstra was hassling me to open there. Lucky I was in still in an expanding mood. This was shop number five, and why not? We were ahead of our targets with Telstra connections, our monthly cheque was growing, and we were riding high in the industry.

As a matter of fact, we made Subiaco our business distribution outlet. It made good business sense. Tim Guest was looking after all our business clients, so eventually I moved his office from West Perth to Subiaco. We had many Shire Councils, large corporations like Woodside Petroleum, Wesfarmers, and many other big mining companies on our books. It made good sense to show a profit and new connections from this new shop. The new Subiaco shop fit-out costs us more than we paid for the entire Phone Shop Garden City. But who cared?! We could afford it; money was coming in. It was the right move.

The Subiaco Central shopping mall management called and offered me space at a reasonable price and there we opened. It wasn't a large shopping mall and Telstra had nothing in the area, so I thought it might be a good investment. All we had to do was add the new location to all our advertising, at no extra cost.

One day a young lady about 25 years old came to Subiaco Phone Shop to buy a cordless phone. I happened to be there that day and they were busy. I helped serve a few customers. Now to be very honest, although I owned the shop, I hardly knew the products. Only enough to get by. I usually called the other staff to help me out or to finish the sale. I sold her a Uniden cordless phone for $159 and she left very happy.

Three weeks later she returned. This time she was angry. The phone was not working. I assured her it would be fixed; I'd take it back to headquarters straight away and get my technician to look at it. I did this immediately. Later, I was told by my technician that the phone had been for a swim in the pool or somewhere which voided the warranty. I rang her back and explained what I was told by our technician.

Well, did she go off the handle! She accused us of telling lies just to sell her another phone. That she was a single mother and "how dare I rip her off" etc. I apologised for the bad news and offered her another phone at cost price.

She wasn't going to have a bar of it. "My boyfriend will come and sort you out, wait and see," she told me.

The next day I got a frantic call from Tim Guest. "Wendell, what have you done to this bird with the cordless Uniden phone?"

"What are you talking about?" I asked.

"John Kizon just came into the shop asking for you. I told him you were not here. Kizon told me to tell you to come here and he would be back in an hour.

STOP PRESS. For those of you unfamiliar with Perth's social scene at the time, Mr Kizon was akin to 'Perth Mafia Royalty'. I didn't need to have a brush with him. This colourful man had regular bad press with alleged involvements with bikies and gangland business, thus he was a household name in Perth. He was blamed for many crimes in Perth which were probably not true. John Kizon, I am sure, is a very nice gentleman and I'm sure that he only wanted to chat with me about buying a new handset (err well maybe not), but I said to Tim, "I'm very busy and I am not coming to the shop today. It is not worth losing an arm or a leg over a $159 cordless phone. Just give him a new phone and apologise on my behalf." Tim Guest was extremely happy with my decision. I never saw that lady again. And I am still alive. God bless.

Panasonic Court Case

We used to sell the very popular Panasonic cordless landline home phone. You could buy them as single or double-extension handsets. Apart from facsimile machines, photocopiers, and accessories, they also sold the widely acclaimed four handsets version. Alan McDougal was our representative for Panasonic in Western Australia. He was a good supplier for us.

One day a lady came into our West Perth shop looking for one of these home handsets. Panasonic was a good brand and we had very few returns selling them, so we always chose to recommend them before Sony or Uniden.

She was carrying her young daughter on her hips who immediately grabbed everything I showed the mother. One of these inquisitive kids. I explained all the good features of the phone and she agreed to buy it. I placed the phone into one of our Phone Shop carry bags and she left.

About a month later she returned with the cordless phone in two pieces in the same bag. I was astonished. I'd never seen one in two pieces before as they were made very sturdy.

"Did you drop in from a high ledge or something?" I asked.

"No."

"What I can do, is replace it with a new handset and give you a big discount." "No, I want you to replace it under warranty." she insisted.

I thought it was rather presumptuous of her to expect a replacement when you could clearly see it was dropped and that's what happens when you drop phones. To keep her happy and to show her that I cared, I said, "Allow me to confer with my service manager Derek. I'll be back in a few minutes." Then took the item out the back and showed it to him.

He said with a big smile, "Was this thrown up into the air and someone forgot to catch it on the way down?" I explained what the customer told me. He showed me something else I didn't see.

"Look, a dog has also been chewing on the antenna. The antenna is destroyed, so even if the phone was not dropped and broken in two, the customer would have to replace this phone regardless" explained Derek.

I went back out front and explained all this to her. She was not impressed.

She threatened that I either replace it, or she'll report me to the Ombudsman, or someone like that.

Disappointed I said, "You have that right and I wish you luck." She left the store.

Later Derek said to me, "I think this customer was trying to pull a fast one on you!" I agreed with him sadly.

A few weeks later, in the mail, I got a summons from the courthouse. I opened the letter which summonsed me to appear at the small claim's tribunal or similar, (I don't remember the name exactly). I showed the letter to Deirdre who had already been informed about this situation and knew the facts.

She said, "It's your time. Is it worth going to court for a lousy $190?" According to me, yes, it was.

I went to court on the said date and took my service manager along to explain and to give the magistrate his expert opinion. I saw the lady standing outside. She glanced at me with a rotten look. I smiled back but thought to myself, I won't be so nice to you when you lose this case. I won't be offering you a discount anymore!

When our turn came, the charge was read out and the case proceeded. The Magistrate smiled at her with the baby in her arms, bowed his head down and looked out over the rim of his glasses, and asked her to give her evidence for this case. Well, talk about acting, this woman deserved to be on the *Bold and the Beautiful* TV series for being able to cry at the drop of a hat. Before she uttered her first sentence, she started crying without any good rhyme or reason.

The magistrate offered her some tissues, and when she stopped crying, he asked "Was it ever dropped from a great height?" She claimed the phone did fall off the coffee table, which was only about a foot or 30cm from the carpeted floor. She then went on with the "I'm a poor, single mother" yarn. I was bamboozled and irritated he was letting her spill out all this bullshit.

One would never throw up in public, unless one had been food poisoned, or you overindulged in alcohol, but this was the one occasion I felt like throwing up.

The magistrate asked to look at the Panasonic phone, which was passed on to him to be examined.

He uttered some words, looked at her and said, "Yes, I see what you mean."

It was my turn. He took his glasses off and looked at me "Mr Parnell, what have you to say in your defence?"

I asked, "Would it be okay if my Service Manager spoke of the problem, he could do it much better? I am untrained in the technicalities of the phone."

"No, I want your version of what happened. You are the proprietor are you not?"

"Yes, I am sir." I said, "But......."

He cut me off, "No Mr. Parnell, you tell me, in your own words about what you think happened to the phone." I was getting the message things weren't going my way. I told him the whole story from start to end, as you have already read.

He took his time looking at the phone.

He then said, "In this modern age of technology, one would think the manufacturers would make their products with more durability. As for the teeth marks, this innocent child would have never meant any harm to this phone."

This case had taken all of 15 minutes; it was crunch time. An answer was coming. Was it going to favour me, or her? I wasn't very confident anymore. The magistrate was writing something down and taking his time. I was starting to sweat a little as I was getting more rattled as the minutes passed. Finally, after deliberating for a few minutes, the verdict was read out.

"I find this case in favour of the plaintiff, therefore Mr Parnell, you are to fully refund the plaintiff the original invoice price, and furthermore, you are to pay all court costs" the magistrate announced.

I certainly didn't agree with the magistrate here. In the twelve years we'd been trading, I was taken to court on five occasions. I won the other four, this one was a no-brainer case. People always think we try and cheat them. This was the only case I ever lost. I took it on the chin.

The following day, our friendly representative from Panasonic, Alan McDougal came for a visit. I'd never mentioned this to him before, but I had to tell him the court case story.

He was shocked by the news, and said "Wendell, why didn't you tell me this earlier?"

"It was a no-brainer, Alan; this was wilful damage, and the judge knew it."

He said "No, I meant if you had informed me of this in the first place, I would have given you a new replacement phone for free and saved you all that trouble of going to court." Thanks Alan. Now you tell me! You can't win them all.

Chapter 27

Melbourne Cup Competition at Garden City - 1999

My old mate and the best Telstra rep I met in my time with Telstra was Geoff Ridgwell. One morning he walked into my shop at West Perth with a big smile. We were now called Phone Shop.

Geoff said, "Wendell, there's a competition coming up that I think you should partake in. I know you have an artistic flare from your musical background. You're going to love being in this artistic competition."

He went on, "And if you win, we're going to send you to the Melbourne Cup. There are only three winners from each State."

Now those words caught my attention. I'd never been to the Melbourne Cup and of course, I would love to go.

"What do you have to do to win a spot for the Melbourne Cup prize?" I asked.

"It's easy. About two months before the Melbourne Cup, we are doing a huge promotion on TV, radio, and the newspapers. The artistic part of the promotion would be that all the strip dealers do something fancy in their stores. Whether dressing up your shop or anything fancy to attract people. We will be promoting it heavily through the media to try and get customers to come into your shops and do a Telstra connection or buy a mobile phone from your store."

He told me about the dealers from other stores were already planning their strategies. The end decision on who went to the Melbourne Cup depended on the best presentation and artistic content within their shop. And as always, how many phones were sold or how many Telstra connections were made on that day, the usual catch.

"Hey Wendell", Geoff asked, "Would you like to win a spot to go to the Melbourne Cup?"

"Geoff, I'm *going* to win a seat, I already know it," I smiled with excitement.

When Geoff left, I quickly rang my dodgy brother, Ben Stuckey, and told him the news.

"Ben, put your thinking cap on, when I visit you later today, we can discuss it further."

That afternoon I went to Garden City and met Ben.

"Ben, we need to do something outrageous, outlandish, outstanding because if we only depend on sales and connections, the big boys will win hands down. They have the upper hand with many shops." We discussed many ideas but still felt behind the eight ball against the bigger dealers.

I told Ben we could spend hundreds of dollars dressing up both shops. But I didn't like our chances knowing the bigger dealers could easily outspend us and win hands down. Their connections daily outran us.

Then my artistic side kicked in. I thought, why waste money and time on decorations in both shops? We could put up more signs, streamers, and balloons, only to throw them away later. Why not instead hire six real jockeys to be present at the Garden City shop on the day the judges were going to inspect various shops to pick some winners? Ben thought it was a marvellous idea.

I rang the jockey club at Ascot Racecourse and inquired about hiring some apprentice jockeys. They needed to be fully dressed up with whips in hand and stand outside our Garden City Phone Shop between 12pm-2pm, Simple. They agreed to send six apprentice jockeys at a cost of $900 ($150 each). I was happy and hoped they wouldn't let me down. I spoke to Ben at Garden City about my idea that afternoon.

"Why six jockeys, why not six other good-looking entertainers?" Ben suggested. Good one Ben, I like your idea better. We needed variety. I rang some of my friends and managed to get five entertainers and kept one jockey to keep within the theme of the Melbourne Cup.

I got my friend Patti Broad to dress as one of those women in the Caribbean style dress who wore fruit on her head, an Elvis Presley lookalike, a Rugby League player, a Grand Prix racing car driver, and a professional golfer, all at a cost at $600. This saved us $300!

THE CREW FOR THE MELBOURNE CUP COMPETITION STANDING OUTSIDE OUR GARDEN CITY, BOORAGOON PHONE SHOP

I had to make sure that Telstra was going to do their rounds and inspections on the day I contracted these people. Geoff and I were good mates by now, so I asked him for a special favour.

"Firstly, I need to know what day you guys are inspecting the shops. And secondly, make sure you bring your State Manager Jim Woods here between 12-2 pm on that day," I insisted.

"I'll just tell him Wendell invited us to have lunch with him on that day at 1 pm." Geoff assured me. What a friend.

That day, to go the extra mile, I gave in and bought lots of balloons and streamers and put up plenty of signage which made the shop in Garden City look like it was party time.

At exactly 12 pm, the six entertainers walked slowly towards our shop. How did I know that? We could tell by the customer's reaction; something was going on. You never saw such a spectacle. Five entertainers all dressed up, and one jockey with a cap on and whip in hand in a shopping centre! They looked very colourful and by the time I greeted them we were starting to draw more people and attention.

One thing I did forget, I was supposed to mention to the shopping Centre Management of our exploits that day. They soon came around and asked me what the hell was going on. I explained the reason and they reminded me the next time to ask permission in writing.

Then one of them said, "I hope you are not bringing real horses into the shopping centre, are you?" I assured them I was not. Phew!

The crowd was building and the kids were being handed balloons by the entertainers which in itself caused a commotion. It was all going as planned.

Lo and behold, meandering at the back of the crowd, I saw Geoff Ridgwell, accompanied by Jim Woods (State Manager), with a big smile. He waved at me enthusiastically, and I was sure a prize was in store for me. I went and had lunch with them. Jim Woods was so impressed, he insisted Telstra pay for lunch which was another bonus. Remember, it was me who asked them for lunch. And guess what? I went to the Melbourne Cup, hooray!

Rojan Josh won the Melbourne Cup; my horse ran second last. You certainly don't win them all.

Chapter 28

Belmont Forum Little Shop

In 2006 we when we took over Meencomm Communications, we shifted their entire stock, furnishing, offices and a very large safe. Yes, every single item I paid for went to West Perth, all moved by a Scottish friend Colin Richmond. He lived in Kalamunda, a distant outer suburb of Perth. I was surprised, when one day, out of nowhere, I got a call from Colin.

"Wendell, do you know of the Belmont Forum shopping centre?" he asked.

"Yes, but I don't go there, why do you ask?"

"I'm pulling down a trinket shop, and I was thinking of you. With all that extra Meencomm Communication shelving you have leftover; this shop would suit your business perfectly. I thought before I pull everything down, I'd give you a ring." I thanked him for thinking of me.

He continued, "I know the management here well. They regularly appoint me to disassemble shops. I'm dismantling a shop that went broke. They have not paid their rent for six months or more. It would be a shame to take all these beautiful slat walls and furnishings to the tip. They hardly put it up for sale."

I was curious. "You have caught me at a good time. I'm free and Belmont is only fifteen minutes away. I'll race over now and have a look".

"Okay, I'll have a morning tea break and wait for you."

I got there about 10.30 am and met Colin opposite the Strand Bags where the empty shop was. I had a good look and thought wow, he was right about all the wastage if pulled down.

"If anyone re-fits this shop, it would cost a lot of money to rebuild" he said.

I agreed with him. Replacing the plate glass windows and the roller shutters was at least $10,000; forget everything else. Just add Telstra display cabinets and get lots of their signage and you'd have a Telstra-looking shop for next to nothing. What shall I do?

Colin then rang Jill from Centre Management, who popped over within fifteen minutes. Colin introduced us. Jill asked if I was interested in leasing the shop.

As usual, I put my thumb and pointer finger to my chin, pulled it a few times and lied, "It's not quite what I'm looking for, but I can consider it."

"Why don't you come to my office, and we can have a chat," said Jill.

Before we left, I whispered into Colin's ear not to pull down the good bits he knew I needed. I could do a deal here straight away.

He winked at me and said, "Righto."

I sat down in Jill's office while she got me a coffee. I rang Deirdre and told her what I was up to and she reminded me we had just bought two other businesses recently and the bank was keeping close tabs on us.

"Babes, I'm going to pull off the biggest coup here since the Phone Shop takeover. I'm going to steal this shop from them," I reassured her.

Jill came back and it was business that I wanted to discuss. Jill told me Colin had mentioned to her I bought Phone Shop Garden City, Meencomm Communications, and Eyelevel Communications recently and I was expanding aggressively.

"Congratulations Wendell. What do you think of our shopping centre?" Jill asked.

Now, I was on TV regularly, operating in the Garden City Booragoon and Karrinyup shopping centres which were classed as A-grade centres compared to poor old Belmont Forum, a B-grade centre. She knew that too. So, I thought why not pitch for as much as I can get?

"For starters, what's the rent and outgoings," I enquired. She told me. I was mildly surprised, a little less compared to the other two centres I was paying rent to. She mentioned that they would welcome a Telstra dealer in their centre. Just what I wanted to hear.

"Hmmmmmm, what about that shop? You must want some money back from the rent they owe you?" I probed.

"If you are really interested in opening in Belmont Forum, I will talk to the owners straight away and ask if you can have all the fittings and furnishings for free."

"What about Colin, I would want him to stop work straight away and he might lose money over our immediate deal?"

"He would be paid as he quoted a flat fee," she reassured me.

I rang Colin and asked him to stop work. I excused myself and went and had another look at the shop. Yes, he was right, the shop re-fit would cost $20,000 to $30,000. There were lots of stands, furnishings, and good fittings worth a fortune, and all mine for free. What a coup!

I went back to Jill and told her some white lies; I said I had spoken to my partner but there were three conditions I wanted to add. First, we would take the shop as is. Secondly, I wanted to include in the three-by-three-year lease that there was to be no other Telstra dealer allowed to trade there during my lease agreement. Finally, I wanted three months' free rent. She said she would put it to the owner.

I went back to Phone Shop West Perth and told Deirdre the story and I rang Ben too. Both listened to my story and wished me luck. The demand to lock out Telstra would be hard; the rest was achievable. I felt confident and comfortable that the deal might work. I remembered the deal at Garden City when I didn't have the experience to demand such things. I would wait and see.

I got a call from Jill early the next morning and she said, "Wendell I have good and bad news. Which one first?"

I asked for the bad first.

"Well, the owner wants you to open four weeks from today as he has lost enough from no rent in the past six months. And the good news, he has agreed to your terms." Jill said.

"Call me when you have the contracts ready, and I'll open in four weeks." I had to inform Telstra about my takeover, and they were happy as they were also looking for one of their other dealers to open there, but too late buddy. Wendell jumped in first, again!

For us, this was the easiest shop to open. Ninety percent of the shop was there; all I needed was a sign for the shop. I rang Colin and told him the news and thanked him profusely. I also employed him to rebuild this shop and to bring certain items from West Perth; the remains from Meencomm Communications to deck out this new place. It worked and we opened four weeks later.

Unfortunately, it didn't take long for the burglars to figure out there was a Telstra mobile phone shop operating in the Belmont Forum shopping centre. There were lots of opportunities for these thieves but how would they break in? The shopping centre had guards in patrol cars patrolling around the outside perimeters and on the inside.

Numbers against phone thieves

By Kate Gauntlett

UP TO 70,000 mobile phones have been stolen in Australia in the past year but industry representatives have warned thieves and stolen phone buyers that a number identification system means they will lose out.

Phone Shop retail chain managing director Wendell Parnell said thieves broke into his Belmont Forum shop on Monday night and left with 70 phones.

"We've been hit nine times in six years," he said.

The 70 stolen phones, mainly Nokia, are worth about $35,000, or $500 each. Mr Parnell expected people would be offered them on the black market for about $50.

He warned those tempted to buy a cheap second-hand phone.

"Serial numbers on mobile phones mean you can trace the stolen phone to a person using it," Mr Parnell said.

Police Sgt Mike Gough said people whose phones were stolen should give their phone's international mobile equipment identity number to their carrier.

The identification numbers are recorded inside the handset by makers and transmitted whenever the phone is used.

Carriers have access to a database which registers stolen mobile phones' numbers.

The Australian Mobile Telecommunications Association keeps the database and alerts police when a stolen phone is used. People buying a second-hand phone can check on the AMTA "findaphone" Web site to see if their phone is stolen. AMTA spokesman David Black said that since the database was set up last March, 69,000 phones had been reported missing.

It is not known how many illegal users have been caught as a result of the new system, which relies on the cooperation of carriers and police.

The AMTA and carriers are discussing complex technical and legal restrictions of blocking use of a stolen mobile phone.

$35,000 loser: Phone Shop chain managing director Wendell Parnell with some of the types of phones taken from his Belmont Forum shop on Monday night. Seventy phones worth $35,000 went in the raid. PICTURE: ROD TAYLOR

ORIGINAL PAPER ARTICLE ABOUT THE BREAKIN AT OUR BELMONT FORUM PHONE SHOP

I got a call from the centre guards at about 2 am advising me that there had been an entry into the shopping centre, and it was the Phone Shop that was broken into. I couldn't figure it out as the shopping centre was well guarded.

As usual I attended to see what the damage and mess was. Ben also arrived within minutes of me. The security guards were there and could only watch from the outside of the shop. I had to open the roller shutter doors to inspect the damage and loss inside. The thieves smashed the Telstra display cabinets and made off with lots of mobile phones. The break-in was discovered by the security guard on his rounds, but strangely no alarms went off. This was most unusual. We didn't have an alarm system in that shop. Rarely was the shopping centre ever broken into. The outer parameter shops facing the street were targeted from time to time.

We cleaned up the shop as we were experts by now; five break-ins in West Perth. Read the write-up we got in the article provided.

Now here's the report from the shopping centre the next day. They claimed that the burglars climbed onto the roof from the eastern corner of the shopping centre, cut a hole in the roof and came down into the shop from the roof, directly above my shop, took what they could and left the same way. The police who attended the next day were baffled as to how they got to the *exact spot* considering our shop was right in the middle of the shopping centre. Where were the guards?

Maybe nowadays you could use your mobile phone's GPS to get an accurate hit, but in those days, it was not possible. The police suspected some inside help but came to no conclusions. All the monitor alarm's sensors were placed in the entry points and nowhere else, thus no alarms went off.

There, go figure out how these things can happen. The Centre Management assured me they were installing alarm sensors in the roof cavities of the building immediately. They learned for free, at my cost.

Chapter 29

Telstra Opening at Garden City

Telstra was now starting to open their own branded 'Telstra Shops'. They were bigger and much slicker than ours. They had the money to spend. Back then, we were all called *strip dealers* as we were not only in shopping centres, but out on main roads or strip somewhere out in the suburbs. So, when I bought the Phone Shop at Garden City, in the elite suburb of Booragoon, I was Telstra's hero. They were very happy that I was going to sell their goods and services there. I was also upholding the Telstra name at the Karrinyup Shopping Centre.

Then came the bad news. I heard from our dealer manager that Telstra was looking at opening a rather large store in Garden City, just 100 metres away from the Phone Shop. They were also opening a store in the Carousel and Karrinyup shopping centres. Can you imagine how I felt? It was like being hit by a bus.

We were being encouraged to open our own branded name shops in major shopping centres, only to find out Telstra themselves was now our competitor. Not Optus or Vodaphone, but our Lord and Master. Seriously? How stupid to have two Telstra-branded shops in the same shopping centre. One called Phone Shop, Telstra's Premium Licensed Dealer, fully authorised and representing Telstra. The other one simply called Telstra Shop, our new competition. This was the next biggest shock I encountered, apart from the One-Tel episode. Telstra was going to open in opposition to me.

I approached Mark Bradbury, our state manager at the time. He was apologetic but explained to me that the new Telstra's rollout strategy was beyond his control.

"Why are you opening in opposition to me? Why don't you just let me open that as a Telstra Licensed Shop? I'll close Phone Shop down and we can have one Telstra Licensed Shop rather than have two Telstra outlets in the same shopping centre," I pleaded.

"Wendell the thing that worries us about you running the Telstra Shop is the rent. You are now paying only $5,000 a month. Our new Telstra Shop is going to jump to $15,000 a month, which you might not be able to afford." I don't think Telstra would have opened any shop knowing they might lose money on it. We were the guinea pigs already.

He admitted to me that the shop was going to be three times bigger than the Phone Shop. The news of Telstra opening its new branded Telstra Shop was frightening. We were Phone Shop licensed by Telstra; it just didn't make sense.

The new shops would obviously impact my business in a negative way. The average person would go directly to the Telstra Shop, rather than deal indirectly with Telstra through us. Mark and I had several meetings and disputes over the next four weeks because they insisted, they were opening. Getting them to trust me to open it fell on deaf ears.

Telstra had done their homework and knew the market much better than me. Would they open a shop knowing they might not succeed? Not likely. They had data from their national network shops and already knew the killing they were going to make. Also killing my business at the same time. I even considered challenging them in court.

I flew to Melbourne to have a talk with Mark's boss with the hope that he would see my logic, but I didn't get anywhere with him either.

By this time, I was becoming disillusioned with Telstra, and I even considered exiting the telephony industry because it felt like my whole world was crumbling down. I tried my best to persuade them but didn't get anywhere:; finally had to accept defeat.

One day Mark Bradbury came for a visit with Rob Engelbrecht (RIP) our new area manager. (Geoff Ridgwell had moved on by now). Mark looked worried.

"What have I done wrong this time?" I asked in jest.

"I've just been informed by our leasing department that you have stopped Telstra from opening at the Belmont Forum shopping centre," he said sternly.

This was a pure victory for me, because for once I had the upper hand here in the Belmont Forum shopping centre, thanks to the lesson I learnt at Phone Shop Garden City. I didn't have the experience back then, but now finally, the shoe was now on the other foot.

Telstra wanted me to change my lease wording with the Belmont Forum shopping centre. I asked Mark to clarify.

"Telstra approached the Belmont Forum shopping centre to open a Telstra Shop and were told that Wendell Parnell, the guy from Phone Shop, had written into his lease not to let any other Telstra operator into the shopping centre for the duration of his lease with the Belmont Forum." The shopping centre had no choice but to honour our lease and contract. Telstra for once were beaten at their own bullying game.

A week later, I got a call from Rob Engelbrecht, my new dealer manager, who informed me that Mark Bradbury and his boss from Melbourne wanted to set up a meeting. They were prepared to come over to my office (at the closest café, Miss Maud's) to try to persuade me.

With nothing to lose, I agreed to the meeting.

We set a date and time and met at Miss Maud's. The first thing voiced was not being able to take over the Telstra Shop at Garden City, Carousel or Karrinyup. They informed me that they'd come up with a compromise that might be suitable for both parties and asked if I would at least listen to it.

"Start talking, I'm listening," I leaned in.

They said the compromise was that I open a Telstra Licensed Shop at Belmont Forum, instead of them, and close the Phone Shop. It was the only choice they had to fulfill their rollout strategy. There was one condition; I had to open the Telstra Shop no later than four months from that meeting date.

"Let me think about it and I'll let you know tomorrow," I replied.

I discussed their proposal with Deirdre and Ben. We all agreed it was better to have one Telstra Licensed Shop at Belmont Forum shopping centre, rather than two Telstra operators as in Garden City. Our Phone Shop lease was coming up for renewal and I had a three-year option. So, I agreed and brazenly suggested Telstra chip in a few thousand dollars to assist in building our new Telstra Licensed Shop. My excuse was that I had just spent $30,000 refurbishing Phone Shop (a slight exaggeration), which would be wasted. Telstra didn't have much choice but to agree. They threw in 20% towards the cost of building the new Telstra Licensed Shop. The shop to build cost a staggering $200,000 - the cost of a four-bedroom home out in the suburbs - back in those days. It was quite strange because once we built the Telstra Licensed Shop as agreed within four months, we still had a six-month lease on our other Phone Shop situated 100 metres away.

Ben was now managing the new Telstra Licensed Shop in Belmont Forum and overseeing what we call the 'little shop' around the corner'. So, when a customer came into the Telstra Licensed Shop and if they were unhappy with the price, Ben would recommend to them they try the other little Telstra Shop up the road. He would tell the customer they always sell things a bit cheaper or for less at the Phone Shop.

If the customer wanted to buy a leather case that Telstra Licensed Shop was selling for $39 and thought it was too expensive, they would be redirected to Phone Shop. Ben would quickly ring Phone Shop and describe the customer coming. 'Tell the guy he can have it for $36, three dollars cheaper'. The Phone Shop would always make the sale. Vice versa, if we couldn't get a sale or connect out of the customer from the Phone Shop, we'd send them to the Telstra Licensed Shop. In legal terms, it was against the Monopolies Act. What we were doing was tinkering on illegal, but we got away with it. You can call it being naughty.

Chapter 30

Becoming Disillusioned with Telstra

The realisation the end was near began to appear the day I learned Telstra was preparing for a huge rollout in every major shopping centres all around Western Australia.

Telstra advertised in the newspapers looking for new Licensees. If successful, they would be given a license to operate a shiny new Telstra Licensed Shop which were increasing in popularity.

A new wave of business-minded people were on the hunt. By now the word was out that owning a Telstra Licensed Shop was the way to go. There was big money to be made. The writing was on the wall.

As time went on, the floodgates opened. There were more and more Telstra Shops and Telstra Licensed Shops opening in shopping centres locally and in all major towns including, Albany, Bunbury, Kalgoorlie, Geraldton, Busselton, and other smaller towns. Just like McDonalds, they were popping up everywhere.

I knew I had had enough. Even if I wanted to expand, I would have to go into more shopping centres as Phone Shop. Then Telstra might decide to put another Telstra Shop or Telstra Licensed Shop next to me. I wasn't going to take that chance, so I stopped expanding. The Telstra expansion continued all around Australia.

Some local strip dealers were thankful and praised me for the clever stunt I pulled over Telstra with the Belmont Forum shopping centre lease.

Some smarter strip dealers were also planning to move into shopping centres after seeing my success at the Garden City shopping centre with Phone Shop. Once Telstra gave me a Telstra Licensed Shop to operate in Belmont Forum, other strip dealers were asking for the same rights.

Little did they know, Telstra was trying to get rid of all strip dealers, including me! That meant all the strip dealer shops ending with the word "Communications" were going to be shut down. They only wanted to have Telstra Shops owned by Telstra, or Telstra Licensed Shops on the scene. The Licensed Shops were now going to be owned by smart businesspeople, that was their game plan.

Chapter 31

Had Some Big Wins 2001 Smashing Telstra's Glass Window

It was a ridiculous, shameful and stretched relationship between Telstra and all their strip dealer partners and the Telstra Licensed Shop licensees. This was the very reason why Donald Black from Phone Shop never wanted to sell mobile phones. I can understand his reasoning, but I'm also glad about his decision not to convert to Telstra. If he did, I wouldn't be writing this story today.

Somehow, it was always a lopsided disadvantage to the dealers. First, you'd have to buy the mobile phones from either Brightpoint, Roadhound, TelePacific or Telstra. Then you'd sell it to the customer for zero dollars. They must sign up for a $50 or higher plan. You then send a copy of the contract signed to Telstra at 242 Exhibition Street Melbourne. Telstra would then process it and send you back the original costs of the phone you purchased. That's one department. Another would send you a $30 connection fee, and another would send you the monthly airtime commission cheque. All these monies owed would arrive one month later, and sometimes much later. That made our cash flow very tight.

All this can work providing you had a good cashflow to begin with. Even though Telstra gave you credit, depending on the size of your dealership, and the time of year, there often were periods when Telstra owed you more rebates than you had credit. Let me tell you about one of those occasions.

It was in the middle of November 2001 when I found out we were selling more products of Telstra than ever. Our TV advertising certainly was making a dent in our stock cage. Ben, Deirdre and I had an emergency meeting as stocks were depleting fast. Also, knowing Christmas was only four to six weeks away, we had to act fast. Ben got me the stock report, whilst Deirdre got the finance report. Deirdre told me we had used up all our credit with the distribution centre at Telstra. Ben complained and told me we were low on stock. Not a good position to be in, especially when the best sales months were coming up.

Gone were the days when we used to buy 10-20 mobile phones at a time. We were now buying them by the pallets. There are 100 mobile phones in a pallet. If the average price was $500 each, then the pallet costs $50,000. We were receiving at least one pallet per week, sometimes two. Remember, we had six shops to supply, and Christmas was only six weeks away.

I put an order in for 300 mobile phones, thinking if we didn't sell them all by Christmas, we would move them early in January 2002. We waited two weeks before Ben informed me, we needed stock as we were running low. I rang the distribution centre and asked when I should expect to receive my order. I was informed my order was still there, they were waiting for clearance of my credit limit. I immediately spoke to Deirdre and asked what was going on? She said we were over our credit limit with the distribution centre. Our limit was $150,000, and the stock was going to cost $250,000.

"How much were we owed in rebates?" I asked her.

"Roughly $280,000." was her answer.

I rang up my State Manager and explained everything to him. He was very sympathetic and said he would ring up and find out what was going on. Fifteen minutes later I got a call back from him. He told me exactly what I already knew. He said he had rung his National Manager, but he was in a meeting.

"It's 10 am, the 16th of November, and even if the stock left Melbourne today, I'd have to wait another week for it to arrive. We are getting very low on stock here" I informed him.

"I'll call you back soon." It was 11 am and I was getting impatient and worried. He called me back and said the distribution centre won't release my stock until I paid my account in full.

"Mark, we both know I'm not exaggerating when I say Telstra owes me more than I owe them."

He agreed but was helpless. I asked him who his National Manager was?

"David Bickett," and Mark was kind enough to give me his direct number.

I rang David Bickett, and similar answers, the same thing happened, it was out of his control. It was 12 pm and can't tell you how stressed I was. I thought, I must talk to the No 1 man in Telstra, he definitely should be able to help me. So, I rang David Thodey's (CEO) office in Melbourne at the Rialto building, Telstra's headquarters. They put me through to his secretary Rayeleen Olds. She was a lovely lady, who calmed me down. Before she calmed me down, this was part of the conversation:

Rayeleen: Good Morning, David Thodey's office, this is Rayeleen Olds.
Me: Hello Rayeleen, this is Wendell Parnell and I'm the licensee of the 'Phone Shop Group' (Group sounded better, we had six shops) in Western Australia.
Rayeleen: Hello Wendell, how can I help you?
Me: I'd like to speak to Mr Thodey please.
Rayeleen: Sorry, he's in a meeting all day outside of the building. Can I take a message?
Me: No Rayeleen, but whatever I say here and now, I want you to make notes, so Telstra can't say later that I didn't warn them. I apologise if I was rude to you in the first instance, I'm emotionally upset (I was really livid).

I explained everything that I had done that morning, including talking to the distribution centre, talking to my State Manager, talking to his boss David Bickett, and now talking here with her.

Before she could say anything else, I threatened, "I'm getting a baseball bat, and I'm going to your head office in Saint George's Terrace Perth, and I'm going to smash every plate glass window I can find."

She was silent, must have heard the desperation in my voice, how emotionally charged up I was.

I continued, "Before I do that, I'm sending all the TV, radio stations and newspapers this message I wrote earlier" I read it out to her:

"At 2 pm today, a very desperate Telstra dealer, who is very emotionally distraught, is going to smash all the plate glass windows in the Telstra building at their Saint Georges Terrace headquarters. 'That should get someone's attention,' I shouted at her.

Then I said to her, "Please help me, Rayeleen, for I'm desperate." **Then I burst into tears and cried like a baby.**

She said she was disappointed and very sorry to hear what I had just told her. She went on to tell me, David Thodey would also be upset too, to hear all this.

Then she said, "Did you know since David became the CEO of Telstra, David has changed and improved the culture of many things within the Telstra Cooperation structure. He has done many things to give Telstra a better image, we are a much better company now, much better than before." She was really trying to be helpful.

"Please give me an hour to get back to you, I promise you, I will ring him immediately and send him a message just in case he doesn't answer. Please be patient and wait, I'll see what I can do." She put me at ease, and she calmed me down. After hearing all her wise words, I thanked her for listening and stopped my sobbing.

It was 12.30 pm and I was getting ready to go out and do what I promised to do. Deirdre was not happy with my intention but agreed to send the email out to the media as soon as I left my office. Within 30 minutes of my call to David Thodey's office, I got a call from my State Manager.

He said, "Wendell, I just got a call from my national dealer manager advising me to inform you that the distribution centre is going to release your order immediately." I nearly broke down and cried again. It was like being on an emotional rollercoaster.

Ten minutes later, I get a call from the distribution centre advising me my order was leaving Melbourne today. The release of the mobile phones was an important symbolic gesture from Telstra to us. Half an hour later, I got a call from Rayeleen. I was so thankful to her for what she had done for me. She said it was her pleasure to help, and that David Thodey was a very good CEO at Telstra. How could I not agree? Another lesson learnt – sometimes those ladies who answer the phone can wield a lot more power than you think. Thank you Rayeleen,

I doubt Telstra wanted my story to be seen Nationally on the evening news. I'm not even sure if the media would have shown up to cover my insane threats, but I am sure about one thing, I would have carried out my mission as promised, for I was a desperate man, and desperate men will do desperate things.

We Had A Telstra Win

Deirdre was forever challenging Mark Bradbury, our State Manager for the money Telstra owed us; this went on for months. She believed that our records were true and correct; they showed Telstra owed us a lot of money for all the returned stock we had made over a twelve-month period. They never recognised our submissions, nor paid us, or gave us a credit note for the money owing. Nor did they recognise various connections and connection commission, and therefore the handset rebates we were entitled to never showed up. This happened constantly.

Remember, Telstra are a very big organisation and had different departments we had to deal with. There was the airtime commission division, connection payment division, handset rebate division, distribution division, and the returns department. All these departments acted independently. Stupidly, all of them didn't speak to each other. Therefore, we were dealing with five departments, all at the same time.

Here's the way things operated: Telstra would announce new connection plans. We would buy stock from the distribution centre to correspond with expected sales aligning with those plans. Thus, we would sell the stock to the customer on a plan as either a new connection, or existing customer on new plan with or without handset.

Then we would have to send the paperwork to Telstra to have the finances recognised and number of sales attributed to our business. That department would then send on the appropriate figures for which we were entitled to be paid. Then that division would confirm to the payment division, who would then, hopefully pay us what was owed for the particular period. They also imposed a timeline for us to claim upon. If we were late, they would not recognise the connections, commissions, rebates and subsequent monthly trailing commissions to which the business would be entitled. However, if Telstra was late with their payment, we had to suffer, wait, and reclaim it repeatedly, and that could take months.

Deirdre's problem was finding the outstanding amounts accumulated, which was growing monthly, Telstra was not acknowledging nor paying it. We ended up in the downward whirlwind spiral of cash flow issues. This was due to their non-payment of what they owed the business.

To Deirdre's recollection, Mark Bradbury was not very helpful to our business when it came to this ever growing, increasingly, problematic situation.

Eventually, Mark Bradbury and his cohorts, finally agreed to pay up after many requests. If we gave them a figure of what we knew was owed, he would ensure the amount would be paid in good time. Almost a trick question-you show me yours and I'll tell you mine, scenario. Can you believe it?

Now, Deirdre could prove the connections and outstanding connection commissions. She could prove the handset IMEI (mobile handset serial numbers) being sold by our business which should have triggered the handset rebate. However, the problem was our business had no way to quantify the airtime trailing commissions owed. Only Telstra had access to this calculation, and in those days, with the complexities of prepaid sales and plan sales crossovers, we had no way of knowing what each customer spent per month on airtime.

The conundrum was how to come up with a fair result for payment? What we believed to be fair, the amount we calculated for this component, Telstra did not agree. This was an ever-growing, staggering, outstanding amount of money. So, we developed a formula based upon what we received at the time, for the period of time stemming from the initial connection and/or sale of handset. We applied it to the invoice we raised which Mark Bradbury had said would be paid.

Our belief was Telstra had no idea either. Or if they did, they were playing a game of cat and mouse with us. Anyway, whatever figure Deirdre and our accountant arrived at, especially if Telstra agreed to it, she was suspicious. Maybe she had grossly undercalculated it. It was difficult to quantify the hours she had invested in nursing this whole project on to a conclusion. Maybe we should have added on another few thousand dollars towards her time? Deirdre's work hours, not to mention stress, had increased significantly.

However, in the end, Deirdre and I agreed, we had to move forward with the business and thus submit a claim at a figure which was doubtful, but acceptable. With these suspicions in mind, Mark Bradbury signed off on our claim. We waited, with bated breath, to see the money in our account. Once sighted, Deirdre was able to apply it to all the outstanding's. A big sigh of relief for poor Deirdre. Another headache was put to bed, another headache was resolved peacefully at that, a large victory thanks to Deirdre. We finally received the $158,000 owed us. Bastards.

A Big Brightpoint Refund

One afternoon, Bill White, our representative from Brightpoint, brought this gorgeous lady into our shop by the name of Rina. He said she was the new representative for Western Australia. We already knew he was transferring over to Sydney soon. He was introducing Rina to all the dealers and making sure she knew where all the shops were located. He did make mention to Rina as a joke, to watch these two dodgy brothers, meaning Ben and me.

I said to Ben, "I'm sure we will have to help train her as we did Bill", and Ben agreed. Rina was extremely helpful to our business, especially to Deirdre. They got on very well. We would see Rina, two, sometimes three times a week. Much more than we saw Bill.

One day Deirdre said to me that Brightpoint had stopped our trading account. I was curious as everything was running smoothly, and we were making money.

"Why?" I asked Deirdre. She told me that we apparently owed them $84,000.

"Do we?" I asked. Deirdre said, "Well sort of" but it was like the Telstra story. Brightpoint owed us money and we owed them money. It's a struggle when all are suppliers were based over East. Every time we sent something back for repairs or warranty, we waited patiently for their response. If we didn't get an acceptance notice from them within two weeks, we had to follow them up again, with a phone call. Mobile phones do break down. And believe me, we sent at least 10-20 back to our suppliers each week. When you had sold thousands, it's only about one percent. All dealers had the same problem.

Over a long period of time of us sending back unwanted stock, DOA (dead on arrival) stock and broken-down mobile phones to Brightpoint, the cost tallied up whilst we waited for our credit notes.

I rang Rina to come over and have a meeting with Deirdre and me. She obliged and came around that day. As usual, the three of us went to Miss Maud's and had coffee. I listened to Deirdre explain to Rina what the problem was, and Rina agreed to investigate it. In the meantime, I asked, "Where do I get my Nokia's from?" Rina said she would investigate this matter straight away. I had to get stock from other suppliers at a slightly higher cost. Never mind, we should have this problem sorted by next week I thought. I was wrong.

Deirdre had to dig up everything she had already submitted over the past few months. More work for us when the problem was on their end. It was going to take weeks to find all the paperwork, as we normally sent all our filing papers to a warehouse in Guildford for filing, a suburb six kilometres away. There was a huge paper trail involved in this business. There were always four copies for everything we sold. Everyone had to have a copy. One for us, one for the customer and one for the supplier and one spare just in case.

Rina confessed confidentially there might be a problem on their end. The young guy employed in their 'send and received' department was not filing and registering the returned goods as well as expected. Somehow, there was going to be a delay in working through this problem. Rina managed to extend our credit until the problem was solved. This took about two months. Deirdre had to prove every cent we claimed for. This was done successfully over time with the help of Rina. Finally, Brightpoint agreed to pay us.

Deirdre was so happy to see the end of this taxing paper trail, she had other work to do. Can you imagine $99,000 worth of credits lost? Thank you, Rina. Another one bites the dust.

Citibank

Because mobile phone shops were an emerging industry, no one knew how to predict the rapid growth of our business selling Telstra handsets, and other communications products. Banking, and your faith in your business bank manager, could make or break you. After starting with the Westpac Bank, moving to the Commonwealth Bank of Australia, then the National Australia Bank, we finally ended up at the famous Citibank, Let me tell you, the exercise of changing banks can be a nightmare. Ask Deirdre.

The issue was, these were the early days of online transactions and banks, who offered wages and invoice payments online had software was that was dicey and sometimes unreliable.

Remember in those days it was dial-up (internet service), not bigpond or Wi-Fi. Wi-Fi today is running on 5G, and we have the privilege to use it today. Most people reading this would take it for granted to have fast internet service like it's your birthright. In those heady, early years, we had to suffer, and without choice, had to rely on the most unreliable services of dial-up.

Anyway, as I was saying, we ended up with Citibank. They are a business bank, whereas the others in those days were more consumer orientated. Citibank offered personal services and many products and solutions for growing businesses.

With Citibank, we were able to establish a line of credit, as well as personal credit cards and cheque accounts. The credit card account was under my name. Deirdre had a secondary card. I eventually had to issue a letter to Citibank in Sydney issuing her an 'Authority to Act' on my behalf.

Unbeknown to us, we were not meant to use the personal credit card for business purchases. Funnily enough, it was Citibank themselves who each month, assisted Deirdre over-the-phone for her to execute the payment of huge amounts of money to various suppliers. Some ranged from $90,000 to $150,000 per month. We opened our account with Citibank mainly because we had to pay one of our wholesalers, Brightpoint, a large sum of money at the end of each month, thus we ended up with so many Qantas frequent flyer points.

It took them three years to realise we had accrued millions of points with Qantas which we had to use up. I knew sooner or later someone was going to find out it was illegal to use our credit card in that manner, so I booked business-class trips around the world. We finished up using four around-the-world business class trips. The fifth one, Covid came along and screwed it all up.

A little story about Scott Pollock, the Branch Manager of Citibank in St Georges Terrace, not the one located towards Adelaide Terrace. What happened was this. Telstra, in their wisdom monitoring the rapid growth of our business compared to other dealers, issued an edict that we were obliged to show them the statements of our bank accounts. Of course, we challenged them on the authority of this request and refused. I pushed it back onto them to go and find out for themselves. I consulted my solicitor and instructed Deirdre to consult the bank.

Now, Scott Pollock our bank manager did not agree with this breach of our privacy. He wrote a letter to the effect that Telstra's contract with our company did not contain any instruments that entitled Telstra to see our personal, or company bank statements. Telstra backed down from this bullying tactic for the time being. They later factored this in as part of their due diligence on all new dealers before they entered the Telstra business agreement.

From then on, everyone had to comply with this new rule but not us. Thanks Scott. Also, thanks to our amazing accountant, Joe Versaci. He showed us a way to be able to lever off our banking history, for us to obtain another loan to buy our next home in East Perth.

Dharma and the Tax Office

Our in-house accountant was Dharma. A Sri Lankan man who got his accountant's degree at the age of 48. Clayton, another Indian employee working as a salesman at West Perth had asked us if we needed an accountant. Clayton was very observant and saw Deirdre was overwhelmed with paperwork.

Yes, she controlled the back of the house and by now needed help with the bills and keeping track of monies owed. We now had lots of companies on credit, and it was way too much for Deirdre to handle by herself. Dharma was ever so grateful we gave him a job. He was married with several children and his wife ran a day-care centre from their home.

Even though Dharma was a qualified accountant, Deirdre patiently had to guide him on what she needed. She trained him on all of Telstra's money trail.

Typical diligent Asian worker, he would always arrive ten minutes after we arrived in the morning at 8 am. And he would always wait until we left, which was 6 pm. Most days we'd have to kick him out early.

In 1999/2000, the Tax Office advised us and the whole country we would be undergoing a massive change to our sales/wholesale tax system. Whereby before we paid 22% sales tax upon invoice, it was now being changed to 10% and re-branded as 'GST' or gross sales tax. This would represent 10% of the invoiced goods and would be added at the end of the invoice of the goods as a separate figure as 10% of the net sale. The company would then follow suit and add this on to the customer's invoice. This posed two massive conundrums for every business in the country, not only ours.

We had to stocktake and calculate the value of the 22% previously paid to suppliers. Followed up by a claim of the total already paid to the supplier. This had to be written into the company's annual accounts which resulted in an audit by the Tax Office in a later year. We passed with flying colours thanks to Dharma's expertise and Deirdre's guidance. There was a lot of work involved but they nailed it alright. What we didn't mention was, we purchased many goods at no cost from Meencomm Communications and Eyelevel Communications. So, we received lots of extra money back from those goods that were useless to anyone, but the rubbish tip.

Then we modified our point-of-sale system to accommodate the new way of charging the customer and flagging how much GST we collected. If the customer was in business, they could claim back the 10% they had paid us. We in turn, had to calculate and remit the 10% GST we collected from the customer. So, every business in the country effectively became a tax collector and tax remitter at the same time. The massive problem created for us was what Telstra owed us from before the changeover date. This conflicted with the date they actually paid us. The tax problem and conundrum were finally sorted out slowly and surely as time went by. Thank you, Dharma and Deirdre.

But you can imagine the stress this caused not to mention how boring and tedious this work was becoming. Deirdre and Dharma went to sleep and dreamt of numbers. It seemed to be all work and no play.

Part 2

Chapter 32

The Tide Turns

One day I got the shock of my life. Let's Talk Communications, owned by the UCMS group from Sydney were fishing around to expand into Western Australia and got in touch with me to arrange a meeting. They wanted to buy all our Phone Shops (situated at Belmont Forum, Karrinyup, Garden City, Subiaco, and our Head Office in West Perth). This was the first time someone wanted to swallow me up – until now, I was used to doing all the 'Pac-Man like' chomping.

A gentleman by the name of Omar Ozizi came to our West Perth office for the meeting. As requested, and in accordance to due diligence, we had to share all our profit and loss papers, our taxation submissions and our stock reports. We had never done that to this point, total reports for six shops. It was an arduous job to collate for poor Deirdre as she and Dharma were responsible for gathering all that information. In those days, the software we had to use at our disposal was developing. Omar visited us daily checking to make sure we were providing him accurate figures. Because we had never sold any of our businesses previously, we had to get used to providing everything they asked for. As much as the numbers drove Deirdre crazy, she was very protective of our business secrets and figures.

During this week, Omar stayed in Perth and talked to several other dealerships, so I found out. Finally, he seemed satisfied with all the information he had gathered from us. He rang me up on day seven and announced that he was going back to Sydney to present to his board of directors, the results of the due diligence which he had performed on our company.

Each day after Omar left Perth, I waited anxiously for him to ring me. I was desperate to get out. I have had enough of Telstra in opposition to us in all our main shopping centres.

The call finally came at about 11 am one morning. "Wendell, this is Omar (he had a strong middle eastern accent), I'm in Perth, when are you free to talk?"

"How about lunch?"

He agreed. I picked him up at his hotel and we went to Coco's restaurant in South Perth. I felt relieved sitting in front of him at least I would get an answer, one way or the other.

As I held by breath in anticipation, Omar began, "They were not totally happy with your figures nor fully interested in buying you out."

My jaw dropped. But he continued, "I might be able to convince my bosses if the price was right." He sounded like he was on my side.

He said, "You know these big companies, they just want to swallow you up for as little as possible. I know you are a sincere man and I like you; I'm going to fight for you." I smelt a rat.

We discussed many things about the marketplace, about businesses going broke and the many takeovers being made by Fonezone. Now here's an intriguing subject that I never thought of. Let's Talk communications were also a big player in the telecommunications market over East. I think they were in competition with Fonezone at the time, buying up small mums and dads' outlets, and Telstra strip dealers. This way, they would have a large presence in the marketplace and would have enough clout to make good profitable negotiations with Telstra. I now saw their strategy.

We finally got down to the price. Omar had already asked me what value I put on Phone Shop, so he knew. He waffled on for a few minutes and made me an offer. I wanted $$$$$$$ but they offered me $$$$$$.

I wasn't happy with the offer but agreed to call him later after talking to Deirdre.

After lunch, I dropped him off, raced back to West Perth to see Deirdre and told her the news. She looked disappointed. We had worked too hard and didn't want to go down the tube, which I saw coming. The writing was on the wall. Ten years had gone by rather quickly. Keenly we glanced at one another, and with emotions flaring, acknowledging how passionate we were about our small empire; with these new 'Telstra Shops' opening everywhere, I predicted we would go bankrupt if we didn't sell. Our business was something we built up from scratch. It had become our life, and after many, many hours of blood sweat and tears, workload increasing daily, it was being taken away from us. It certainly felt like it. We discussed the matter for a couple of hours. My last words to her were, "If you don't want to sell, I'm okay with it. But let me tell you my gut feeling, we should take the money and run. I want out, I've had enough."

I told her they were offering us less than what we wanted, but you know what, that would still be enough money to give us a comfortable lifestyle for years to come. Anyway, we still had the Telstra Licensed Shop at Belmont Forum. That was making a decent amount of money, and she wouldn't have to work so hard anymore.

"Let the bigger players fight it out with Telstra in the shopping centres. If these guys want to take over our business to have a bigger share in the marketplace, I'm okay with that." I concluded my proposal to her and waited for her reaction.

After a few moments I could tell she knew this was for the best. I had convinced Deirdre, and she accepted with clear emotion then business head kicking in, my decision. Good.

I called Omar and accepted his offer. The deal was done. Relief was on its way. Thank goodness for UCMS.

We had to call a general staff meeting the following Friday and invited everyone to attend our head office in West Perth after work. Because it was usual for us to have monthly meetings, they must have thought we were calling it early.

On Friday, I bought two cartons of beer, cans of coke and other soft drinks from the Hyde Park Hotel and ordered many buckets of Kentucky Fried Chicken. I also made a trip to Coles down the road and bought chips, nuts and orange juice. Because of distance, not everyone arrived at the same time. So, the early arrivals could have a drink and nibbles. All our shops closed at 5.30 pm, so some staff were 30 to 60 minutes away. We had about 45 staff coming or thereabouts. We didn't invite the Belmont Forum staff because we were keeping that shop.

Between 6.30 and 7 pm, everyone arrived. I sent Dharma our accountant, and some staff to collect the Kentucky Fried Chicken next door. I offered everyone a drink and we had something to eat. I called for attention from everyone and there was silence. I was a bit choked up but had to keep my composure.

"Everyone, I have some good news and some bad news to share with you" I announced.

When I had everyone's attention, I said, "The bad news is, after ten years of building up this Phone Shop business, Deirdre and I have decided to sell our business to Let's Talk Communications. But the good news is, you all still have your jobs for at least six months with the same wages as today. That was part of the deal I negotiated with them. They are based over East and don't have staff here. There's no way they will replace you immediately. If anything, they need you more than you need them. Omar will come around starting Monday to interview you; therefore, you can negotiate your own new wages with the new company if you want." I didn't want to elaborate too much more and told them we are out in two weeks.

There was disappointment on most faces, some cried, and some were happy for us. We had a good team. After I got paid from UCMS, I gave all the staff an extra week's pay for their loyalty and hard work. We also paid them their wages and holiday pay. They were very happy with our kindness.

After we settled and on the last day of trade, it felt like the noose was finally taken off from around our necks. We were so relieved to sell our business and get out, but emotionally drained at the same time.

Nine months after the sale, the UCMS Group ran into some trouble and had some financial problems. UCMS were the parent company of Let's Talk but they were also involved in many other things. Apparently, from the amount of money they lost, metaphorically speaking, they were already a company teetering, when they approached us to sell to them. They eventually went bust and I was so relieved we made the right decision to accept their offer when we did. I must put it down to pure good **luck**, again.

Chapter 33

Belmont Forum New Refit 2002

With the Telstra Licensed Shop contract, you are obliged to refurbish your shop every four years. It's a staggering amount of money you must spend every time that happened. You must pull down your complete shop and build a new one according to their new design. It had been only four years since we built a newly designed shop in Belmont Forum.

We usually got a notice from the Telstra Shop design team, advising us that a new design shop was being rolled out soon. We had to have many meetings with their designers. Every shop was different, so according to what shape and size your shop was, they'd re-design and remodel their new look to fit your shop. (How nice of them)

Our shop was 100 square metres. I flew to Melbourne once to make changes to suit our back office. This space they called 'back of house' stored all our stock, and it was where all the administration took place. We had to submit all our plans and designs to the shopping centre management. They also had to approve what we were doing. If it did not suit the shopping centre look, they had the right to disapprove it and it would have been back to square one. I'm sure the Telstra design team had private discussions with all shopping centres before rolling out their new designs.

So, after a lengthy and arduous period of negotiations with Telstra and the Belmont Forum management, we had clearance from everyone for the go ahead. We were officially the first cab off the rank, ready to roll out the new look.

As this period drew near, our Telstra license was up for renewal. This happened every two years. We weren't too worried about the renewal because apart from a few minor disputes, we were in harmony with Telstra. We carried on business as usual and concentrated on building our shop as soon as possible. We gave our shop fitters all the designs from Telstra and gave them the green light. Fortunately, they were available and agreed to start work immediately.

Apart from building the interior according to Telstra's specifications, they had to pull down the existing shop and take it to the tip. Telstra came to the rescue by providing us with a pop-up cart. This cart was designed for this very purpose. It was rectangular shaped about 20 square metres. We placed the cart right in front of our current shop and didn't have to pay rent for space. Normally they would have charged about $800, but we still paid the normal full rent during renovations.

We had to reschedule all our staffing rosters because we couldn't accommodate everyone in that small space. The staff was aware of what was going on. Some took leave and somehow, we managed to keep everyone happy.

In those days there was no Sunday trading. So, over the weekend, we got our staff to shift all the stock and equipment into the new storage area. There was a lot of work involved in this project. Everything was methodically and successfully shifted by midnight Sunday. The pop-up shop arrived early Sunday morning and we worked on getting that shop functional by the end of late Sunday night. Everything was working well, in theory but the following morning was going to be the big test, as we had never been in that position before.

Monday morning Ben arrived at 7 am and we put the final touches to the new shop. Small but functional. This was a five-to-six- staff operation. Our full staff was 12, including Deirdre and me.

The staff had to get used to standing outside the pop-up shop and greeting potential customers as they walked pass. No explanation needed; everyone could see what was happening. The day progressed well with a few hiccups as expected. Ben and the staff worked hard and made sure everything ran as smoothly as possible.

Late Monday afternoon I got a call from Telstra's design department advising that they had a crisis meeting over the weekend about us modifying the current model shop front. I explained that I had already started work on the new design we agreed upon. They insisted we halt all work and look at the new design. I couldn't believe what was going on. Verbally they gave us the go-ahead and so we did. Although I must admit, they had not officially signed off on the paperwork. So what was I to do? Wasn't a 'man's word' good enough anymore?

Work continued as tradies had to board up the shop with timber, strip all the walls, shelves, back-room offices, and pull everything down. Everything was going to be brand new. It was sad to see them sledgehammer the thick glass windows which originally costs us about $25,000. Yep, smash and take it all down to the rubbish tip, which was the first stage.

First thing Tuesday morning I was at Telstra's head office in Stirling Street, Perth. You can just imagine the frustrations going on between Telstra and me. Admittedly, these poor guys in Perth only found out about the changes the day I did. But they had to wear their Telstra hat and deal with me accordingly. We argued for hours as their new design was going to cost me another $20,000, and I wasn't going to budge. It became a Mexican stand-off.

In a tactical move, they politely reminded me that our license was due for renewal in three months. I was now more insulted by that statement than the shop design changes. I spoke to my lawyer and said to him, "Maybe we might have another One-Tel situation on our hands." As always, he asked me to keep my cool and wait and see what happened next.

Work continued and I just ignored their demands. The shop was finished in four weeks, and it looked good. We spent another weekend shifting everything back into the new shop and on Monday morning started to trade as usual. Telstra didn't mention anything more about the shop design. But sure enough, a couple of months later, when the license was due to be renewed, they mentioned it again and asked me point blank "Are you going to comply with the new shop design?"

Nope, I was not going to do anything more than what was done. In true Wendell fashion, I simply said, "If you don't renew my license, I'll be seeing Telstra in the highest courts." Maybe I had a case against them, or I was plain lucky, but nothing more was mentioned about the shop design, and they renewed my license.

I do believe that from that experience, Telstra must have put a black mark against my name and the end of my relationship with Telstra was coming to an end. It was only a matter of time.

Chapter 34

Ben growing wings – 2002

Telstra was holding its Annual Licensee's meeting on the Gold Coast at the Hyatt Resort in Coolum, Queensland. On this occasion, they requested that the managers of all Telstra Licensed Shops nationally, accompany their licensees on this occasion. We had to fly on a Friday, to attend the conference all day Saturday and Sunday. Then fly back Monday or stay a few extra days at your own expense. A quick trip for all of us. Apart from the accommodation, food, and drinks, we had to pay for our own airfares. Unlike the old days when they paid for everything, including airfares.

We had enough notice to accommodate their request. Ben and I packed and flew to the Gold Coast first thing Friday morning. Not just us, but most of the West Australian Licensees were on the same flight. There were about 300 of us from all around Australia attending the conference. The resort was fully booked out by Telstra.

On the plane, Ben had a sleep, and I watched a movie. When he woke up, we got some beers and started to have a chat. Ben then went on to tell me that he and another Telstra Licensed Shop manager from Joondalup called Paul Hart were planning on going into business together. I was taken aback and asked him what type of business.

He explained that he wasn't resigning but planned to do this part-time. They were going to contact all the Telstra Shops, including the strip dealers, offer to buy all their traded-in second-hand mobile phones for $50 or less, refurbish them, and sell them on the Internet. This disturbed me.

"Both of you have a day job, so how are you going to have time to run a business that requires a lot of man-hours?" I asked.

"We are planning to do this after hours and on our days off."

"Ben, this is a conflict of interest. What if a customer comes into our shop looking for a second-hand mobile phone? Are you guys going to offer the customer what we have in stock, or are you going to offer the customer what's in your stock?"

He told me it wouldn't affect anyone because they were mainly offering their stock on the internet.

I didn't like it one little bit. By the time we finished our beers, it was time to land on the Gold Coast.

"Let's continue this conversation after we check in at the resort. We should find a quiet bar somewhere, have another beer, and continue." I suggested and he agreed.

After we landed and checked in, I called Ben and said "Let's go for a walk around the Golf course and have a chat." We ended up walking on the beach. It was about 5.30 pm and the weather was about 24c. That was the better option, as most of the bars were full, being a Friday night.

Ben had now been working for us for ten years or more and was managing Belmont Forum during this period. Maybe his wings were starting to grow. Admittedly, our relationship was starting to frail a little by this time as Ben wanted more autonomy.

The one thing I can say about Ben, is that he was very thoughtful and creative. He would always surprise me on my birthday. He would come up with a different gift for me each year. There are so many years of memories, I picked the one below. It signifies our development in growth by the growing number of shops in each business card. I have kept all his gifts. Could be worth millions one day lol.

ONE THE MANY CREATIVE BIRTHDAY GIFTS FROM BEN

Naturally, I was concerned about Ben's new business venture but more concerned about the conflict of interest occurring. I tried my hardest to make sense to him, but as I said, maybe he was coming of age and his tiny wings were starting to flap. There was no way he was going to change his mind. I gave him all the logical reasons why he should not enter this business partnership whilst being employed by us. But he kept insisting he needed to try something new. I could see the end was near. We walked back to the resort in silence.

I rang Deirdre with the news. Naturally, she didn't agree with him either. We spent an hour discussing this matter.

I said to her, "Let's wait until we get back and the three of us will have a meeting about it."

The conference speakers waffled on as usual: Telstra explained all the new plans to come and how the new rollout was going to make us more money etc. I usually got bored at these conferences at the best of times, but now all I could think about was Ben's new venture.

The one thing I can say is, Telstra always put on exquisite food and lots of drinks. No alcohol during the day, but at night, yes, with dinner and a band playing in the ballroom.

A couple of other Licensees and I ducked down to the Casino without anyone knowing. We tried hard not to have a late night at the Casino but that only worked in theory. We got back at some ungodly early hour of the morning, struggled out of bed a few hours later, and went back to the conference for some intensive training, with red eyes. The rest of my Gold Coast stay was a blur. I couldn't concentrate on anything at the conference, except for possibly losing Ben.

We tried our best and were cordial, but the strain on our relationship was certainly present. I think we had fun there on that weekend, at least we tried to. We usually won something, even if it was only a door prize, at most Telstra gatherings, but this time nothing. Serendipity?

There were plenty of new Licensees to talk to and meet. On the last evening, we were given some souvenirs to take home and we packed up and all returned to Perth the following morning. That was probably my worst weekend away, ever.

Deirdre picked me up at the airport and Ben got a lift with some other Licensee. I did offer him a lift but I don't think he was ready to meet Deirdre just yet. They got on extremely well during the past ten years. Deirdre highly respected Ben and I think vice versa. Obviously, the question in the car on the way home was, what was the outcome between you and Ben? I had to confess, nothing. I had a premonition his end was near. Ben could have been our son, or that's what it felt like. He was twenty years younger than me. Same age as my daughter.

It was not easy, we couldn't get used to knowing that someone so close to us over the years was growing wings, and about to fly off. It was not a good feeling.

On Monday, work continued as usual. Deirdre and I were in West Perth and Ben in Belmont. We agreed to meet on Thursday night for a chat about our future, as there was late-night shopping.

On Tuesday night at about 7 pm, there was a knock on the door at my house in East Perth. Deirdre went downstairs to see who it was. We lived in a three-level house. I was watching the news and Deirdre came back upstairs with a letter in her hand.

"Ben dropped this off, his father was waiting for him in the car, engine running," she sighed.

Deirdre opened the letter; we had already guessed. It was his resignation letter. We were understandably devastated, shocked but not surprised. We both felt a bit numb, sad and had a stiff drink. Finally, the bird has grown its wings and was ready to fly away. It was hard to imagine Ben leaving, but it happened.

I went over to Belmont Forum the following morning to see if I could persuade Ben into staying but he was not budging. I tried hard but one knows when one must step back and accept the situation, take the blow on the chin, and walk away.

Ben left two weeks later, and we gave him a farewell party. We kept track of his movements through our Telstra contacts. I don't think that second-hand mobile phone business ever got off the ground. Maybe it was the first move he needed to leave us. By then our business was running full steam ahead and I didn't have much time to think about not having Ben around anymore. We employed Neil Randle to run Belmont Forum. He was an ex-Telstra employee who managed another one of Telstra's Shops. It worked out perfectly for us.

We attended another Telstra conference. This time in Perth. It was a smaller affair and all the West Australian Licensees attended. During the conference, Telstra welcomed all the new Licensees and announced that they were opening another Telstra Licensed Shop in Midland. This suburb was about six kilometres from us in Belmont Forum. It got up my nose a bit as we had a lot of the country people visit us and buy mobile phones. Great Eastern highway ran a few kilometres past us, and we got a lot of trade from the passing traffic. Telstra said the new Licensee wished to stay anonymous for the time being.

SOME OF OUR ORIGINAL BUSINESS CARDS

One day our dealer manager dropped in and informed me that Ben was the new Licensee for the Midland Telstra Licensed Shop. I was surprised they had kept it so quiet. If anything, I was upset and jealous, yes jealous. Why, this little whipper snipper upstart that I trained was going into competition against me, was he?

"I'll teach him a lesson or two" I had all these bad thoughts running through my head. As I said, I was angry and more jealous of him than anything.

Then I had a flashback. I remembered vividly ten years ago Tony Raj saying the same words as I just did, about me going into competition with him. The reality hit home, it was time to let go and I felt a bit better. At least I had Ben for ten years, not like the ten weeks I gave Tony Raj. Yes, everyone must find their path in life, some end up in a caravan park and some go on to better things. Both Ben and I belonged to the latter group.

Midland opened, and then Ben opened another shop south of Perth in a suburb called Success. Ben did very well. Ben and I somehow got back to talking again and life continued with no regrets. We still maintain a good friendship today. As a matter of fact, we are going to celebrate Ben's fiftieth birthday in Bali, sometime in March 2023. I'm sure we are going to have a hoot of a time.

On the 1st of July 2024, Ben and I are going somewhere special together, just the boys, to celebrate the opening of E.T. Phone Home 30 years ago. I hope we don't get robbed again on our first night! LOL.

Chapter 35

Sean was Popular in Belmont.

I must tell you a story about our most popular staff member named Sean. His grandparents were from India, so he was a third-generation Australian. He had a fair complexion, a well-built physique, and was always well-groomed. That got him noticed. You could see he had a bit of an Indian look about him and a very handsome young man he was. I think Sean was about 22 years old. Believe me, all our staff, the management in the shopping centre and all the customers used to love this guy. He had this charm about him that was as genuine as the day is long. He got on with everyone, especially the customers who would walk into the shop.

When Sean had a day off, some of the staff would say, "I wish Sean was here." When things were quiet, he would make us all laugh, or he'd be teaching someone how to do something. He had fascinating stories. The girls in the shop found some of his stories riveting. He was the life of the party, that's for sure, and we adored him for that.

Sean had a chat with Deirdre one day and explained to her he needed to go to the bank for a loan to buy a motorbike. What he needed from us was a letter of recommendation for his character, his work practices, his income, and of course how long he had been working for us. This was an easy task for Deirdre, so she typed a nice letter for him to take to the bank.

She then sat down with Sean and asked, "Why do you want a bike, why not a car?" He just had his heart set on a bike and he excitedly told her the make and model. I don't remember the name of the bike, but I can tell you one thing, it was a big bike with a 750-cc motor. Deirdre was shocked and concerned but he soon put her mind at ease. That was Sean.

Still, Deirdre said, "Sean, you know you haven't got your license for a bike that size. Why don't you go and buy something smaller, like a 150-cc bike? When you learn to ride that, maybe you can graduate to a bigger bike one day."

But he was insistent and had his mind set on getting this motorbike, and of course, he charmed his way into Deirdre's heart. "Okay, but don't tell me I didn't warn you," was her final caution.

After picking up his letter from Deirdre, he left the office and went to the bank to apply for his loan. He had to wait for about three or four days and then he got the good news he was waiting for.

The following day after picking up his motorbike, Sean came to work a bit earlier than his usual starting time. On that same day, three other staff members were there early too, which was most unusual. There was a reason for that, Sean had brought his motorbike to work for the first time and wanted to show it off. This he did successfully for about two weeks. Every day in the morning, then either before during lunch or after work, everyone would go out the car park and have a look at his bike.

Even customers he knew would say, "I saw your bike out there and it's a beauty." Then the novelty finally wore off and there was no more talk of his bike.

Deirdre and I went to Bali for a few days holiday and I got a phone call from John, the manager of the shop. At first, I didn't accept the call.

I said previously to John, "When you ring me, and if I don't answer hang up, count to ten, ring me again. If I don't answer hang up, count to ten and ring me again." This was a secret code between us. Only after the third ring I would pick up the phone, because it wasn't cheap. In those days a call from Perth to Bali was like $13 a minute. So, after he rang three times in a row, I rang him back.

"John, I know you wouldn't ring me unless it's urgent, so what's the problem?"

He said mate, "We are all shocked and very sad here at the shop. Sean was killed in a head-on motorbike accident about 2 am and we just found out from his parents." Talk about being in shock! I couldn't believe it and felt like I had the breath punched out of me. When I finally had the courage to tell Deirdre, she burst into tears. It was a tough day at Belmont Forum and for us too.

On the day of his funeral, with respect for Sean, Telstra permitted us to open the shop for only half the day to allow all the staff to attend.

We had a big notice on the front door explaining briefly what happened to Sean. Needless to say, it was a very sad day for his parents, his girlfriend, all his friends who were there, and for all our staff. We were all dressed in our Phone Shop uniforms and I'm sure that's what Sean would have wanted.

And that story is the saddest thing that ever happened to us in the history of our E.T. Phone Home and Phone Shop history. Goodbye Sean (RIP).

Chapter 36

Belmont Forum Ending 2010.

With Ben leaving, Sean passing, seems the timing was right to wind things up. We were now in our fifteenth year in business, I felt it was time to say goodbye to another chapter in my life. I started to look for buyers for my last Telstra branded shop in Belmont.

I had a couple of major dealers interested. They spent hours of my time trying to figure out the $1.5m in goodwill and stock I was asking. But Telstra was still growing and everyone was asking, "When will the bubble burst?" That was the million-dollar question.

Everyone thought I was selling because the end of mobile phones growth was near. Little did we know that it would continue growing for another ten years. But everything I told any new buyer was the plain truth; it was a well-established, and financially, a well-earning business.

Today, there are no more strip dealerships, or 'mum and dad' owners like in the beginning. Telstra had enough of us, the very people who helped them grow at the beginning. We all invested heavily by taking risks to get them started, but we were now getting moved on.

Ben, being well-known and highly regarded by Telstra was the very first person I offered the sale of the Belmont shop to. Midland was about six kilometres away so a perfect marriage for the Eastern suburb's corridor. But at the time, Midland had only been open for about 12 months and that may have restricted and frightened him financially. I'm sure the asking price also put him off, as it did others. He declined.

Buyer 1

There was this chap called Finn, from South Africa. He was the first real prospective buyer. Someone working in Telstra gave him some inside information that Belmont Forum Telstra Licensed Shop may be up for sale. Finn came charging in like a wounded bull. He sounded like he was prepared to write me a cheque the next day.

I met this guy daily at Miss Maud's for a whole week. He would ask hundreds of questions. He brought along his laptop daily and wrote down everything I said. I gave him as much information as he asked for. I let him talk to my accountant and gave him our tax returns and our daily sales figures, everything he requested. Well, to say he was a time waster was being nice. Finn finally made me an offer for $500,000 plus stock.

"According to my figures, your business is too expensive," he announced.

I told Finn to go find another $500,000 or more, otherwise please quit annoying me. What a fool.

By the way, for the record, from the first day I met this South African guy, it took another two years to finally sell our Telstra shop. Yep, two more years of profit didn't worry us, plus wages, not bad indeed.

Buyer 2

Next was my then-shop manager John Brown. He had no money, so I made an agreement to finance him. Think about this one, why would I want to finance a business unless I was guaranteed it was solid? This business was so solid, I had nothing to lose, I knew that. I was willing to take that risk.

The deal went something like this. We would sell him the business on paper, but everything stayed in our name until the business was fully paid for. I gave him five years. Can you imagine owning a business in five years without having to pay anything upfront? I knew from our figures it would take that long to pay off. The business was growing each year. Don't forget that he and his wife would also earn a decent wage from the business. He was our Telstra dealer manager for about two years before I offered him a job.

I approached Telstra with my plan. As usual, there was the official paperwork needed by Telstra from us requesting our sale to John. Then John had to do his due diligence with Telstra. I'll cut it short. It took about two months of paper trail back and forth to Melbourne and back. Finally, I got a notice advising me that Telstra had turned down his application.

Now you won't believe this next story:-

John worked for us for about two years. When he left Telstra to come work for us he didn't have a car, so we bought the car that Telstra provided him as part of his wage sacrifice. This vehicle we bought from the Telstra Fleet operations. We wrote a cheque from Talbora Pty Ltd. The car was also registered in Talbora's name. That was part of our agreement to have him work for us and be our manager in Belmont Forum. We also opened some internet cafes in various shopping centres around the metropolitan area. Thus, the car was important.

One Monday, about three days before Deirdre and I were going on a ten-day holiday, one of my staff told me that John and another staff, an Indonesian student, were going to Jakarta on Friday. I was not told about this by John. I approached him and asked him if it was true? He said yes, there was an opportunity for him and his friend Robert Gib to open a business in Indonesia selling cheap light globes made in Thailand. The reason the Indonesian staff was going along was to be his interpreter. By the way, the Indonesian staff's uncle worked in the Indonesian Government's Ministry department. He was going to engage John and Robert to change all the light globes for all the Government buildings in Jakarta.

I said to John, "I'm going on holidays in four days, now you are going to Jakarta in three days and taking one of my staff with you." I asked, "Who's going to look after my business?"

John said, "There's nothing to worry about, I have taken care of everything, and I will be back in a week." He said, "I will appoint my wife who will run the shop whilst I'm away. I can also run the daily business from there, it's not hard."

I couldn't believe what I was hearing. Firstly, none of the other staff were trained to manage the store. Telstra and I had an agreement that the Telstra Licensed Shop was to have a senior member (manager), Deirdre or myself at the shop each day to represent Telstra to their customers. No one else.

I then asked him, "Why did you not mentioned this trip to me?"

He said he knew I would think it was crazy and object to him going to Jakarta. He saw an opportunity to make some quick money at my expense. Great John, well done.

I took Deirdre to Miss Maud's and told her the whole story. She was shocked. She reminded me of the Telstra agreement.

"Yes, I know. We really don't need this type of situation right now."

"What are we going to do?" she asked.

"He should be sacked for this," she said. "Taking leave without permission and at short notice and taking an important staff member with him."

"The first thing to do is cancel our trip. We will go and replace John and that will keep Telstra happy."

I said to Deirdre, "We are being blackmailed here and we are not in a position to sack him."

Anyway, a week was not that long I said, "So let's shut up and put up with his bullshit."

One week went past and no John. Then an email arrived apologising for his delay in returning.

The excuse he made was, "Red tape was taking longer than expected." He promised to return in a week. Now the second week went past and still no return of John.

I said to Deirdre, "I am now in a position to send him a facsimile."

This is what I wrote, "John you have abandoned your position at work, and taken leave without permission, therefore I am dismissing you as our manager." I also sent him a message to return the keys to our vehicle.

He did return six days later and went straight to the unfair dismissal commission and lodged a complaint against us.

The following week received a phone call from the unfair dismissal commission wanting an explanation. They wanted us to re-employ him AND pay him his past fortnight's wages! I explained the story to them and stood my ground. They said they would talk to John and get back to me.

A few days later I got their call advising me they were going to take me to court over this matter. I felt like telling them to 'F off' but I didn't.

Instead, I said, "Sure, I'll see you in court."

I later got another call from them saying John didn't want to work for us anymore, so would I please pay him his holiday pay? I agreed to pay the holiday pay but refused to pay his past two weeks' wages. Finally, they said, "Okay, but the holiday pay must be paid by the end of this week." I agreed.

Just when I thought this whole debacle was behind me, we found out, when asked, John refused to return the car keys. He insisted that the money for the vehicle came out of his redundancy payout from Telstra. Deirdre found the cheque butt and the bank statement that clearly showed the $26,000 for the vehicle came from our bank account. He had no proof of him paying for it.

I went to the Police and explained to them the situation. They went to see him and asked him to return my car. He told them it was his car and he had paid for it. This they reported to me the following day. The Police said it was now a civil matter, take him to court. There was nothing more they could do, end of their involvement.

Deirdre was not well at that time and was hospitalised. I stopped everything I was doing and explained to Telstra that I sacked John and Deirdre was in hospital. Telstra agreed under the circumstances, that they would allow another reputable, long-standing staff member act as manager for the time being. I went to the shop daily between attending to Deirdre in hospital and making sure business was operating as usual.

After about two weeks when Deirdre was feeling a little better, I suggested we take John to court and get our car back.

Tough little Deirdre agreed and said, "Let's not waste any more money on a lawyer, we'll go to the courthouse, get all the forms we require and fight him in court."

That we did. John got himself a lawyer by the name of Chris S. They dragged the case out for three years. I won't go into detail or how many court appearances we made in that time. All I can say is that finally we appeared before a magistrate, his lawyer put up a good defence, but it was us, yes us, who were not lying. Thankfully the magistrate saw through John's lies and awarded the case to the plaintiff.

He was ordered to repay us back the $26,000 plus interest which came to $31,000. The following day I got a call from John's lawyer claiming that John wanted him to appeal and take the case to a higher court. I explained we were very tired of all this drama; Deirdre was not well again. If we prolonged this case another six or twelve more months, it could kill her.

So, I spoke to his lawyer and said, "Here is my offer, Chris, pay us $20,000 and let's call it a day." We had checked current market value.

He said he would talk to John and get back to me.

He rang me the next day and said I could come to his office, pick up the cheque for $20,000, and transfer the car into John's name. We were so relieved, Deirdre cried bitterly and that was the end of that.

To end this story about John; John and Robert's business venture failed in Jakarta. Nothing ever developed – they didn't make a quick buck or become millionaires. Much later I found out from Telstra that they rejected John's application for my business for reasons only known to them. I cannot disclose what I found out, but I wonder if he tried the same tricks on them? Also, I'm not sure whether his lawyer ever got paid. For months after the court case, we received many letters posted to John. He also rented an apartment from us (at cheap rent) thus how we received his mail. I did open one of his correspondences from his lawyer. I won't mention the money owing.

Buyer 3

My two dear friends from my younger days in Burma/Myanmar were Rudy D'Cunha and Eugene Sweeney. I've known these guys all my life. We all lived and grew up in a town called Thingangyun, about eight kilometres from Rangoon/Yangon. Both their sons were employed by me for years. I had a meeting with them one day and I suggested they look at buying my Telstra Shop in Belmont Forum. It was an obvious scenario; buy the business in partnership and let their sons run the business for them. It would also give Rudy a job as manager.

Eugene's son, Fabian, had worked for us for three years and was already a manager in our business. Rudy's son, Nigel, was a representative with years of experience working for another large Telstra company and for us. Both guys had a ton of experience between them. It was the perfect marriage. Everyone was excited except for one thing - the price.

Eugene and Rudy were not used to dealing in hundreds of thousands of dollars. Eugene owned his own taxi, was very comfortable, and made a decent living. Rudy was working for Telstra in Osborne Park in the strip dealer section. He was the manager and on a good wage. Back then these guys were in their late fifties, and I was sure they would own their houses by now.

The amount of $1.5m in goodwill and stock was never on their radar. It was a shock to their system. But they finally realised, it was a 50/50 buy-in, which reduced the figure to $750,000 each, which sounded much more achievable.

They had a meeting and advised me that they were interested, (which I was happy about) so we set up a meeting. They asked me many questions about the profitability and longevity of the shop. After they were satisfied, they spoke to their accountants. I had to give them all our banking details, our tax returns, and as much as their accountant wanted to see. I even had two meetings with their accountant. He gave me the third degree every time. Even though I understood he was protecting these guys, I was getting annoyed with all the questioning. It was clear as daylight that all the numbers added up.

"Then why are you selling a profitable business?" I was asked. That was the $64,000 question on everyone's lips. Telstra had to know everything I told these guys. I couldn't stack the figures even if I wanted to, because Telstra would pick up any false figures or connections in the buyer's due diligence paperwork. The buyer was well protected in their investment of buying Belmont Forum by Telstra's involvement in the sale. This was as good as it gets.

To ease their concerns about the accuracy of monies taken weekly, I offered Rudy a position as manager at Belmont Forum. He was working at Telstra, at their Osborne Park strip dealership. So, it made good sense for him to come and work for me, see the daily sales, get a feel of how things worked there, and bank the daily takings. There you have it, couldn't have been a better solution for all. Rudy took up my offer and resigned from Telstra immediately and became the manager of Belmont Forum. We continued our business negotiations between the three parties, that is Rudy, Eugene and me.

They spoke to their lawyers, accountants, to their wives and to their banks. I had to submit more letters to Telstra advising them of the sale of my shop to these guys. They then had to be interviewed by our State Manager. Rudy was well known to him. It seemed all went well in the interview. Now, all we had to do was compile all the due diligence paperwork required by Telstra, and I thought we had a deal.

I was wrong.

The reader must understand one thing, money never bought you a Telstra Licensed Shop. Yes, it was important you didn't go bust financially in the first six months and embarrass Telstra. More importantly, you had to prove you could run the Telstra business daily. Like I said earlier, these guys, Rudy, Fabian, and Nigel were experts in Telstra affairs. So, everything being equal, they should have been in Belmont forum three months from the first day I submitted my letter of sale to Telstra.

It wasn't that easy. I took at least six months of rewriting their business case. Someone in Melbourne was still not convinced they were the right people to run a Telstra Shop. After about six months of negotiating, my friends got sick of Telstra's attitude towards them, so they pulled out.

I was so close to selling my shop, I would have bet anyone there was a sale happening here, 100% guaranteed it was going to happen. There you go, our Lord and Master Telstra, is a law upon itself. The deal was off. FML.

I knew that Telstra wanted to get rid of me, and I wanted to drag it out as long as possible. What all buyers didn't quite understand was that Telstra had to approve the sale. They had the final say.

By that stage of lessons learned, it was understood that Telstra wanted a solid business case, and it wasn't going to be easy, it was getting harder if anything. The new process was, I had to talk to our State Manager first about any new buyers. Then he would analyse my case, and if he approved, it had to go to his boss in Melbourne for approval. The only thing my Myanmar friends had going for them was, both of their sons were Telstra experts, including Rudy, a long-time Telstra employee. They were more than suitable for this business. There was a game being played by Telstra, which I found out later.

Buyer 4

Rina and Bill White were the last and best candidates around that I could think of. They were also keen to buy a Telstra Licensed Shop. After finding out that Rudy and Eugene had had enough, I rang Rina and gave her the news about Rudy and Eugene pulling out. She was excited and came around that afternoon. I met her at Miss Maud's and started talking about her interest in the shop. I then told her the asking price and she shivered.

Rina and Bill were well known throughout the telecommunications industry here in Perth. Bill was also a known Olympic swimmer. He was the first West Australian representative for the company Brightpoint from Sydney. A large and good company to deal with. He was around for about two years. At first, when he first dropped in to introduce himself to us, Ben and I both picked up that this guy knew less about mobiles than we did. We got on very well with him. He was a good learner and representative for Brightpoint.

He could read and see through the Dodgy Brothers (Ben and me). We had our own ways and methods of dealing with representatives. We'd initially try and give new representatives a hard time but always managed to become friends later. Bill was a keen and an enthusiastic worker. Brightpoint must have noticed his talent and transferred him to Sydney.

Rina said, "As you know, Bill has been asked to be transferred to Sydney."

I said I knew that and asked to have a meeting with him the next day.

Back to square one. My last hope was to encourage this couple into buying Belmont Forum. To my surprise, at the meeting the following day, I saw two people who were over keen to talk about the sale. Try to understand, here are a couple in their thirties looking for opportunities to go into business to improve their future. What a better way was there, than to continue in the industry they knew best.

The first question asked was how much? We know the answer already, $1.5m. It was a rude shock, but that was the reality if you wanted to jump into a successful business. I explained that even though the price was steep, they could recover every cent and more in five years. Then, if they wanted to sell, they could ask the same price, or more, depending on how much they had increased the business. Can you imagine being able to repay that amount of money in such a short time? It was a certainty for purchase if nothing had changed in Telstra's plans in the future. Nothing changed for eight years after 2010.

They were ready for the challenge. I told them there was another problem: To make certain that everything I told them was correct, Bill should quit his job with Brightpoint and start as manager in Belmont Forum asap, just as Rudy did. It made sense. They were going to discuss it and get back to me.

A few days later I got a call from Rina. "Yes Wendell, we're up for it. Bill is giving Brightpoint notice and can start work at Belmont Forum in two weeks."

I was happy to hear this.

The ball was rolling, the hard work began again. The first thing to do was to inform Telstra of the prospective new buyers. As they were known to Telstra, it was much easier just to pick up the phone and advise Mark Bradbury, the State Manager. I had to follow that up with an official letter of request.

Rina and Bill owned a house in a suburb called Mount Hawthorn. Houses there were expensive, so borrowing was not going to be hard. They advised me they had a meeting at the bank in a few days, but in the meantime were talking to their accountant. As usual, we had to provide profit and loss papers, our lease contracts, our current license duration remaining, and many more things all accountants need to see. This was now an easy job to accomplish. Deirdre had done these many times in the past 12 months. She did her usual best and provided as much as requested.

They had their first interview with our State Manager which went well. Now for the long due diligence paper trail. They worked very hard to comply and submitted every detail Telstra needed to know about them. They wrote a very impressive letter to Telstra detailing their past experience and present. I know because I read it.

All paperwork was sent to Telstra's head office in Bourke Street Melbourne. Meanwhile, Bill started at the Belmont Forum Telstra Licensed Shop as manager. Telstra are not the quickest in replying to these types of affairs. There were lots of phone calls between Telstra and the Whites. I was kept in the loop of what was going on because I saw Bill daily. The time it took Rina and Bill to get a second and final interview in Melbourne, took about four months.

Finally, they were summoned to Melbourne for that last interview. We were all excited because this was it. After this interview, you got a letter saying whether you were successful or not.

They flew to Melbourne and had the interview and came back the next day. We met at Miss Maud's, and I wanted to know how things went. They were happy with the interview, and it was a relief after six months of negotiating. I wished them good luck and shook their hands. Now the waiting game for the final answer.

A week later, Bill came in one morning looking like he had not been to sleep the night before.

"Are you unwell?" I asked.

"We received the letter. We regret to inform you that your application was not successful."

It was devastating news. These guys had their finance approved, the talent required to run a Telstra Licensed Shop, the right age and had the energy and enthusiasm one could ask for. WHY WHY WHY?

I immediately rang Mark as he had already been informed by his Head Office of the outcome. He wasn't privileged to disclose any of Telstra's business to me. I was so desperate I flew to Melbourne the following day to try and persuade Telstra but failed. They would not disclose their reasons for their rejection. End of story.

Rina cried and was in no mood to meet me to discuss the possibilities of what went wrong. We finally met, the four of us, Deirdre, Rita, Bill, and me at Miss Maud's. We had lunch and tried to nut out what was the reasoning for the disapproval of their application.

Rina came up with the possible answer. During their interview, apart from many questions, the $64,000 question was asked by Telstra. "Why are you two not married?" This unsettled Bill a lot. He almost told them to F off.

Rina said, "This might have got Telstra's nose out of joint, but no one really knows." If I had to guess, and only guessing, I believe that Telstra's ulterior motive was to put an end to more mums and dad investors owning a Telstra Licensed Shop. That is only my opinion, but in the long run, I think I was right.

Rina met Bill whilst working for Brightpoint in Perth. Thankfully Bill got his job back at Brightpoint and went to Sydney to later become the National Accounts Manager for Brightpoint. Rina also got a transfer there. They went on to have two beautiful daughters. The last I heard was that they are still happily living together in Sydney. I'm sincerely sorry it didn't work out.

I want to summarise my 100% honesty to everyone. Back when I was trying to sell Belmont Forum, here are some facts to read and consider:

1/ The asking price of $1.5m was justified. Ask anyone who is an accountant, they will tell you it was not overpriced. Money back in five years? Yes.

2/ All three buyers, John, Rudy, and Bill managed the Belmont Forum shop and got first-hand information on the daily takings. They knew my numbers were all correct and true.

3/ The Telstra Licensed Shop is still operating today. From 1998 to the first of May 2023.

4/ I don't take delight in mentioning this to you guys but should any of you have been successful in purchasing my Telstra Licensed Shop, you would have paid off your loan in five years as I predicted, and you would have made at least $1.5m to $2m in the **risks** you took.

You'd be smiling today. Your dreams would have come true. It was just as I predicted. Everything I said was true, you now know my position back then with Telstra, as read in this book. We told no lies and took no prisoners. Deirdre and Wendell are honest people.

Fonezone

Buyer 5

Fonezone was a Queensland-based company. I first met David McMahon, the owner of Fonezone at the Adelaide Grand Prix. He had five shops then and knew the strip dealer market pretty well. He was expanding with his wife, Maxine. They were expanding rapidly, had the full Telstra backing, and were buying up all the small mums and dads' investors, with Telstra's blessing. Just what Telstra wanted. Telstra's grand plan was to deal with one or two big players who owned hundreds of strip dealers and Telstra Licensed Shops. Fonezone got so big; they listed on the stock exchange as Vita Group. Their shares hit $1.85 in 2018. Today, their shares were 11 cents when I last looked. (03/01/2023)

Vita Group/Fonezone ended up buying the Telstra Licensed Shop in Belmont Forum from us. They knew we were on the way out with Telstra, so they had the upper hand in this deal. They offered us $$$$$$ and we settled at $$$$$$. If you go back two years on our asking price of $1.5m, it's just over half of that. But add on the two years' of profit we got while negotiating, then we almost got what we wanted in the first place. Not forgetting two years of extra pay. Nothing to be ashamed of. Any goodwill profit, plus stock, was still good money.

That was the end of Belmont Forum for us.

If you are exhausted reading about the sale of this shop, imagine how exhausted we were in the thick of it! We were ready to come up for air after all the years of hard slog.

It was end of an era. This was the end of 17 years of our lives devoted to the telecommunications industry. Even though the buyout price was healthy, we still had mixed emotions. We had to learn to let go. I had to let go. For me it was not just about the money; it was about the sense of community we had nurtured around us. We had become friends, (and still are to this day), with many of our staff and other shop owners, and other Licensees in the Telstra world. It was time, yet sad, to say goodbye. Goodbye.

Telstra ended up buying out the Vita group for a few $$$$$$$ dollars in the end. It seemed that now, after all those years of hard slogging done by the mums and dad investors, the tirelessly working strip-dealers, and their very own unwitting partners, Ben Stuckey, Licensed Telstra Dealers, the Wendell and Deirdre Parnell's, and Vita group, all have been bought out by Telstra. Finally they didn't need us anymore; maybe it was their plan all along? Their long-term strategy worked. But who cares?

"Boom Boom Boom Crash Bang Bang," cried the drummer boy Wendell. What can I say, except Thank you Telstra and E.T. Phone Home. You were the real stars of this book.

THE END

Wait, you want more? Great. Read on to discover 'Where are they now?' and other titbits about the industry in the final chapters.

WITH BEN STUCKEY EX-STAFF DOING WELL

Chapter 37

Where Are They Now? - Ex-Staff Doing Well

To conclude, I'm happy to tell you, some of my ex-staff have gone on to do bigger and better things for themselves since their apprenticeship in our business. Many chose to be anonymous. Like I was telling you, I had no experience in the retail sales business, and whatever I ended up becoming was simply learned from the day-to-day business that went on at the E.T. Phone Home, Phone Shop and the telecommunications industry. I'd like to name some of the staff who are doing well today.

Ben Stuckey

He went on to own several Telstra Licensed Shops. He had a large one in Midland and another one in a suburb called Success. He also had another Business Centre in Midland. Ben sold both and got out. He too was sick of Telstra's bullying. He sold to Vita Group for a good profit, at the right time. He now runs a business brokerage company and is semi-retired. He commutes between Perth and Bali monthly. Lucky Ben. Best of both worlds.

Tim Guest

This man was always ambitious, and business minded. It was only a matter of time before he flew off from our Phone Shop division in

Subiaco. He slowly built up his business over the years, a huge financial advising company called Infinite Wealth. He now owns and operates a large enterprise, which is doing extremely well. Good Luck Tim.

Neil Randle

He used to work for Telstra. When I found out he was leaving them, I rang him up and offered him a job as our manager. He said several other dealers had approached him too. He liked the way we operated and accepted my offer. He had strong leadership qualities which we needed. At some Telstra meetings, Neil would always give his opinion, and naturally, Telstra never appreciated his comments being ex-Telstra staff. Neil now lives in Tasmania. He told me that he recently got his degree in accounting. We keep in touch.

Charisse Parnell

My dodgy young daughter. She graduated from university with a Bachelor of Marketing and Media. a. After their university studies, Charisse and my elder daughter Tasha lived in London and New York for two years. They both were in performing arts in Perth, and continued their theatre and dancing pursuits overseas. Upon their return, they both qualified as education teachers. Charisse taught at John Curtin College of the Arts then Rossmoyne High School before opening her own dance studio. The Dance Collective (TDC) started in 2003 with just 63 dancers. This year it celebrates 21 years and has over 800 dancers. We are so proud of her.

Tasha Jane (my other dodgy daughter)

Went on to work in an alternative school in Fremantle educating 'disengaged' young people and helping them get their lives back on track. She studied Documentary Film Making and won awards for Best Documentary and People's Choice Award for her short films in Perth W.A. in 2008. To celebrate the legalisation of Same Sex Marriage in

2018, Tasha became a Marriage Celebrant. She continues to take on lead roles in local community theatre productions. Best of all, Thank God Tasha studied English at Uni as she did come in handy in the end - she gave me some good suggestions and corrected lots of my mistakes in writing this book. Thanks Tasha.

Shane Durrant

Shane didn't come with any telephony experience. When I interviewed him, I felt comfortable with his mannerism. He was very calm in speech, polite, and a bit shy. He was about 23 years old and single. He quickly picked up and learned everything about mobile phones and all the Telstra products we sold. As a matter of fact, Shane became the expert in our shop and knew his way around every product. His knowledge was unbeatable. If a customer had a question you were not sure about, you'd ask Shane. That's how knowledgeable Shane was. He naturally ended up in our management team. I made him the manager of Belmont Forum. He deserved it. After we sold to the Vita Group, he went to work for the Telstra Business Centre and apparently is still there today. He married his long-time partner Darry. We remain good friends today.

Mathew Wall

Everyone called him Wally. We were happy with his services to our company. He was another hi-tech savvy staff. During his time with us, I never knew his artistic skills as a guitarist. Only after he left our employ, I saw on Facebook that this guy was starting to make a name for himself as a leading blues guitarist around Perth. He also made a best-selling album and several other albums. Now, he knew that in my past I was a music promoter, yet he never approached me for any help. On one occasion, I received an invitation to come see him play. That came with a condition. It was $30 to attend the event. Being a music promoter, I'd never paid to see anyone. If anything, it was in their advantage for me to go and see them perform. Until today, I have never seen him play. I wish him luck in his music career.

Siska Presila Fletcher.

A delightful lady. She started working for us at the age of seventeen in Phone Shop West Perth. We had expanded in a big way, and she became Deirdre's personal assistant. She also became one of our managers eventually. Like everyone else, she eventually moved on. Landing herself a job at the Atrium Hotel in Mandurah. She worked hard and worked her way up to becoming the manager of the service department. She trained many staff there and was very well respected by her management. She finally became the manager of that resort. Siska is now working in a town up north called Port Hedland. She is the manager of the post office there. I'm sure she will succeed in anything she does. Another five-star ex-staff of ours.

Kathy Russo

She was an important staff member for many good reasons. Kathy started as a salesperson, learned all about the back-of-house requirements, helped Deirdre with the submission's paperwork for Telstra weekly, and was popular with all staff. We promoted her to manager status. After we sold our business, it was the end of her career in the Telstra Licensed Shop business. Today she is married and has a beautiful girl named Devina. The last time I spoke to her, she told me she was a qualified teacher and couldn't be happier. Good memories.

Danny Wilder

This guy was keen and very young. Always in a hurry to get things done, making many mistakes along the way. I trained this guy through all his mistakes. He was a brilliant IT person. He built us a webpage. He was so talented, but we had to let him go. I liked him a lot. He wrote me a thank you letter a few years after he finished with us. He is capable of anything he chooses to do. I'm sure he won't mind me sharing his letter with you. Danny, you surprised me with the letter. I will always treasure it.

Dear Wendell,
   I'm unsure if you may remember me or not.
   My name Is ▓▓▓ im fairly sure you would remember me but times and change and so do people as you once told me.
   I remember you telling me once 'I hope one day to see you in the street and you tell me you are successful and when that day come im sure you would have grown up and made something for yourself'.
   Well I haven't started a multinational or multimillion dollar business, however I'm working in a job to which is something of a success.
   I have just completed a very thorough training course in the insurance industry; I now work in the city for a company called ▓▓▓▓▓▓▓▓ whom you may be familiar with.
   I just wrote to say I really thank you for help throughout the more immature aspects of my life.
   You were right when you said to me you gave me more attention and assistance than any other of the staff members and at the time you probably have no idea how your discussions and advice changed and reshaped my life. Some of your phrases and ideas have stuck in my mind up till now and im sure will still stay there.
   Something you may not have been aware of was the fact all I wanted to do was be as successful and established as you were/are.
   In conclusion I just want to say thank you.
   ☺

LETTER RECEIVED FROM DANNY WILDER
(REDACTED FOR HIS PRIVACY)

Laura Shockthorap

I met this lady the other day at the bar in the casino. She looked at me and said, "Wendell, is that you?"

I looked at her and I said, "Yes." She asked me if I remembered her. I was trying to figure out who the bloody hell she was.

She helped me out by finally saying, "You remember me? It's Laura."

"Oh Laura," I said,

"Yes, Laura, I remember you, you used to manage one of my shops."

She said, "That's right. You won't believe it, but I'm celebrating tonight because I just graduated by becoming a qualified lawyer." Wow, this is like

30 years later. We had a quick chat and I said Laura, "Congratulations, it's never too late to improve yourself."

Laura said, "Wendell, I must thank you for all the help you gave me and all the lessons about life that I learnt from you." I felt good and said goodbye.

Mosharraf Hossain

This young man from Bangladesh is one of the many Asian students we employed. Honest as the day is long and willing to do anything that helped the business. Another student looking for improvement in life. Always prompt and on time, never took sick days unnecessarily. He is currently working as a lecturer in Accounting and Finance at the University of Western Australia. Now married with three children and got his PR to live in Australia. I am so proud of you buddy.

His future plan is to be a successful educator, by opening a private higher education institution for domestic and international students. Good luck Mosh.

I've heard of so many other staff that are doing well in their new careers, sadly I couldn't name everyone. I wish everyone that ever worked for me, all the very best in life with your health and career.

Sickies

Any proprietor of any business will tell you the same story about retail staff and sickies. These guys are usually aged between 18 and 25 years old, well most of our staff were that age. Most of them are not sure what to do in life or what they want to be. All that mattered at that moment was, they just needed a job to pay the rent and probably go to the pub or go night clubbing on the weekends.

It was a common fact on a Monday, without fail, you are guaranteed that a certain number of staff would ring in sick. You had no way of verifying that. You just hope that the next day, they would bring you a doctor's certificate, which hardly ever happened.

But then as the week went on, some of the staff members would boast about their exploits from the previous weekend. The news would soon filter back to me that some of the people who rang in sick were out of town, having an organised long weekend. That's part of the hardships in the retail business or any business for that matter.

I'm not suggesting that all the staff were like that, just some. People only worry about themselves and not about the company or their workmates as they do in a lot of Asian countries like Japan or China especially. People over there would crawl to work just to make sure they're not letting the team down for the day, sick or not. That's the culture over there. They really do treasure their jobs in those countries.

Thankfully 'sickies' are not my problem anymore.

Ratbag Staff

Finally, we did have some real ratbags that lied, stole, and abused everything we gave them to use. There will always be that element of unpredictable people around. I'm just glad we made it to this side of our business life without any of them totally wrecking our future for us.

Amin, Beatrice, Cathy, Dilmah, Errol, Fletcher, Giselle, Herman, Ivan, Joe, Kelvin, Lola, Martha, Neetu, Olivia, Pandy, Quincy, Robert, Salvadore, Tony, Ulla, Viola, Willy, Xylophone, Yola, and Zenith.

Mobile Phone and Accessory Wholesalers

Roadhound was a huge supplier of Motorola mobile phones. Patrick Lynch was their representative here. He was a lovely man who helped us a lot by training our staff and constantly diligently keeping us up to date with new products. Most mobile phone suppliers would give all of us dealers incentives to buy from them. Example: If you bought, say 100 of their new model mobile phones, in return, they'd give you $2,000 worth of Myer vouchers. We did get our share of Myer vouchers, but the big boys certainly cleaned up. They were buying mobile phones by the hundreds, and we were buying them by the dozens. Roadhound were easy to deal with and we certainly bought a lot of stock from Patrick.

Brightpoint was another major supplier of mobile phones. They were based in Sydney. Rina White was another talented, helpful and qualified representative and always there to help us and train us. After Telstra, we probably bought most of our stock from her, accruing points along the way. I remember Brightpoint taking me to the Indy 500 on the Gold Coast. They flew some of us selected dealers from Perth to the Gold Coast. There were other national dealers included too. They had a Brightpoint tent at the racetrack and as usual, in a good position for viewing, with magnificent food, outstanding wines, and spirits. This package was from paid for by all the points we accrued over a period of time. Rina was always on the ball and we became good friends meeting regularly at Miss Maud's for coffee.

Telstra was, of course, our biggest supplier of all mobile phones. They had the money and power to outsell anyone in the marketplace. Their only problem back then was; their credit department always knew what money we owed them, right to the last cent at any given time, yet they did not concurrently recognise what they owed us in rebates for handsets sold on their plans. This was because their credit department did not speak to their Telstra rebate department on a regular basis, resulting in us constantly having problems with credit. Yet, Telstra's rebate department would usually owe us twice as much as we owed them at any given time. There was a continual battle trying to get stock from them when we reached our credit limit. Telstra was always late in paying us our rebates. Consequently, how were we supposed to find the money to buy stock? Go figure! It is commonly known as a cash flow problem, caused by our Lord and Master, Telstra themselves.

Telepacific also supplied the local dealers in Perth with mobile phones. They were big on the Motorola brand plus a few extra brands like NEC and Nokia. The Nokia brand grew to become the biggest and most popular brand in the marketplace. Nokia even established their own repair centre in Perth. Everything was Nokia Nokia Nokia! They had the market cornered. Back then, you would never have predicted the demise they eventually experienced. In those days, I would have bet any amount of money that there would never be another brand that could come to the market and topple them over. But it did happen. The manufacturer made some silly mistake in the software of one of their 'new Nokia mobile phones, and it took them a long time to perfect it. In the meantime, their competitors overtook them and knocked them off as number one in the marketplace. Today it's iPhone's turn to be on top. I wonder if the bubble will ever burst for iPhone! It will, because nothing lasts forever, especially in the IT world. The lovely Ivana Dobson was their representative here in Perth.

Brightstar from America came late on the scene. They then won the contract for Buying and Distribution of all Telstra's products. They ended up being the biggest player on the market nationally. T-Choice, a Singaporean-based player, had a slice of the market share with Sony Ericsson, Motorola, and LG. This company took market share from all the major players until Brightstar came along and took over all T-Choice's customers. That was the games being played by the big wholesalers at the time. Representing Brightstar was a lady called Peta Grant. She was from Perth 1997. Her role was State Manager for the American-owned Brightstar. Like all representatives of large companies, she was good at her job and was always ready to train our staff. I spoke with her recently and found out she had a bad fall in Melbourne and has been off the scene and in pain for five years with back problems. Get well Peta.

Accessory Wholesalers

Force Technology was the only Perth-based accessory company we all relied upon most. Michael Doust and Jake Minear were two young guys who were very switched on in importing everything in the aftermarket (non-genuine) products range. They were based in Osborne Park and gave me credit from day one. Like some of us, they also grew into a million-dollar concern. Most of all their accessories were imported from China. They ended up with a huge distribution centre here in Perth. They just grew bigger and started to sell their products successfully all over Australia. This year 2023, they celebrate their thirtieth anniversary and are still a private company. Mark Whiting was their representative here. Another brilliant representative who serviced us regularly and was always on hand to help us.

Cellnet was from Queensland. Another accessory wholesaler for leather cases, batteries, antennas, power chargers and car chargers, and anything else that was associated with mobile phones. Rhonda Craig worked for Cellnet in Perth, after a very nice man by the name of Brendon left the company. She was very switched on in the industry. She also trained our staff on her day off on a Saturday morning. I am told Rhonda now works for Microsoft. She has been there for ten years. Good luck to you Rhonda.

Force and Cellnet were the two main aftermarket (non-genuine) accessory suppliers for all the dealers in Perth. If you wanted a leather case, antenna, battery, or any aftermarket accessory, you'd deal with these guys. Even though we had our disagreements from time to time, I have nothing bad to say against any of them. We were all growing together, like a family.

All the representatives from the whole industry were there to help and train our staff on all their products outside of working hours. A big 'Thank You' to all.

Chapter 38

Miss Maud's My Head Office

Miss Maud's is a big chain of Swedish-inspired, quaint, leisure-eating cafes. They sold pâtisseries, good coffee, hot and cold meals, and were famous for their catering platters. The staff were dressed in Swedish designed costumes and wore red caps. Miss Maud was a petite, jovial and astute businesswoman. She realised there was a lack of places for women to have lunch around Perth, so in 1971 opened her first café in Carillion Arcade, Perth City. I met the lovely lady owner when we first moved into the Belmont Forum shopping Centre. I spoke to this friendly lady and told her we were from the new Telstra Licensed Shop.

"If you give me a special deal on coffee, I will conduct all my business meetings in your shop," I asked her cheekily.

To my surprise, she answered "Ok I will", and ordered her manager to enter the set price into their computer a special price of $2.20 for all my teas and coffees. My staff also cashed in on this deal. You'd just had to say, "Press the Telstra button" and $2.20 would show up. It was never a problem for us even with their new staff. They knew which button to press because it had 'Telstra' written on it. The original price for coffee was $3.20 a cup.

Now here's the best part. Over the years as the price of coffee went up, someone forgot to adjust my buying rate. So, from 1998 to 2012, the price gradually went up to $4.20 and we still paid only $2.20 per hot drink.

They also had a larger turnover of staff than us. To my luck, and because I had spent hours at Miss Maud's, I knew all their staff very well. Little did they know, I was interviewing most of them daily during the small talks we had. From time to time, I would poach some good staff from there. I certainly had a racket going on!

Thus, I always refer to Miss Maud's as *my office*. It was an in-joke between all my staff. I bought thousands of coffees from Miss Maud's over the years. It really was the best place for me to conduct business. God Bless her and thank you very much, Miss Maud.

Saturday Breakfast

We used to cook breakfast for the staff working on Saturdays at the Telstra Licensed Shop Belmont Forum. Part of the employment agreement was that everyone working Saturdays had to show up one hour before opening to catch up on all the latest gadgets or information Telstra would send us by Friday. They used to love our breakfast.

There were usually eight or nine staff rostered on Saturdays. I would buy four loaves of French sticks and cut them into three pieces per stick. Now that's a decent size breakfast, about ten inches or twenty-two centimetres long. Deirdre and I would get up at about 6 am and that was our routine for about ten years. We knew exactly what to do.

From start to end, it took roughly an hour to cook the breakfast. We would then leave it in the oven and keep it warm, all wrapped and covered up. I would always cook bacon and egg omelettes. I'd put generous servings of this omelette onto the French sticks, then I would put some lovely camembert or brie cheese over that. We added slices of tomato, salt, pepper, and a good serving of butter. We would lightly toast the bread, so by the time we got to work about ten to eight in the morning, the food was still hot. We also bought orange juice plus a big pot of homemade coffee.

Everybody knew exactly what to expect. At the meeting, they would just go and help themselves. Grab a serviette and eat their breakfast whilst we would go through the updates of the new phone plans and Telstra instructions on new gadgets. I have forgotten to mention we also had vegan and vegetarian staff. We had some Indian and Muslim staff too. The Muslim staff knew that whatever they were eating was not cooked in the same pots or saucepans that the bacon and eggs were cooked in. I bought Red Rooster chicken for these guys. You must respect everybody's beliefs and religion and that we did.

The staff were very thankful because they knew the effort we spent to feed them. It was probably the best breakfast they had all week. Other days if you asked, they would say, "Oh, I just grabbed a muffin, or a slice of toast with butter and that's about it." But with us, they had the full breakfast meeting. Everything was there for them each and every Saturday morning. By the way, when Deirdre and I were away, we bought the staff a similar breakfast from Miss Maud's. But rumour has it, they all preferred our home-made heart-warming breakfast, any day. Looking after your staff was important. We certainly did.

Uniforms & Choosing the Right Workers

I met David Panther through my Malaysian friend Mr. Thanapathy. David imported men and women's clothing. I wanted a smart looking uniform for the Phone Shop team. We were now up to six shops, with 48 staff. It was time we upped the ante with our dress code. Whatever new look we were adopting had to compliment Phone Shop. I was one of the very first dealers to introduce a uniform into the strip dealer network. We bought all the clothes for the staff. This wasn't an easy task because the retail staff in those days were very transient, changing jobs often. It is possibly the same today.

We were very particular in choosing staff back then because we knew their transient habits. When being interviewed, they would tell you what you wanted to hear; they wanted to learn all about telecommunications.

The one thing they forget to tell you is; they've already made plans to go to Bali, or interstate with their friend or partner, in about eight to twelve weeks' time. Usually, they would drop this on you about two weeks before their due date. You either had to say, "I'm sorry you can't have a week off because you haven't accrued any holidays yet," in which case they'd resign, or you'd have to put up with their bullshit. This happened quite often.

The choice was to accept their blackmail and give them leave. Imagine the position we were in. Giving them training for three months, buying them new uniforms, and the nightmare of having to start it all over again in three months was stressful. It probably happened everywhere.

I always found International Asian students the best and most ambitious workers. They would come to Australia to study and strive hard to get a degree to take back home. They would either study at a TAFE course at night or a part-time day course somewhere. I didn't mind the three days a week these guys could give me. That was fine by me. Reliable part-time staff was much more beneficial than unreliable full-timers.

As I mentioned before, many retail staff were wandering and aloof young people. These serious Asian guys were here for learning, not here for holidays.

Chapter 39

Things That Made Life Hell

New Design Chiefs Telstra Didn't Need

Every few years Telstra would bring in a new design executive to revamp Telstra's look. They brought along their influences from their previous workplace. For example, a new female executive (working for ex-British Paints) will be flown to Perth and we were all summoned to meet and listen to her. At this meeting, were told that in our next shop refit to expect changes. We would hear how the world was changing and to suit the newest modern look, Telstra was also going to change its colours.

In the following months, we would get a view of what our shops were going to look like. In the case of this ex-British Paints new leader, our Telstra Shop designs were starting to look whiter and a little more silver, what else did you expect? The same thing happened a few years later. We were lumbered with the same type of storyline from another new ex-Kodak leader. All our shops now started looking a little more yellow and orange, I wonder why? These guys never lasted long. All they seemed to achieve was costing us more money every time we had a new shop refit. It was a joke. That's the one thing I learnt from Telstra, always keep changing your staff, then blame them if what was supposed to happen went wrong. It must have been their fault. Another job justification at hand.

When we tried to mention how these drastic changes were eating into our profit, Telstra would simply shrug their shoulders. I don't want to sound condescending, but I'm convinced that some of the Telstra hierarchy were jealous because they could see we were making a shitload of money, whilst most of them were on average wages, or in their cases, very good wages. You could feel their resentment when you applied for the extra money you were entitled to. Telstra had a slush fund to help dealers where it was necessary. If the smaller dealer needed help, we'd have to grovel like poor relatives, but when the bigger players ran into trouble, it was a different story. Millions were thrown at them.

There's a well-known story in the industry about John Illan, owner of Crazy John's mobile phone shops nationally. He had an ongoing dispute with Telstra about not receiving the correct airtime commissions. This landed him in court with Telstra which cost him a lot of money which he lost. So, he decided to jump ship and took his business empire over to Vodaphone. That deal helped Crazy John's as they had a serious major cash flow problem. So, our Lord and Master Telstra lost a big player, Crazy John's to Vodaphone. Apparently, Telstra had poured millions into rescuing John. They tried not to lose this national player but ended up in court instead and won. What did they win? Unfortunately for John, whilst taking his morning jog one day, he suffered a massive heart attack and dropped dead in the park. He was forty-three years old (RIP).

ICE-Tech, IT Programmers Telstra Did Need

Our State Manager at one time was Mark Bradbury. Although we got on reasonably well, we certainly had our differences. As time progressed, Telstra was starting to move faster than expected, continually changing into another fast gear. Their business was growing faster than they could manage. We were all learning on the job, so to speak. Telstra commissioned an IT company called ICE-Tech to develop a point-of-sale system to integrate all Telstra stamped stores nationally. ICE-Tech was trying to teach us their newly written point-of-sale retail program which they had written for Telstra. The intention was to link the sales of handsets in all the nationally independently owned stores, as well as Telstra-owned stores. This was a mammoth task, believe me.

Sometimes they would learn from us, and vice versa. Between all of this going on, there were a lot of conflicts about stock entering on the computer, and lots of other issues which their programmer had to fix. There were many conflicts about the new system which they brought in for us to use at the point-of-sale. Telstra wanted us to be joined nationally as a group, run by the company ICE-Tech based in Melbourne. We were having major problems nationally because even though each Licensed Shop was owned by an independent company, we were all attached to Telstra and thus were forced to share information.

Telstra hired ICE-Tech to train us on a regular basis, with Deirdre and Ben occasionally traveling to Melbourne for their training. ICE-Tech would then send their IT expert to Perth to train our staff. Even though they were the experts who wrote the program, they learned about many their programming mistakes from us, their guinea pigs. We were all learning. Understanding the daily operations of a Telstra Licensed Shop is critical to writing an effective program. ICE-Techs' program had several flaws, and our staff and customers suffered as a result. Despite our efforts to train them on the industry's intricacies.

There was a significant amount of tension between Telstra, ICE-Tech, and Telstra Licensed Shop dealers. This was primarily due to the frustration of not fully understanding how to operate the new system, and confusion regarding the requirements needed to manage sales effectively.

As a result, there was a lot of back and forth between the parties involved. When one party was unhappy, they would vent their frustrations, which often led to being labelled as a troublemaker. However, it's important to note that this was a widespread issue among all Telstra Licensed Shop dealers. It took several years, but eventually, the system came together. Finally everything ran smoothly after this national point-of-sale was introduced.

Chapter 40

Interesting Short Stories
– Telstra Woo Us

Over the years, I've been invited to many Telstra outings. I could talk for days but I'm going to keep these three short within the next few pages, otherwise it may make you jealous! Telstra had money to woo us dealers and they did this with their big fat credit cards.

Bledisloe Cup Melbourne 2001

I'll start with my invitation to the Bledisloe Cup in Melbourne. In 2003, Australia was playing New Zealand. Australia won the 2003 Bledisloe Cup. Telstra flew us to Melbourne for three nights staying at the Hyatt Hotel. They kept us entertained with day trips to the Yarra Valley, daily lunches and dinners in different fancy restaurants and to top it all off, an afternoon high tea somewhere in the Dandenong's. I had a great time between meals, drinks, and bonding with other dealers from around Australia. There were other activities including an afternoon session of training and lectures (yawn) at their head office in Bourke Street. These sessions were their way to justify the money they spent on us. All tax deductions obviously.

But what more does one want? There were no complaints on our end. Telstra gave us all an Australian green and gold-coloured short sleeve shirt to wear to the game. With the right atmosphere and a few drinks, boy, we cheered our team on to win. I had never been to a rugby match, let alone a Bledisloe Cup. It was a big event for me to absorb. It was a sold-out match and as usual, Telstra had a large corporate box with huge TV screens and with food and drinks that would cost the average man thousands. Shall I say more? I still have the shirt.

MY ORIGINAL BLEDISLOE CUP GUERNSEY

The 2000 Sydney Olympics

Telstra started another competition, but this was the big one. They introduced prepaid phone cards. The market was starving for something new and bingo, our Lord and Master came up with the new $25 prepaid phone cards. Our challenge was to sell as many prepaid phone cards as possible. Five shops in Western Australia with the most sold were going to win a $25,000 package to attend the 2000 Sydney Olympics.

Everyone was excited. We knew we had a good chance because the suburb of Belmont and surrounding suburbs were in a state housing commission area. We were right in the middle of it; the not so affluent area. It wasn't a flash suburb like Booragoon or Karrinyup but had the perfect demographics for these $25 prepaid phone cards. We brainstormed for days and had many meetings on how to sell as many as possible and include a gimmick of course. We never got anywhere close to a bright idea.

We were remunerated $3.50 for every prepaid phone card we sold. Prior to the introduction of the $25 cards, tens of thousands of people were on a $50 or a $100 plan per month. Their average spend was $25 per month, yet they were paying a much higher fee. So, there were going to be lots of old and new customers coming to buy these new $25 cards and save money. They were very popular indeed.

This competition was launched on the 1st of July and was ending on the 31 August 2000. The Olympics were starting on 15 September. The winners would be announced on the 1 September. That gave us two months to sell-sell-sell these suckers to win. It was the start of Telstra's new financial year push. Telstra was losing market share to Optus and Vodaphone. It was their way of winning back or keeping existing customers.

Try as you may, the bigger dealers in Perth were obviously going to sell more than us, purely by volume. I thought we might have a good chance, but we needed a gimmick. What gimmick did we have up our sleeve? We didn't. For once I couldn't come up with one. What was happening to the old Wendell?

We were advised well in advance. We knew before the end of the financial year about this new $25 prepaid card. Our dealer manager came around towards the end of June for an afternoon visit. I took him over to Miss Maud's for a coffee. He advised me Telstra was going to rebate all the dealers, 75% towards their advertising done during the next two months, July and August.

I budgeted $800 a week in advertising for the next eight weeks to promote these cards. We needed to sell 50 prepaid cards per week to break even after the rebate. That's not bad I thought as it meant we would only lose two hundred dollars during the eight weeks campaign. We just needed to sell, four hundred prepaid. Without the 75% rebate, I would not have advertised at all. We would still be obliged to sell the prepaid cards regardless. That was what we signed up for and we had to follow the rules. Not really a good deal, but the Phone Shop name would be down weekly. Telstra was subsidising us heavily, so I accepted.

You had to be smart and book newspaper space in advance as everybody was going to jump in there at the 75% rebate offered. Our dealer manager came back again on the 1st of August, and we sat down again at Miss Maud's for coffee.

I asked him all sorts of questions about how we were faring in numbers. He told me we were about number eight or nine on their radar. There was about thirteen in total. Not looking good I thought.

"What were other shops doing, how were they going, and how many prepaid cards were they selling per week," I asked. He couldn't tell me for confidentiality reasons, I understood that. "But can you at least give me just a little hint?" I asked sheepishly.

"No sorry, I can't," he said, and left.

I spoke to Deirdre and Ben over a beer at the pub next door after work that evening.

"Guys, we are not faring well, little chance of getting into the top five to win that Olympic package. Doesn't look like we are going to the Olympics."

Deirdre said she'd pay and take me if I really wanted to go. How sweet.

"It's okay, forget it. Let's think more about it tonight," I said.

The next morning, I spoke to Deirdre and Ben, "I have an idea."

"What idea?" they asked in desperation.

"How about for the next four weeks we sell all our prepaid cards for $20 each instead of $25? We still have four weeks of advertising left, and currently, we are already losing $25 a week on this deal anyway. We need to do something drastic."

Deirdre and Ben were warm to the idea but reminded me that other dealers might find this method controversial and make complaints to Telstra. I explained that there's no law saying you can't give away your profits and losing $1.50 per card, selling prepaid cards. We are certainly not undercutting other businesses profits if anything we are undercutting ourselves and losing on the deal here. It's our money, not theirs.

"We can absorb all the losses, it's tax deductable, there's nothing to lose here. Okay, so we don't get the $3.50 they're giving us for prepaid phone cards, but I've calculated and done the sums. If we triple our sales in the next four weeks, we might have a chance," I explained.

They both thought about it for a while said, "Why not, let's give it a go." Another risk taken.

During the first month of this campaign, we sold 100 prepaid phone cards. The next month, we advertised the $25 prepaid cards for $20. We sold 700. Two smaller strip dealer friends of mine came and bought 100 cards each from me and they each made $500 profit too. Thank God for that. We lost $3,500 on this campaign.

But guess what? We got into the fifth spot and won ourselves an Olympic Package. Do the sums, for a loss of $3,500 (tax deductable), we won a $25,000 or more package to the Olympics. Better than playing poker at the casino, wouldn't you agree?

The Olympics

Day 1

We arrived at the Perth airport and were met by a representative who recognised us by the lanyard provided to us by Telstra. He was waiting close to the Qantas counter and his name was Daniel. He introduced himself and assured us our baggage will be in our hotel room in Sydney when we arrive.

The Qantas flight to Sydney was enjoyable. Imagine six days and five nights in Sydney for the Olympics. It was the hottest ticket in Australia. When we arrived in Sydney, there was a gentleman standing there with a large Telstra sign. He advised us to stand by as there were more dealers joining us. When the five couples finally gathered, he took us to a ten-seater stretched limousine waiting to take us to the Hyatt Hotel in Sydney. We checked in and our luggage was in the room as promised.

There was a bottle of champagne on ice and a welcome note reminding us that dinner was at 7 pm in the Hyatt restaurant. The restaurant was fully booked out by Telstra and was decorated with the Australian colours green and gold. On each seat was a gift. It was a long sleeved blue and silver raincoat to wear to the games in case it rained. We had a beautiful three course dinner, drinks and then it was time to go to bed and sleep. It was a long day.

THE SLEEVE OF MY ORIGINAL OLYMPIC RAIN COAT THAT WAS GIVEN TO US AT THE OLYMPICS

Day 2

After breakfast, we had the morning to either rest or explore the neighbourhood. The coach was leaving at 4 pm for the opening ceremony. Everyone was ready.

There was a great buzz on the coach. Our hosts were very observant, they watch and responded to our every need. They certainly researched their role, as they knew the answer to every question asked. As we got closer to Olympic Park, the traffic became more congested, people were looking for parking or walking towards the park.

Again, we were met and shown our seats, good ones. Opening night of the Olympics was a dream come true. I can't and won't describe every minute of what happened during the next six hours. If you didn't watch it live, you need to find it on YouTube and watch it. We had a ball and were rather tipsy by the end. That's all I'm saying. Oh, what a night. Before we reached our hotel about midnight, we were told, tomorrow morning at 11 am, a coach was taking us to Olympic Park for our first event, the tennis.

Day 3

Pronto at 11 am, we leave the Hyatt and at 12 pm we arrived at the Olympic Park. We were greeted by Telstra representatives and followed them into a Telstra tent. In the tent, tables and chairs were set up. It was obvious we were having lunch there.

After lunch we were taken to our fabulous Telstra seats. Cannot remember who we saw but it was a great game. At 4 pm we were ushered back to the coach and were reminded the dinner was at 7.30 pm. A coach will leave 6.30 pm. So, like sheep, we filed out of the coach and to our rooms. A short rest and back to work (or so it felt like).

The coach was waiting with engine running, we jumped in and soon arrived at Darling Harbour to a seafood restaurant for dinner. The word was order anything you desire; there was a bottle of champagne in the ice bucket and an expensive bottle of red wine for who don't drink French Champagne. I drank both, three times or more. I can't exactly remember what I ordered, but be rest assured, crayfish, prawns, and oysters would have been some for sure. At about 10 pm we were tired and went home. The following morning the coach was leaving at 11 am sharp.

Day 4

Like the previous day, the 11 am coach went to the same tent for lunch, then shuttled off to another event. This time swimming. It was absolutely magical. Watching swimming on TV you get good close-ups and vision, but it was totally different at Olympic Park; it was live and people screaming. We loved it. After a few hours, it was back to the hotel for a rest, then the coach was leaving the hotel at 7 pm for dinner.

This time we went to Bondi Beach to an Italian restaurant. Same procedure, all the whistles and bells were laid on and we had a wonderful evening with entertainment by a roving piano accordionist and three Italian singers. What a fantastic night we had. The Italian wines certainly helped us along with our singing.

Day 5

This event was in the evening, soccer. I'm a party animal, but the past four days eating, and drinking took its toll, it wore me out. I didn't want to partake in any food, drinks or events.

Deirdre rang her younger sister Louise (RIP) and offered her our soccer seats. Louise's husband was a mad soccer fan. They were delighted with the offer. I told them, to go there when the game started and sit down in our seats. There were different hosts for different events, so nobody would know. Anyway, Deirdre and Louise looked alike. Louise and her husband followed our instructions and had a wonderful evening which included food and drinks.

Day 6

Track and field day. We had to leave a little earlier and this event was held in another part of the park. We still got fed and supplied with food and drinks all day. It was enjoyable but a bit boring for me.

Our last evening in Sydney was going to be a big night. This time, because the restaurant was not that far away from our hotel, all of us walked and found the restaurant in Cockle Bay. The restaurant was on the upper floor and overlooked the whole of the Darling Harbour. What a way to end our trip, at a seafood restaurant.

I calculated that by now we had far exceeded our $25,000 allotment. That didn't stop us from ordering the best. Someone even ordered a bottle of Grange. There were ten of us and we must have dented the Telstra purse. I'm told the bill was over eight thousand dollars. Most of the bill was spent by the ladies drinking very expensive French Champagne. I forgot to mention, the men were drinking 1996 Penfolds Grange (the second bottle). I did ask the publisher to delete the last sentence, but they must have forgotten.

I can't add much more to this chapter, but to say it was an unforgettable experience we had. Would I take another risk like I did with the Telstra prepaid cards? I'd say yes, bring it on anytime, I'm all in.

World Master of Business Conference 1999

Six prominent men were promoted on a tour around the world as a 'must be seen and heard, once-in-a-lifetime experience not to be missed' conference. It was hailed as a feel-good motivational show. It featured Mikhail Gorbachev (ex-Russian Prime Minister), General "Stormin" Norman Schwarzkopf (leader of the Yanks into the Desert Storm Gulf war), Justin Trudeau (ex-Canadian Prime Minister), Rene Rivkin (master of making millions of dollars as seen on TV), Brad Cooper (American filmmaker, recipient of a British Academy Film Award) and Al Dunlap (ex-CEO of many companies including Sunbeam, nicknamed The

Chainsaw, The Assassin and the Shredder). According to the ads, it was supposed to be the most intellectually motivating conference ever produced.

Norman Schwarzkopf, the American General spoke on leadership and was most impressive. He threw in his famous line "Whenever there are three or more people, a leader is found. Every one of you can be a leader. The leader is not often the person who thinks he is!"

Mikhail Gorbachev (RIP)
He might have been more interesting if he hadn't used an interpreter. He did make some significant changes to the world. It was he who tore down the Berlin Wall and showed the West that peace was achievable, especially in those cold war days. For that, we are eternally grateful to him.

Justin Trudeau's theme was focused on "The loop of success." Success builds confidence, confidence creates activity, activity creates habit, habit creates results and results create success. I was completely lost halfway through his delivery. Then to make it worse, he said to be successful, you must remember names. That was my worst nightmare when meeting people. Remembering names was not my forte. Sorry, who was I just talking about?

Rene Rivkin (RIP) smoked a cigar on TV. Always talking about making money. I didn't see him.

Brad Cooper I missed him too.

Al Dunlap (RIP) I missed seeing or hearing him.

As you read further you will find out why I didn't see these last three giants.

I had read in the newspaper that the price of tickets started at $400 a head. Some tickets were over $1,000 each. I wouldn't have gone to that type of conference normally and paid that kind of money unless someone else was paying for it. When I got a call from Telstra inviting me to attend, I jumped at it.

"Yes, I need to learn more about business, I'd love to go," I said.

(The conference was held at the Dome Stadium, at the Burswood Casino Complex. The Dome Stadium has since been demolished and Burswood has changed its name to Crown Perth).

When I got there, I couldn't believe the enormous crowd. There was about 5,000 people in attendance, so I'm told. This seminar was supposed to be inspirational, to open your mind up, to enrich your knowledge in business.

Yes, I agree, the talent that presented was overwhelming. Almost everyone attending that day brought their laptop or a notebook, and most took down notes. Every word spoken was embraced by all and I'm sure the audience was stimulated by hearing their stories. But, motivating me, it wasn't. I ended up going to the Casino next door, halfway through their presentation. I was greeted by the Pearl Room manager Tony Godfrey. He bought me a drink, I played blackjack for twenty minutes, won $100 and went back to the seminar.

These guys had proven success; their status said it all. They were giants in this leading world and had made it to the top. They were telling anyone who was interested in listening how to be successful. People want to hear success stories. Everything written in my book is in plain fundamental business acumen. You take risks, work hard, make smart decisions, and if you are lucky, you hit the jackpot.

Ask the thousands or millions of people who have lost their life savings in business. It's not easy, it doesn't come easy. Learn from reading books from people like me. Luck must play a big part. There are fewer and fewer chances to become a millionaire nowadays. I'm not suggesting giving up. You are encouraged to try your luck but be wary.

I have written my own success story and hope you get something from it. As I always say, there are risks in just being alive. It's easier to take a page from my book than theirs. My story is a more realistic rag-to-riches story. You can listen and learn from these Giants, but six of them, one after the other, all in one hit? Too much for me. How did they make their millions? Correction, in some cases, billions? They all tell you the same story, just as I can tell you. It was not easy, it never is. There is always a risk. For every 1,000 success stories, there are also $10m worth of sad ones. Be careful.

And that's a wrap!

FIN

How
E.T. Phone Home
Made Me a Millionaire, Twice!

STARRING
Wendell Parnell

CO-STARRING
Ben Stuckey

FEATURING
Deirdre Parnell

GUEST APPEARANCE
Tasha Jane - Charisse Parnell

WRITTEN BY
Ubba

CO AUTHOR
DwanneeMa

Photography	Scott Pollock	**Technicians**	Ian and Derek
Telstra Mate	Geoff Ridgwell	**Engineer**	Jason Crane
Producers	Wij and Dij	**Wardrobe**	Panther Clothing Co
Financed by	Talbora Pty Ltd	**Publisher**	Madhouse Media
Cover Artwork	Finn Pollock	**Lawyers**	Chan Galic & Associates
Critic	Indie Pollock	**Music By**	Karma and Hands Off
Sponsors	TheDanceCollective Wendell7.com	**Repairer**	Alltech

Media Perth	Suppliers	Trainers
Telstra Channel 9	Telstra	Patrick
The West Australian	TelePacific	Rita
X-Press Magazine	Brightpoint	Mark
Sunday Times	Roadhound	Ivana
96 FM	Cellnet	Rhonda
Radio 6PR	Force	Peta

Special thanks to :- Donald Black and Joe Versaci

In Perth	In Malaysia	In Melbourne	In Sydney
Shirley Eldridge	Mr. Thanapathy	Gary Gould	Fay Ford

Cast

Andy	Nola
Bill	Olivia
Cynthia	Paul
Dharma	Quincy
Eric	Rayeleen
Finn	Steven
Gina	Theevin
Hilary	Uppie
Indie	Vince
Joe	Willy
Kevin	Xylophone
Linda	Yola
Lo-Anne	Zoe

Shirley Eldridge

First class author, editor, my neighbour, and my friend. She has corrected scores, no, hundreds of my mistakes and who guided me patiently through this book writing process. Thank You.

Shirley's novels to date: -

1 - Twenty-Four Seven
2 - Georgie-Girl
3 - The Rocky Girl
4 - Mima-A case of abduction, rape and murder
5 - Edwin-Flamboyant Australian Pioneer
6 - Woman For Sale

Written by Wendell Parnell ©

About the Author

A Scoundrel, Drug-Trafficker, Nuisance, Low-Caste, Jungle-Bred, Troublemaker, Misfit, Money Launderer, Gigolo, Bigamist, Communist, Gun Runner, Rude Man and an Anti-Social Foul-Mouthed person I am not.

Lover of the Arts, Big Marx Bros Fan, Love Phantom of The Opera, Musician at Heart, Ex-Roadie, Decent Husband, Drummer, Amateur Writer, Loving Father, Health Conscious, Good Cook and Philanthropist I am.

There, you know all about me now. Please spread the word I'm not a bad person.

Wendell Parnell

www.ingramcontent.com/pod-product-compliance
Lightning Source LLC
Chambersburg PA
CBHW051535010526
44107CB00064B/2730